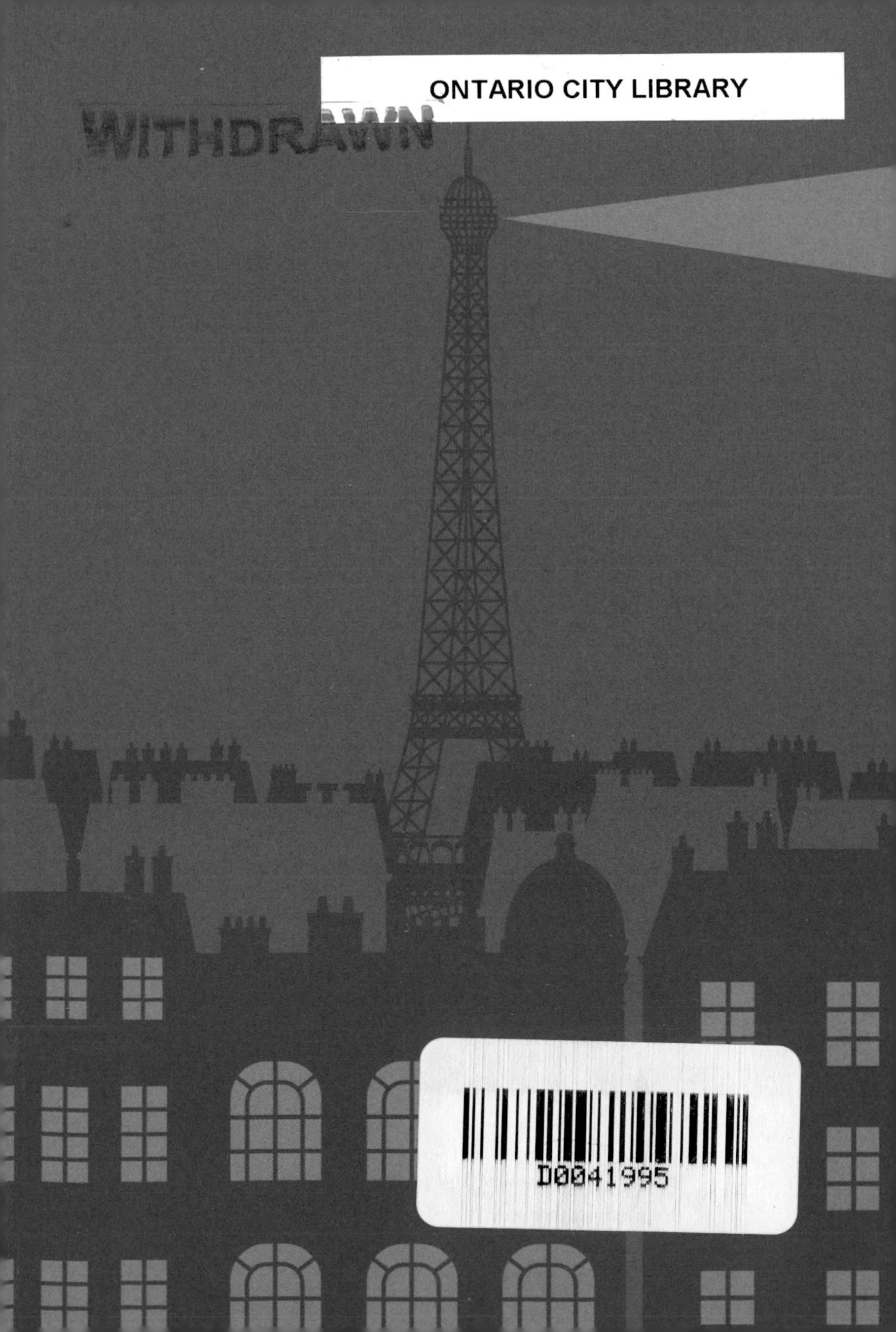

PENGUIN BOOKS

PARIS VERSUS NEW YORK

VAHRAM MURATYAN, an art director
and graphic designer, created his design studio
in Paris in 2005. His work ranges from commissioned
projects in print for such high-profile clients as Chanel,
France Télévisions, Coty x Playboy perfumes,
and La Galerie de l'Opéra de Paris to self-initiated
projects including the box series *Colle décolle et recolle*
and the activity-book collection *J'ai toujours rêvé d'être
un artiste.* Vahram teaches graphic design
and print matter at his former school and uses
his spare time to travel — a lot. In the fall of 2010,
during a long stay in the United States, he launched his
first blog, *Paris versus New York, a tally of two cities.*
parisvsnyc.blogspot.com

VAHRAM MURATYAN

Paris versus New York

A TALLY OF TWO CITIES

PENGUIN BOOKS

PENGUIN BOOKS

Published by the Penguin Group

Penguin Group (USA) Inc., 375 Hudson Street, New York, New York 10014, U.S.A.

Penguin Group (Canada), 90 Eglinton Avenue East, Suite 700, Toronto, Ontario, Canada M4P 2Y3
     (a division of Pearson Penguin Canada Inc.)

Penguin Books Ltd, 80 Strand, London WC2R 0RL, England

Penguin Ireland, 25 St Stephen's Green, Dublin 2, Ireland (a division of Penguin Books Ltd)

Penguin Group (Australia), 250 Camberwell Road, Camberwell, Victoria 3124, Australia
     (a division of Pearson Australia Group Pty Ltd)

Penguin Books India Pvt Ltd, 11 Community Centre, Panchsheel Park, New Delhi – 110 017, India

Penguin Group (NZ), 67 Apollo Drive, Rosedale, Auckland 0632, New Zealand
     (a division of Pearson New Zealand Ltd)

Penguin Books (South Africa) (Pty) Ltd, 24 Sturdee Avenue, Rosebank, Johannesburg 2196, South Africa

Penguin Books Ltd, Registered Offices:
80 Strand, London WC2R 0RL, England

First published in Penguin Books 2012

10 9 8 7 6 5 4 3 2 1

Copyright © Vahram Muratyan, 2011
All rights reserved

Originally published in France as *Paris vs New York* by Editions 10/18, an imprint of Univers Poche, Paris.

Some of the contents of this book first appeared on the author's blog of the same title.

LIBRARY OF CONGRESS CATALOGING-IN-PUBLICATION DATA
Muratyan, Vahram.
  [Paris vs New York]
  Paris versus New York : a tally of two cities / Vahram Muratyan.
     p. cm.
  Originally published: Paris vs New York. Paris : Editions 10/18, c2011.
  ISBN 978-0-14-312025-4 (hardcover : alk. paper) 1. Muratyan, Vahram—Themes, motives.
     2. Paris (France)—In art. 3. New York (N.Y.)—In art. I. Title.
  NC999.6.F8M87 2012
  741.6092—dc23
                                                    2011044058

Printed in the United States of America
Designed by Vahram Muratyan

ALWAYS LEARNING   PEARSON

introduction

After a long journey across continents and centuries — from East to West, from the lands of Anatolia by way of Istanbul, Gallipoli, Thessaloníki, and Venice — my family staked their claim in Paris. I was born in Paris, and yet her culture, her worldliness, her beauty continue to take me by surprise. Growing up in such a seductive place is its own kind of magic. Paris is known for her charming streets, her infinite possibilities, her mystery; I love her for her unpredictable moods, her whimsical nature, the whirlpools that churn beneath her surface calm. She embodies the essence of her people, and I love her despite all her complications, big and small. On a bicycle, by subway, or on foot, I plunge down her bustling, narrow streets, I cross her from *rive* to *arrondissement*, ready to discover what she has in store for me: a conversation on a café terrace, a subtitled Korean movie, a quaint covered market in an unknown neighborhood, a run along the Seine, a jaunt around the city at the first signs of spring. The whole world dreams of paying her a visit; I, in turn, dream of seeing the world. As a child, atlases made me want to zoom out, to encounter faraway places, to imagine alternatives to the life I led, to travel even farther west and move beyond the city my family claimed as home.

Hello, New York. The first time she and I meet, I am five and I am dwarfed by the Big Apple. Later, as a teenager, I experience an exhilarating feeling of sensory overload before the never-ending skyline, the limitless variety of perspectives: Art Deco and Neo-Gothic buildings rising up side by side; the giant shadows of skyscrapers; the bold mix of culinary traditions; the wild enthusiasm of her inhabitants. Like a siren, New York calls to me. In 2010, I decide to live there for a few months to discover whether I can make her mine.

I sit in the New York subway, the train hurtling downtown as a tunnel swallows up the sound of screeching wheels, the air conditioning set at a chilly sixty degrees. I watch the people around me, sketching some poses in my notebook: a worker in coveralls snoozes in his seat; an office girl chats with her colleague, a coffee in hand. Ideas come, go, and come again. I write some down, forget others. I draw an espresso cup facing a giant coffee to go; a bent-over old lady facing a grandmother in jogging pants... A series of pairs take shape on the page, comparisons that I instantly want to share with family and friends, day by day. And so my **Paris versus New York** blog comes into being. Almost overnight, my work becomes a sort of tapestry, weaving connections between travelers, dreamers, and romantics alike. The universal appeal these two cultural capitals have takes me by surprise, and soon more paired images take shape and the blog turns into an experiment for the book you now hold in your hands.

This friendly visual match is dedicated to all lovers of Paris, of New York, and to those who are torn between the two.

vahram muratyan
July 23, 2011

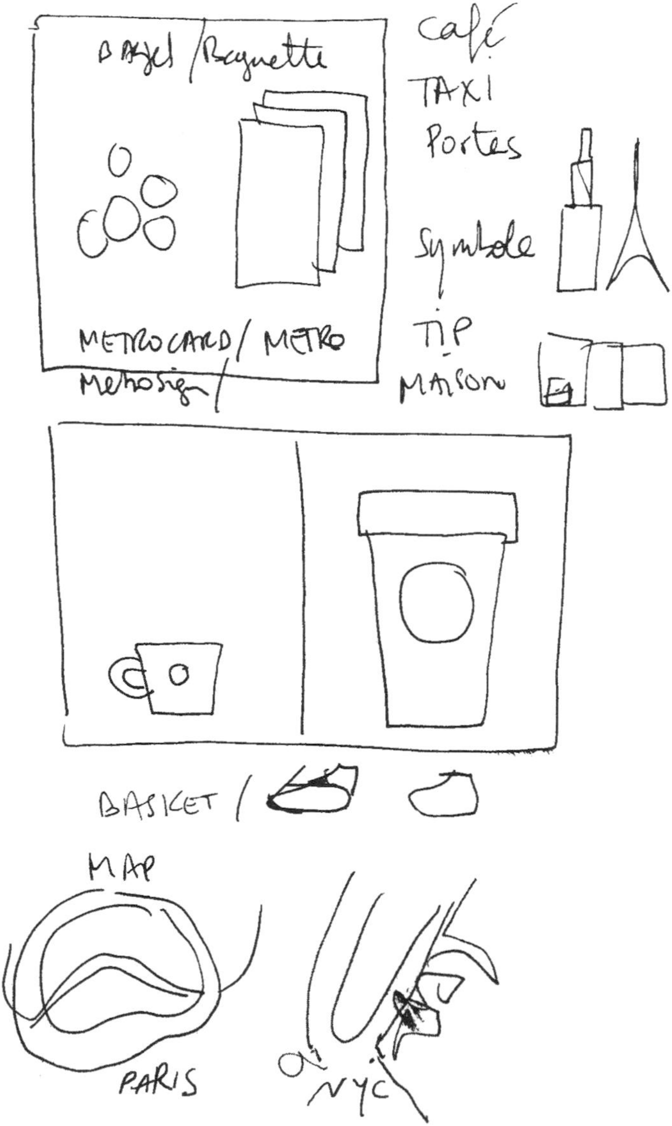
BAGEL / Baguette
METROCARD / METRO
Metrosign /
café
TAXI
Portes
Symbole
TIP
MAISON
BASKET /
MAP
PARIS
NYC

Paris versus New York

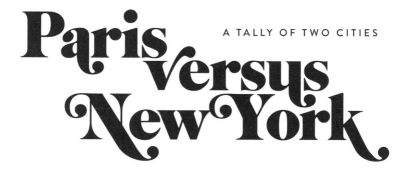

A TALLY OF TWO CITIES

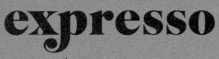

expresso

assis en terrasse

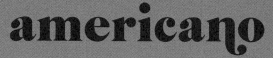

americano

keep walking

quotidien

daily

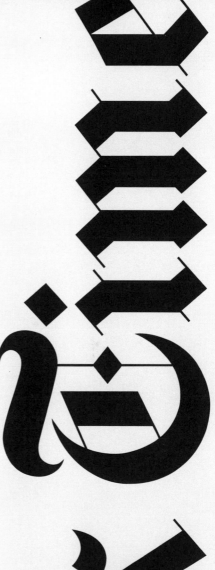

baguette

+ beurre demi-sel

bagel

+ cream cheese

orientation

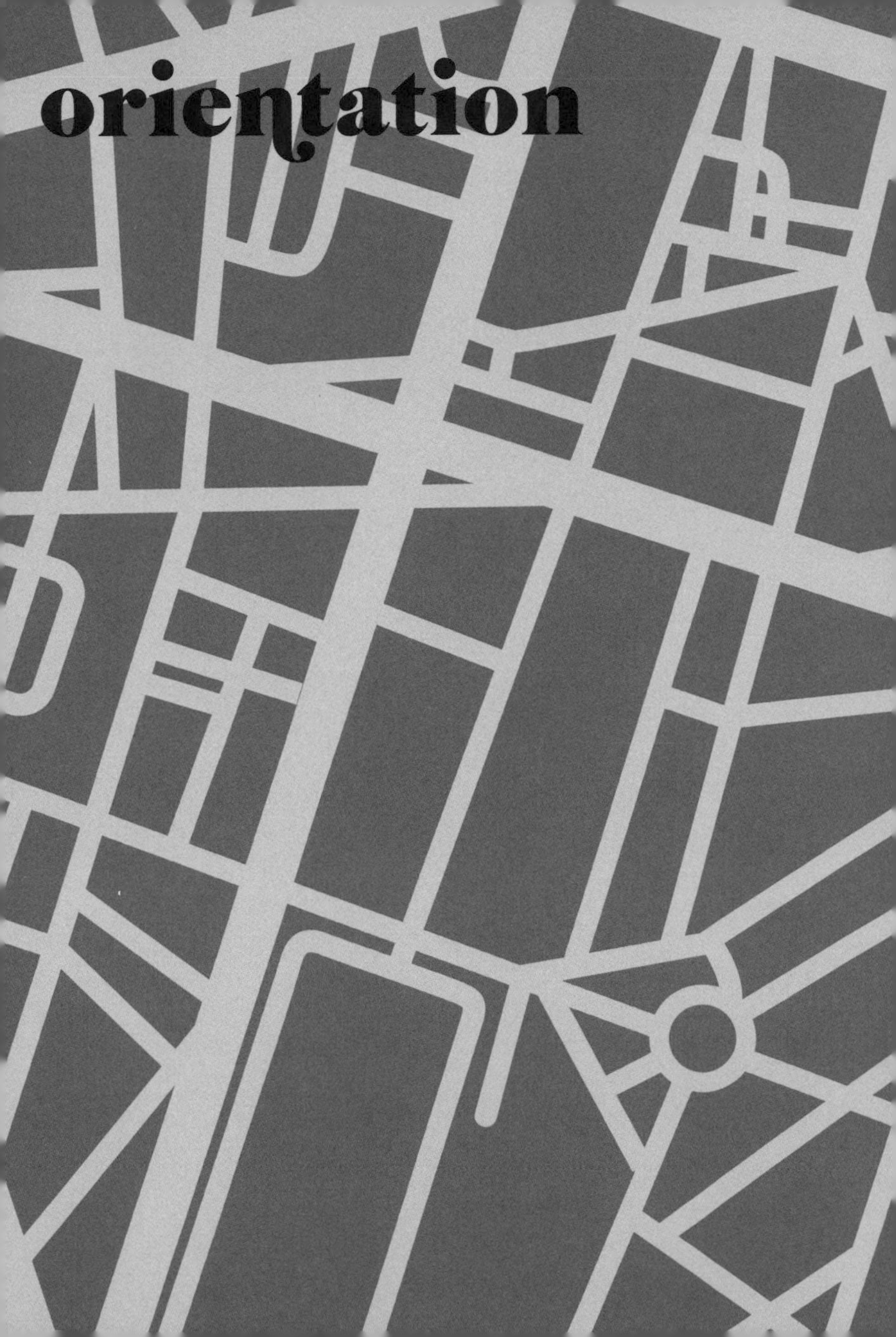

location

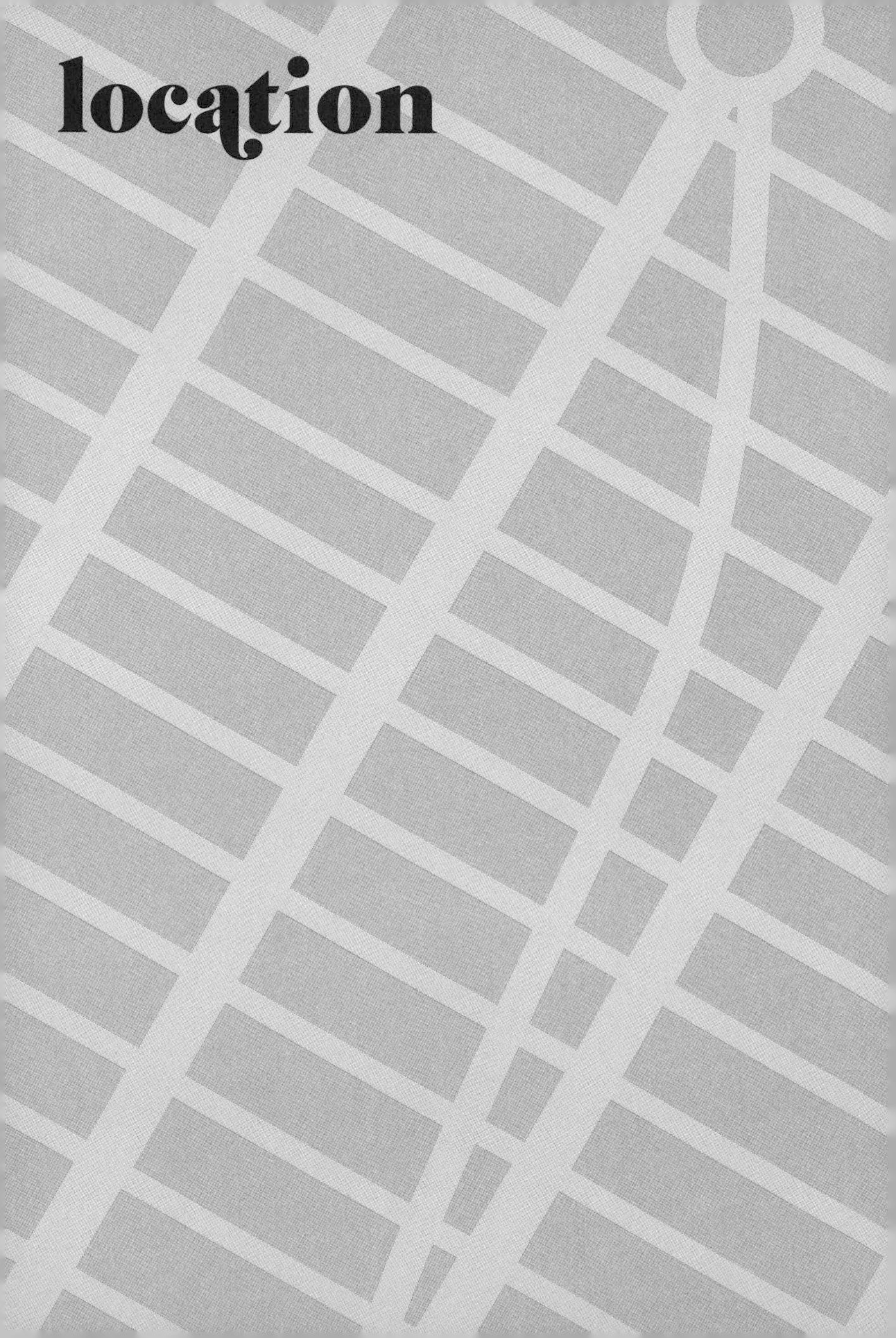

pause

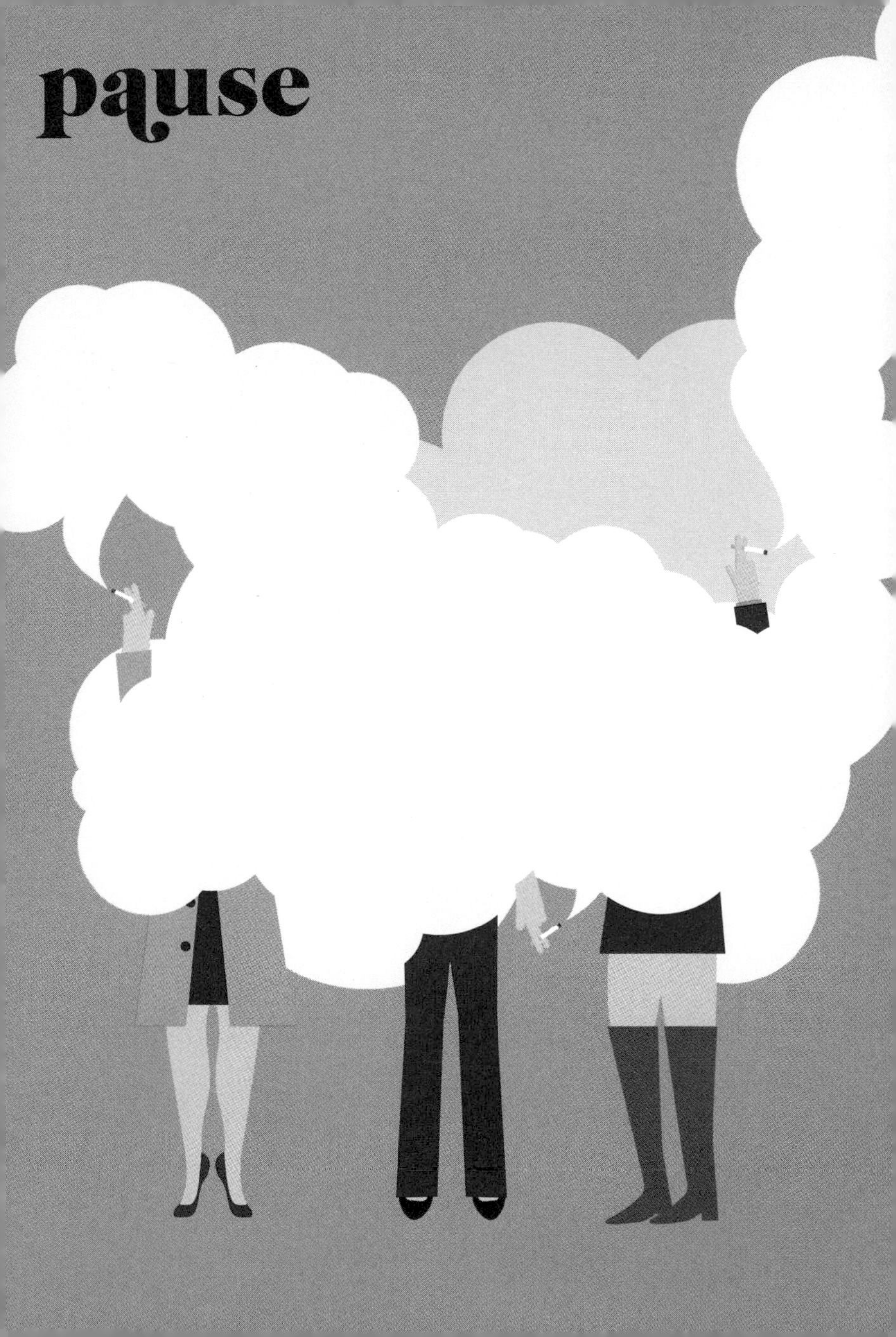

go

métro

subway

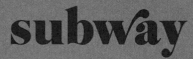

ville Lumière

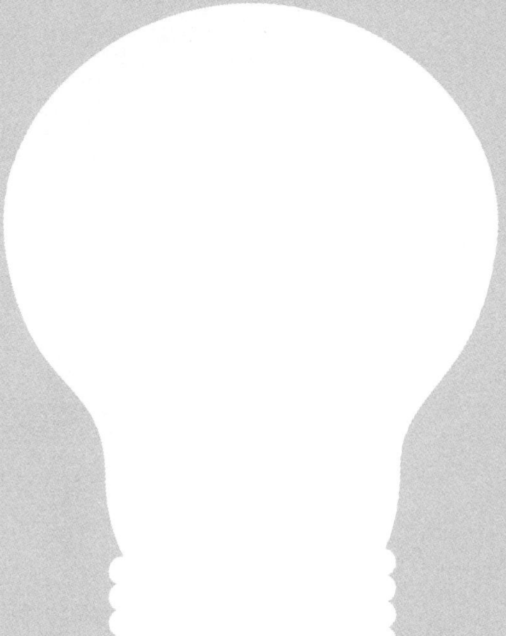

Big Apple

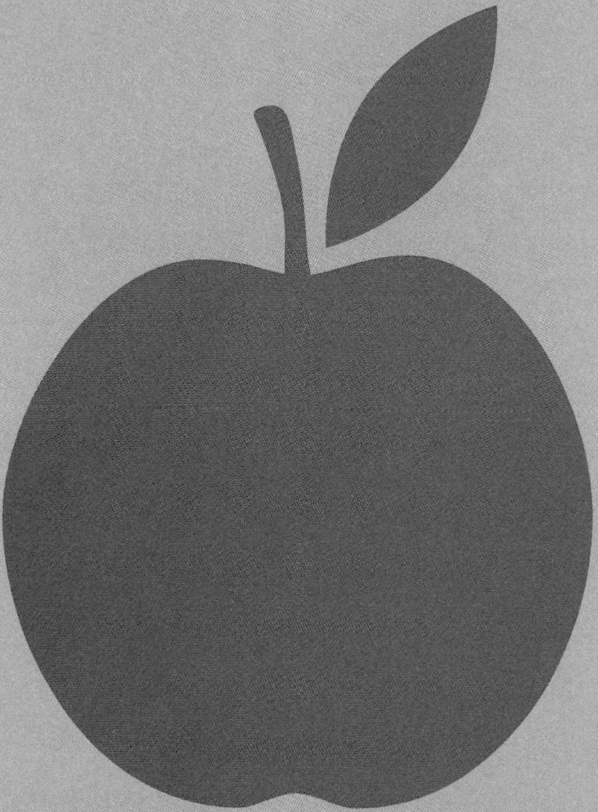

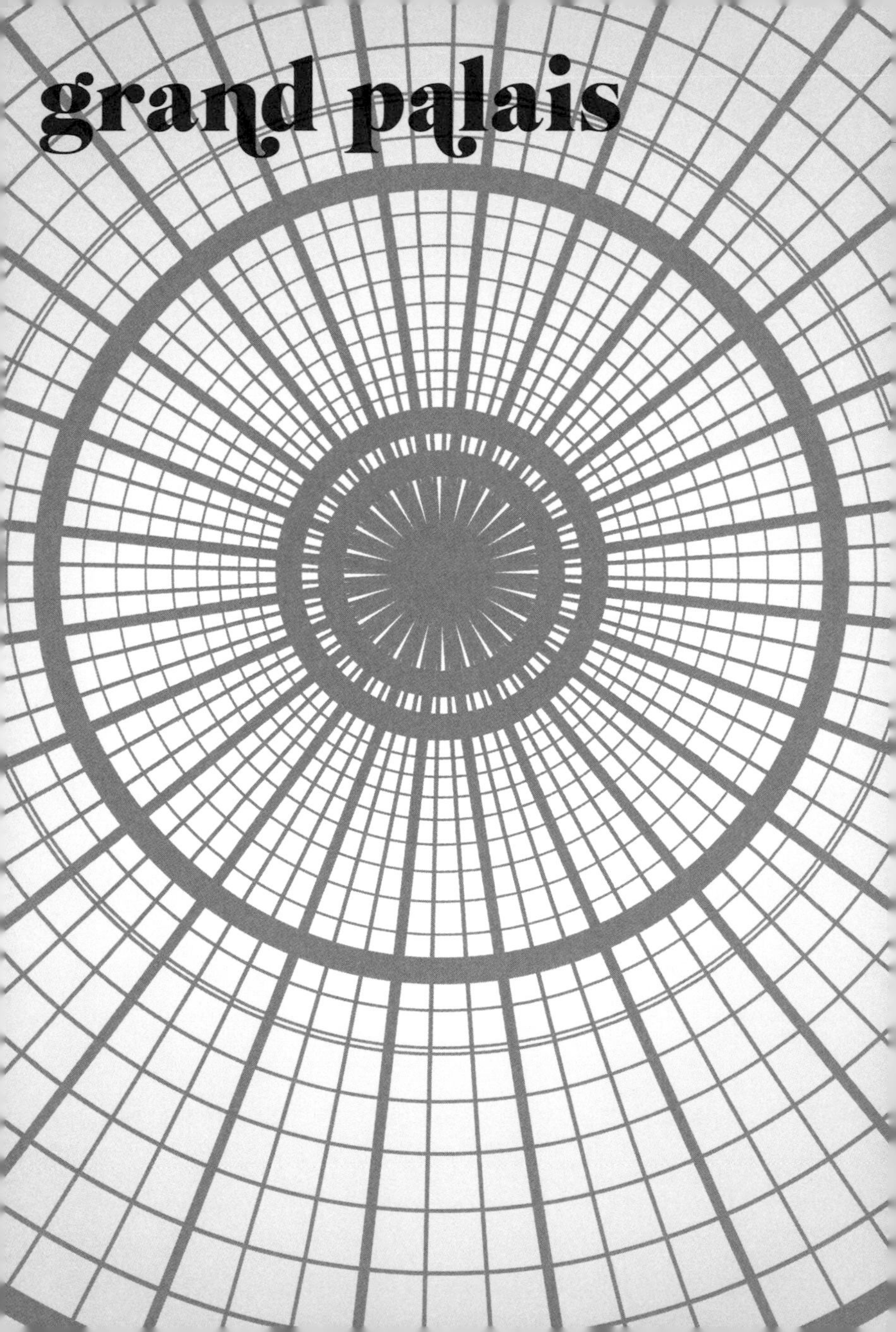
grand palais

grand central

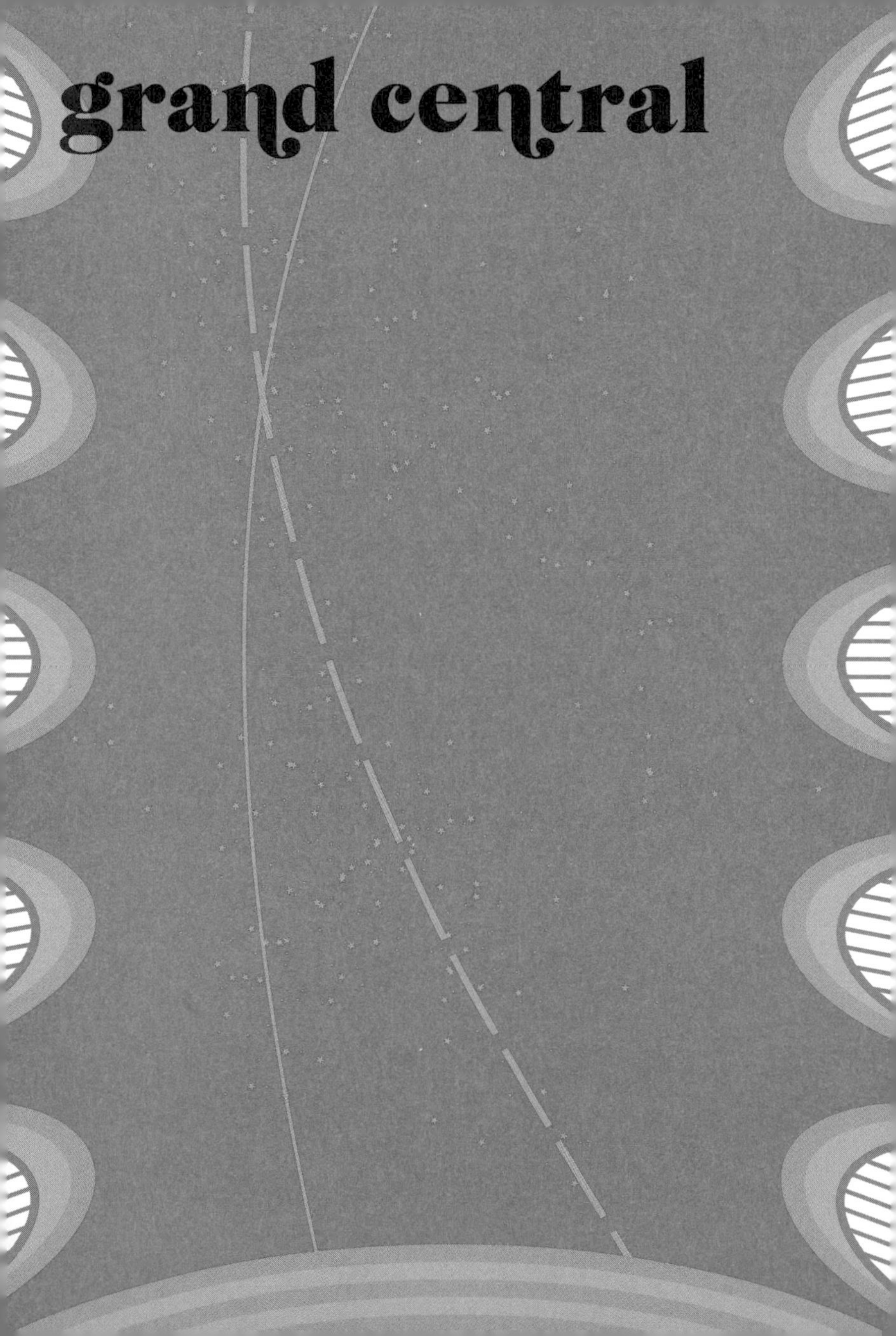

coulée verte

de la bastille au bois de vincennes

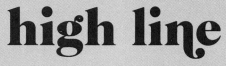

high line

from the meatpacking to midtown

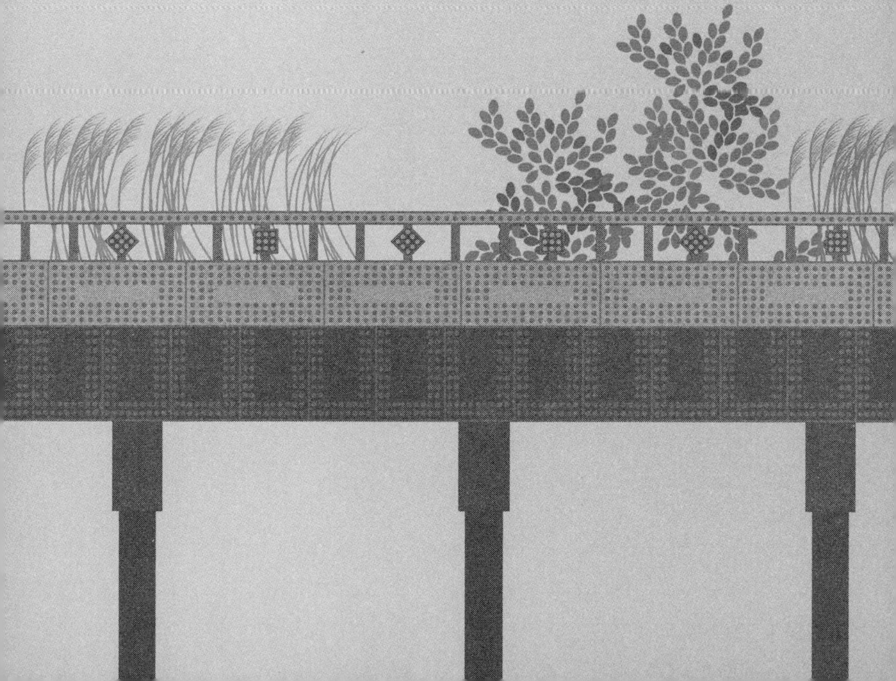

double file

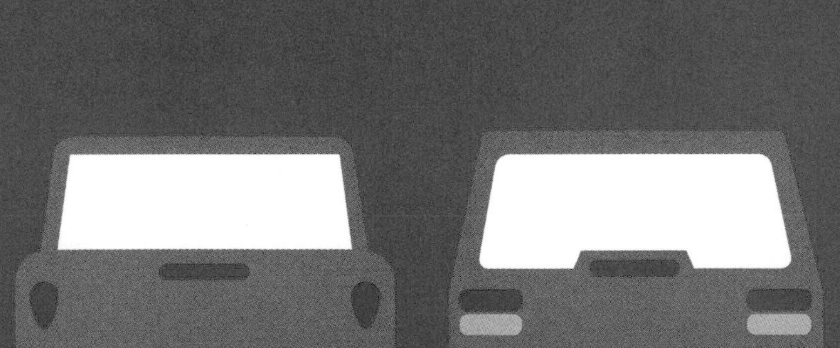

high rise

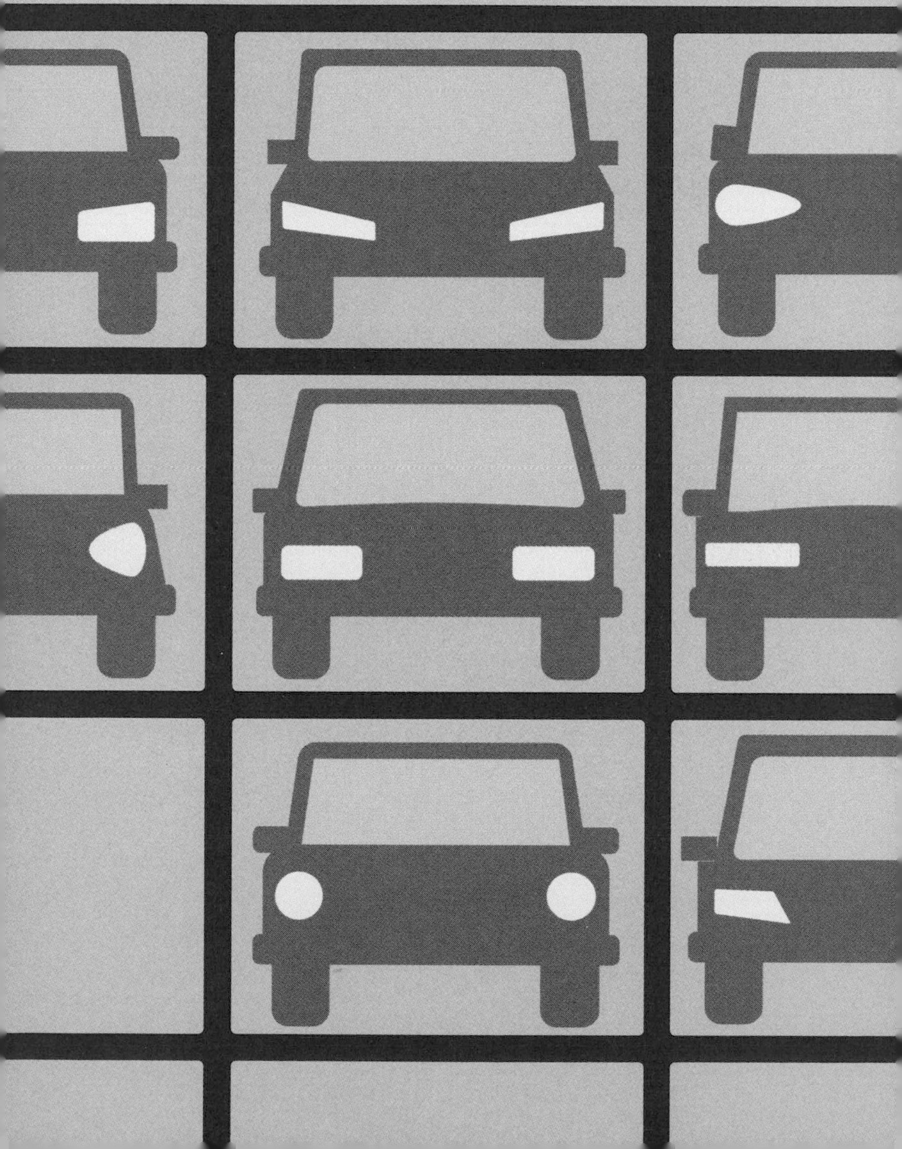

hiver

cinq centimètres et c'est la panique

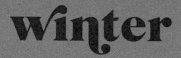

winter

alternate side parking has been suspended

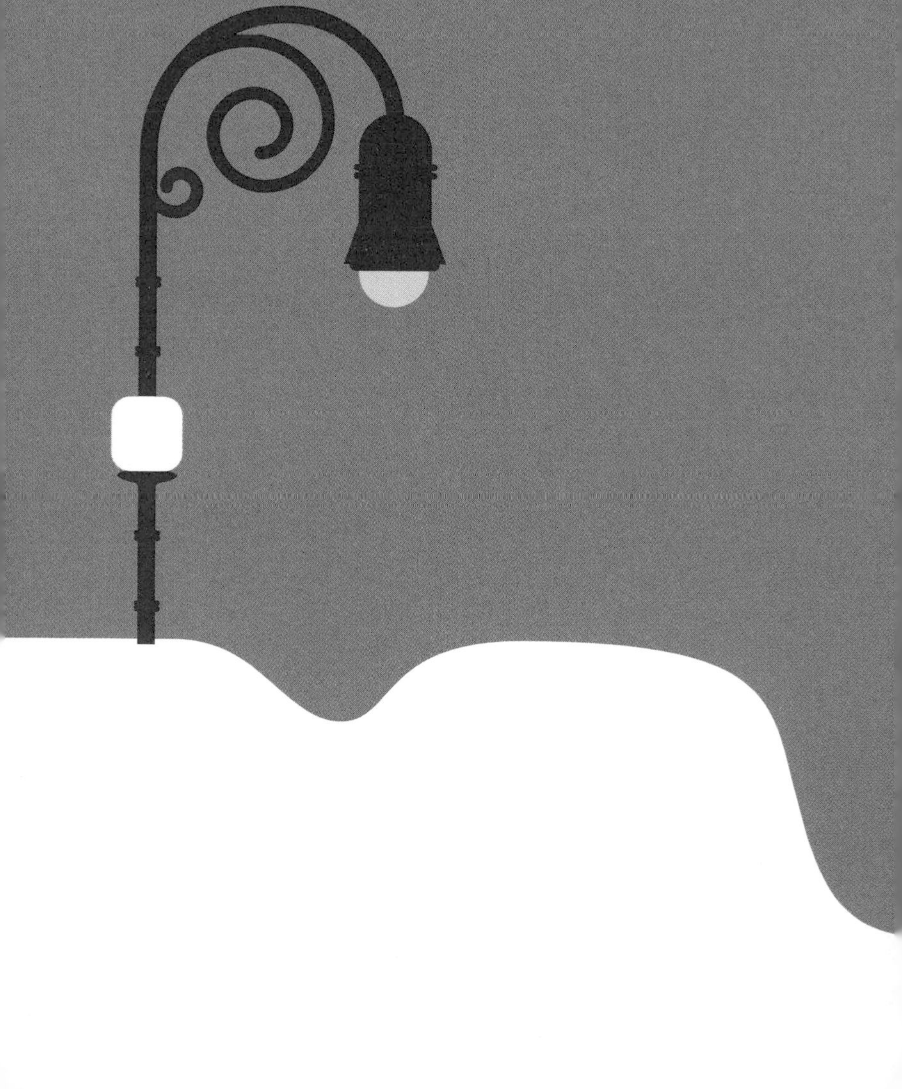

vieille dame

au parc monceau

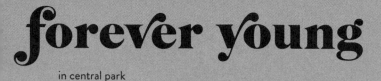

forever young

in central park

attendez

don't walk

traversez

walk

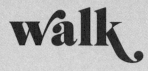

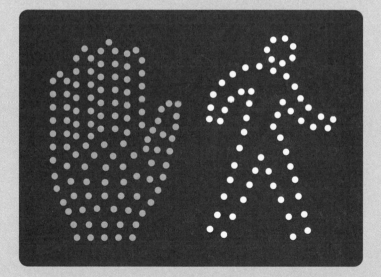

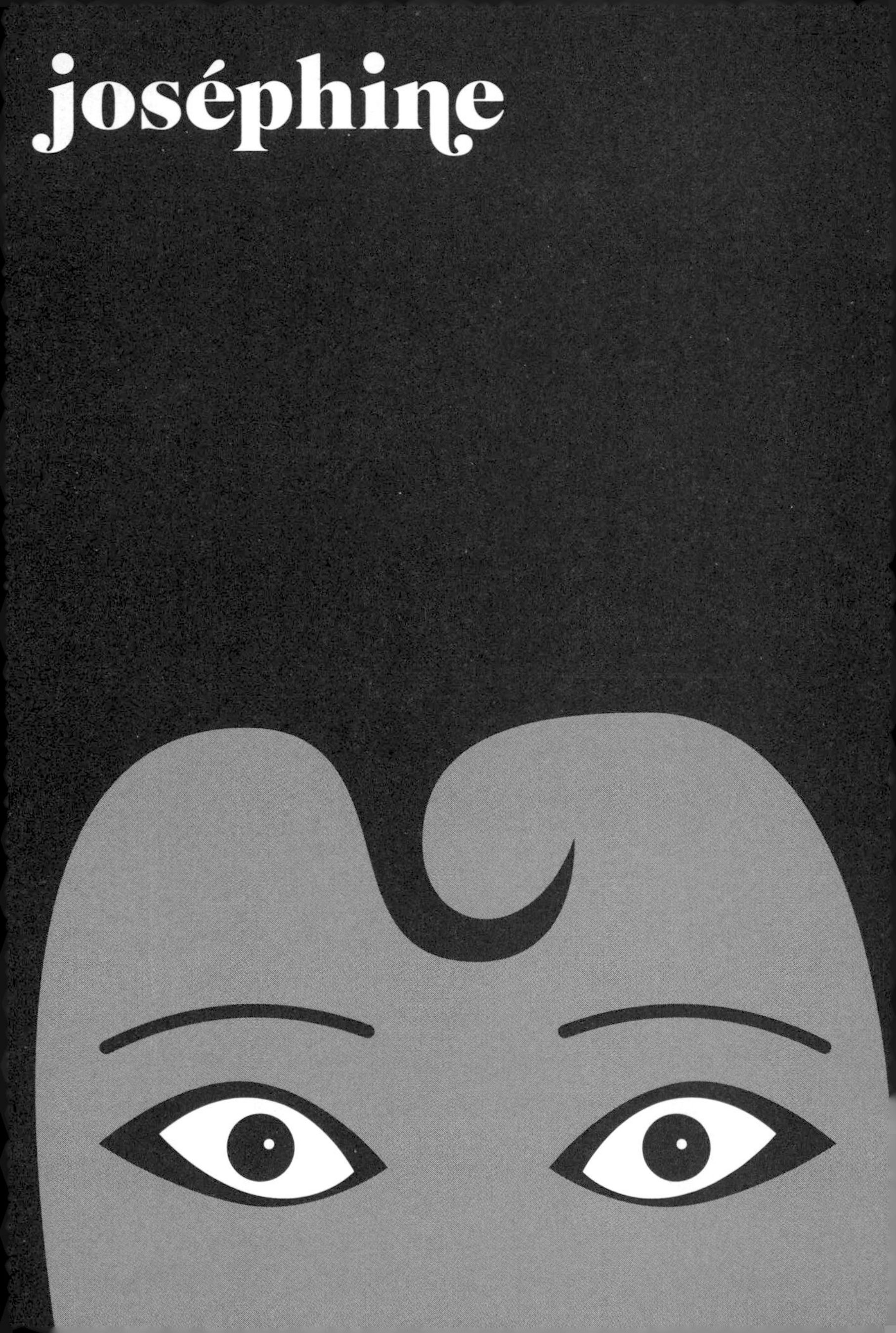
joséphine

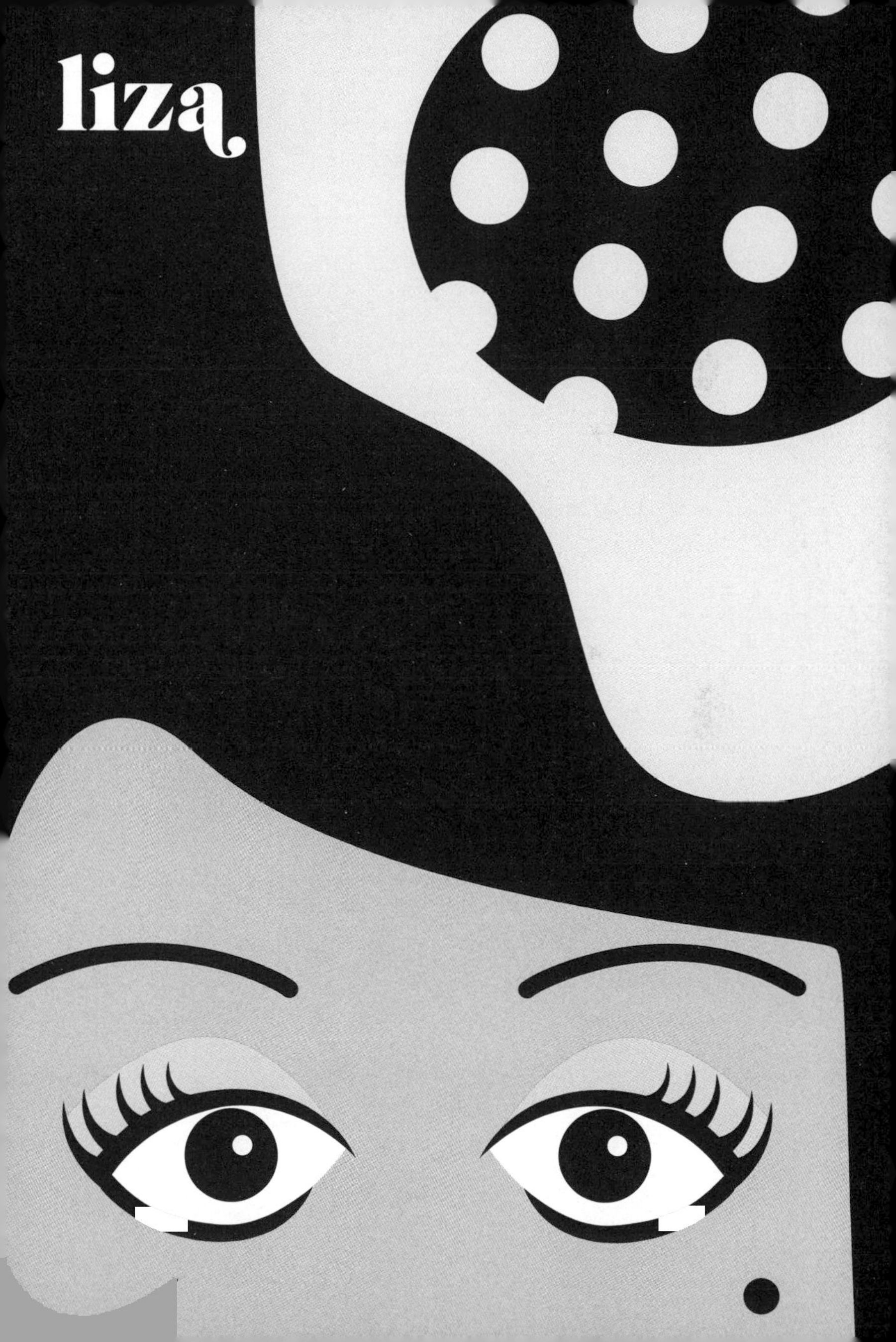
liza

pierre de taille

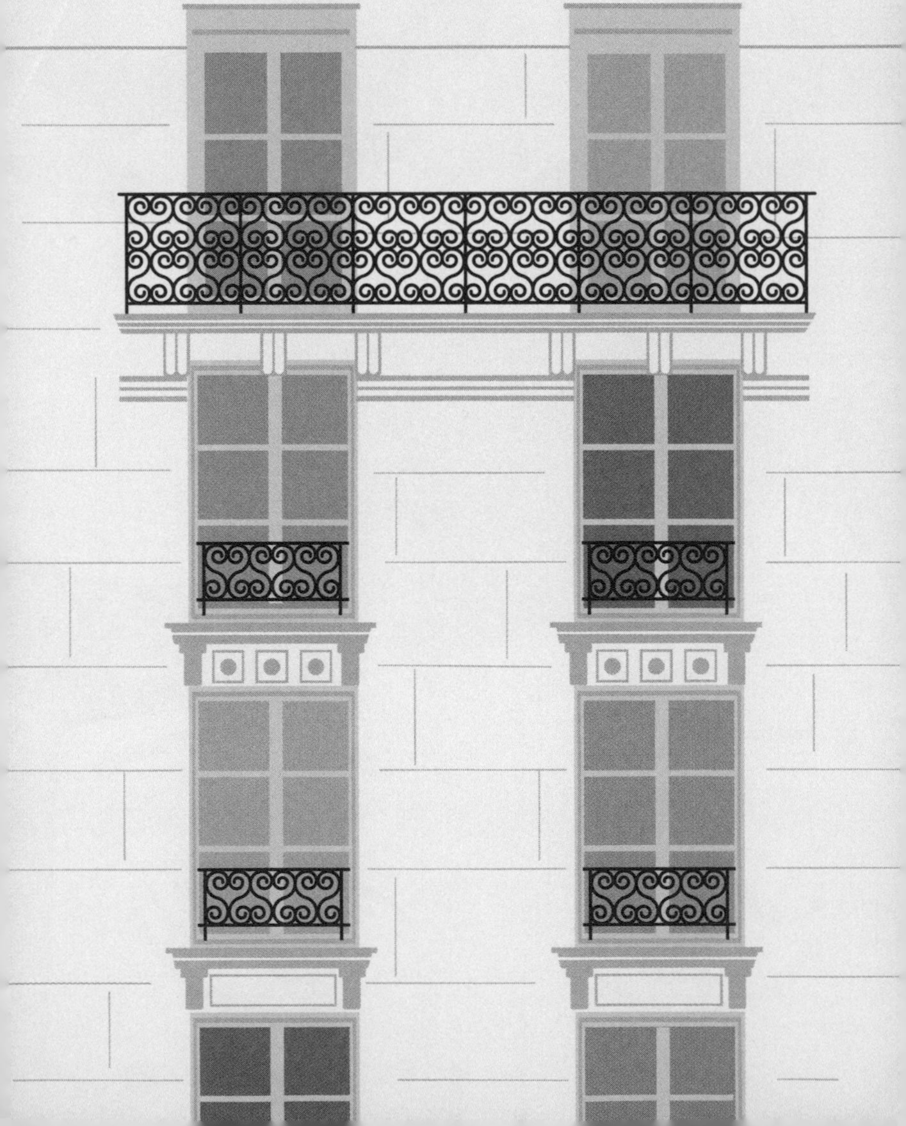

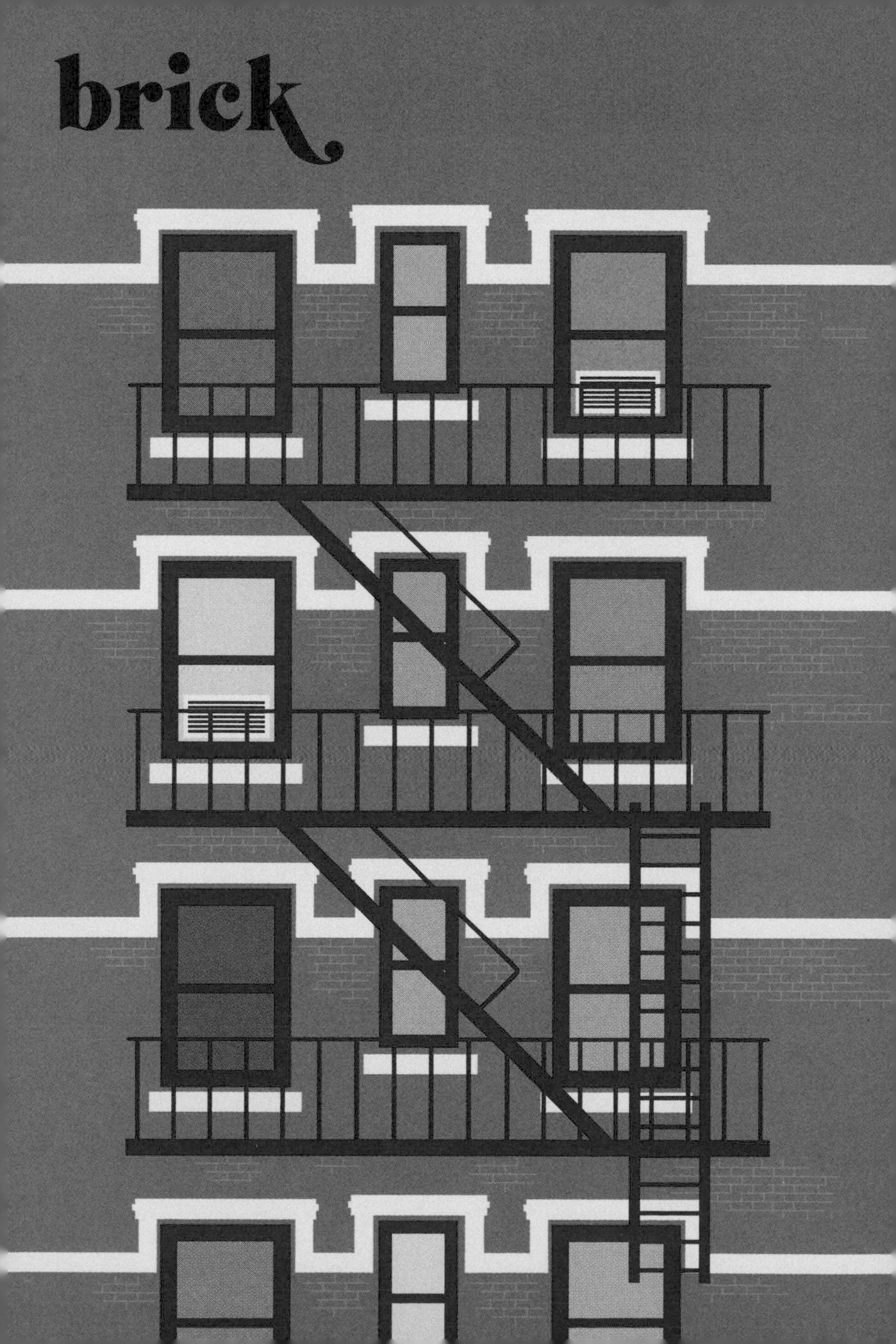
brick

amélie

à montmartre

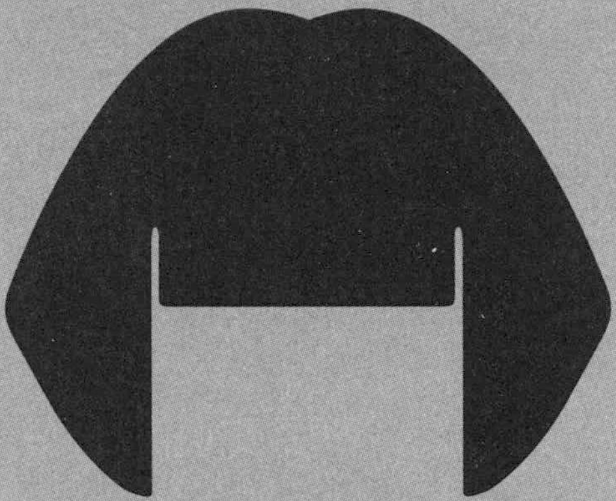

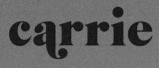

carrie

in the upper east side

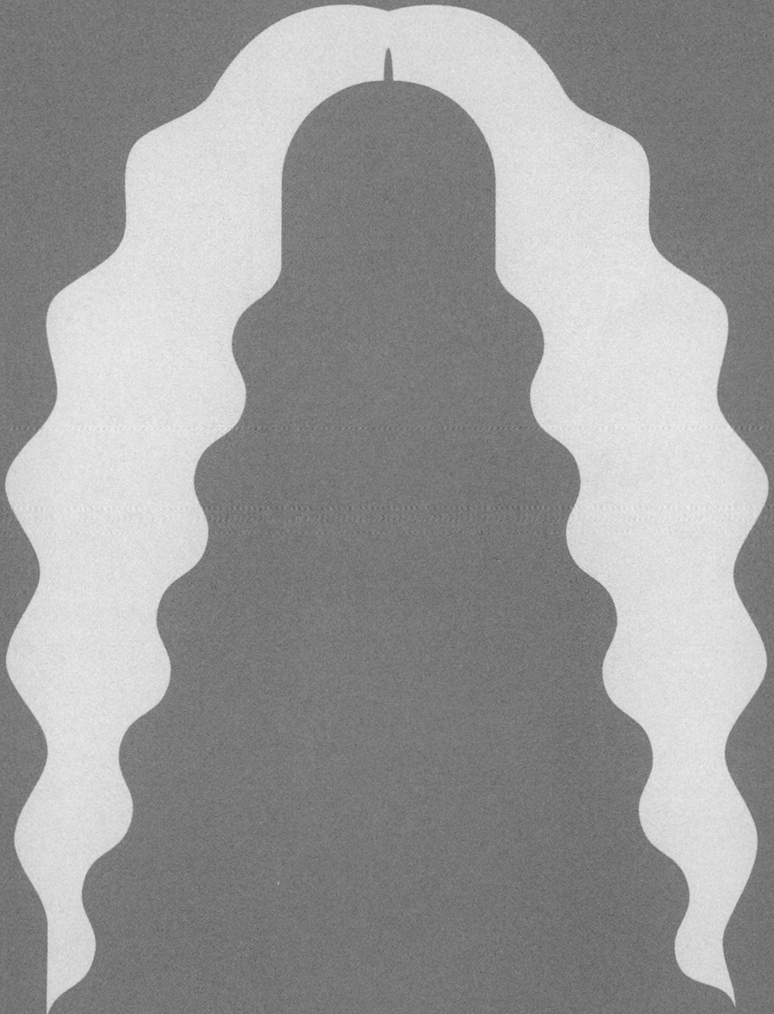

macaron

cupcake

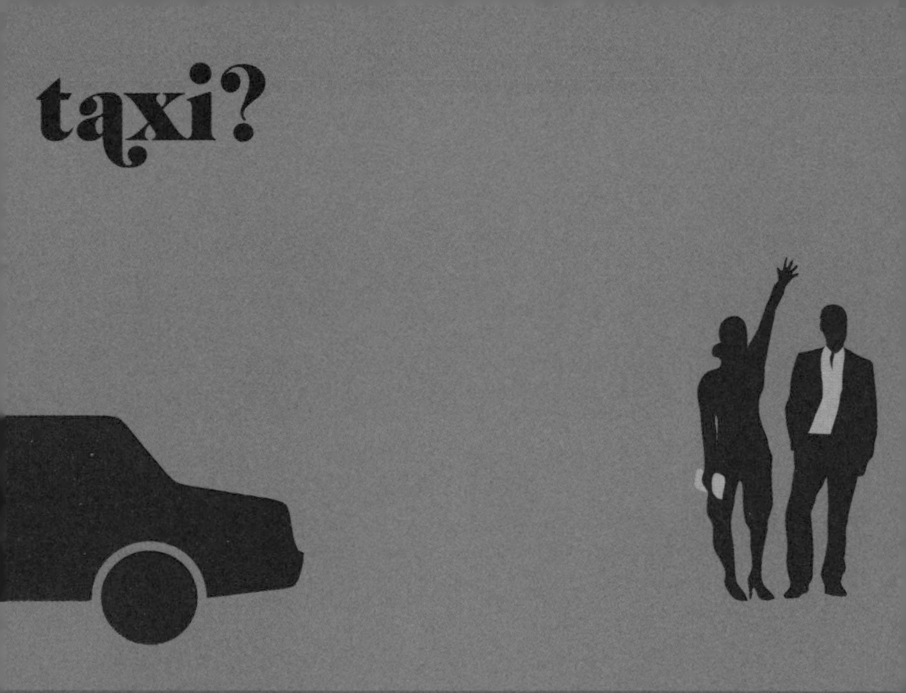
taxi?

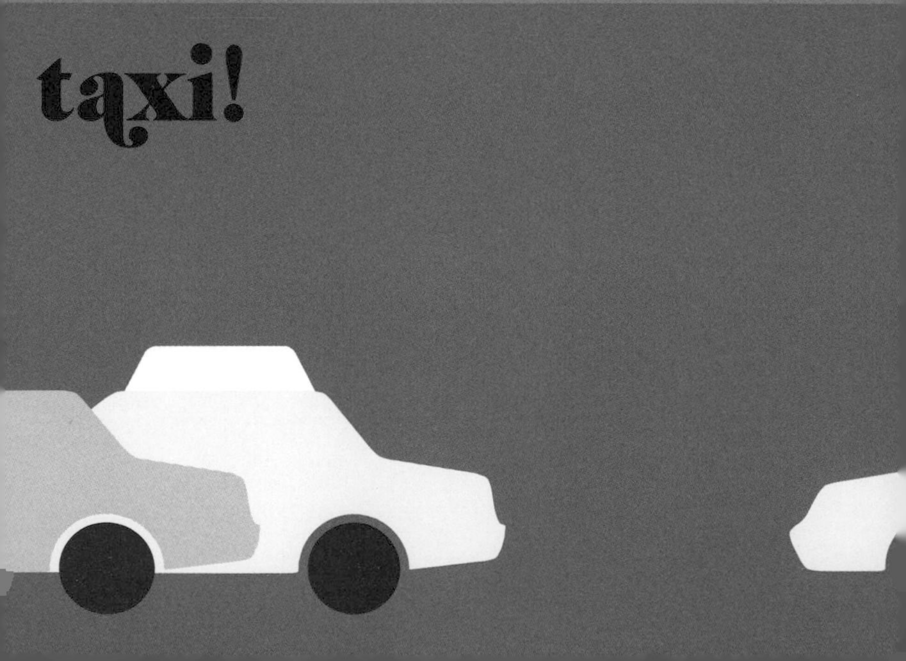
taxi!

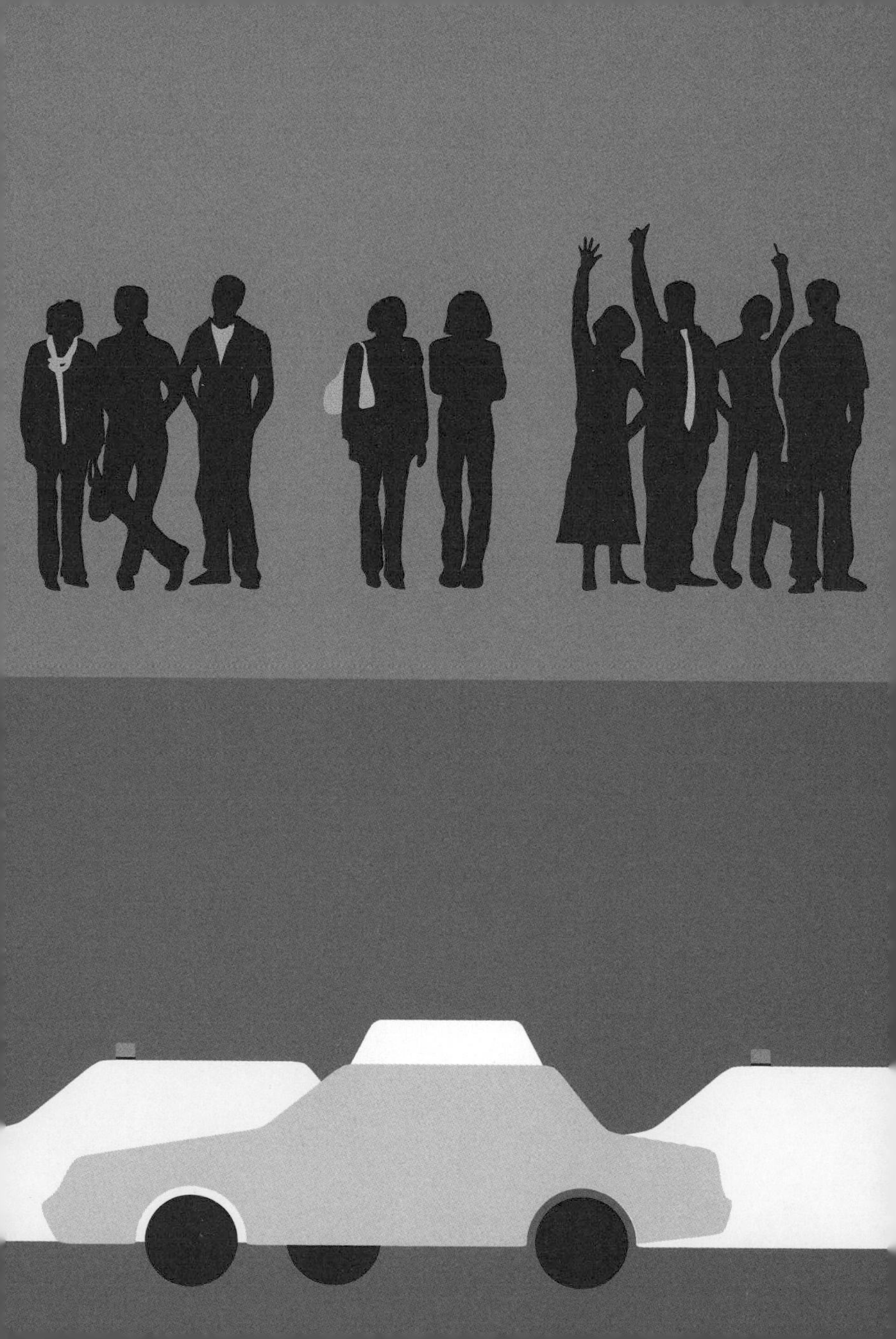

depardieu

le dernier mêtro

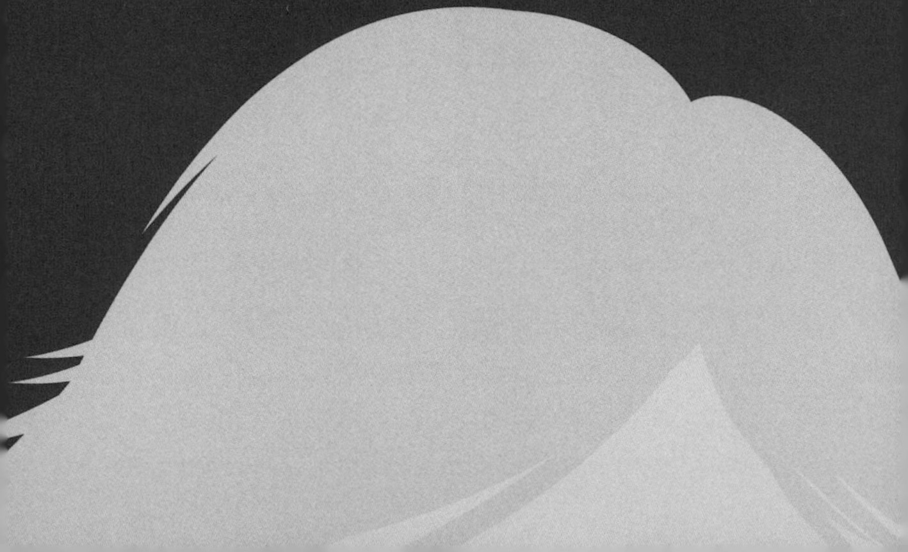

de niro

taxi driver

truffaut

les quatre cents coups

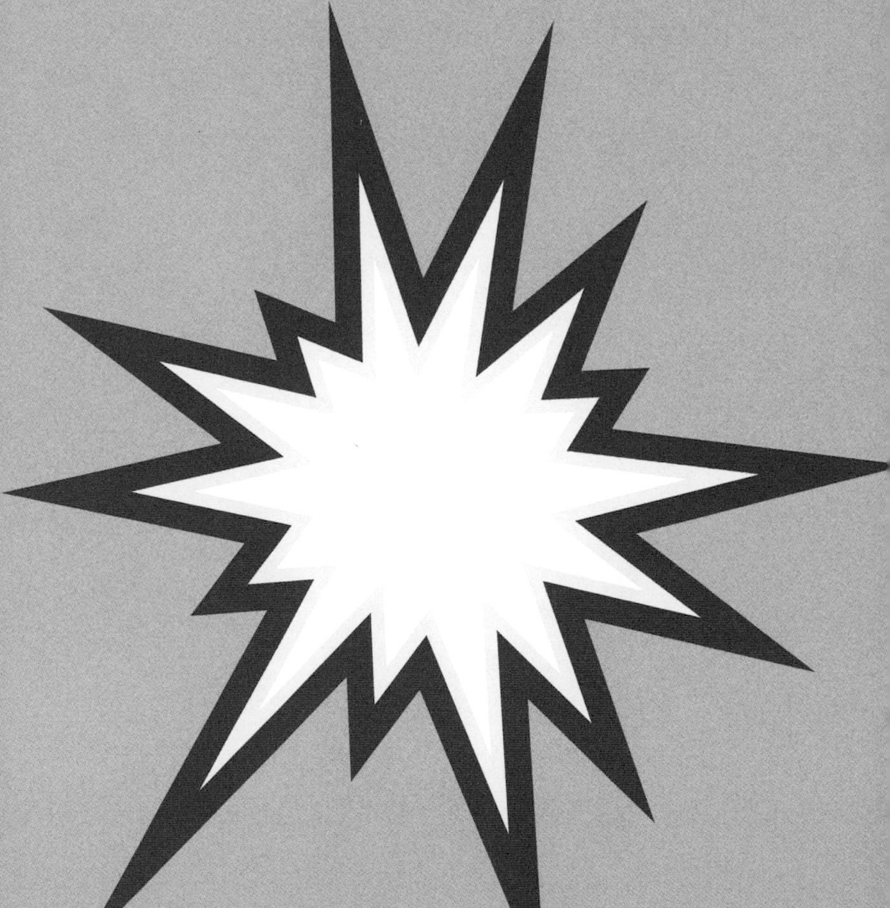

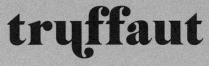

scorsese

mean streets

samedi soir

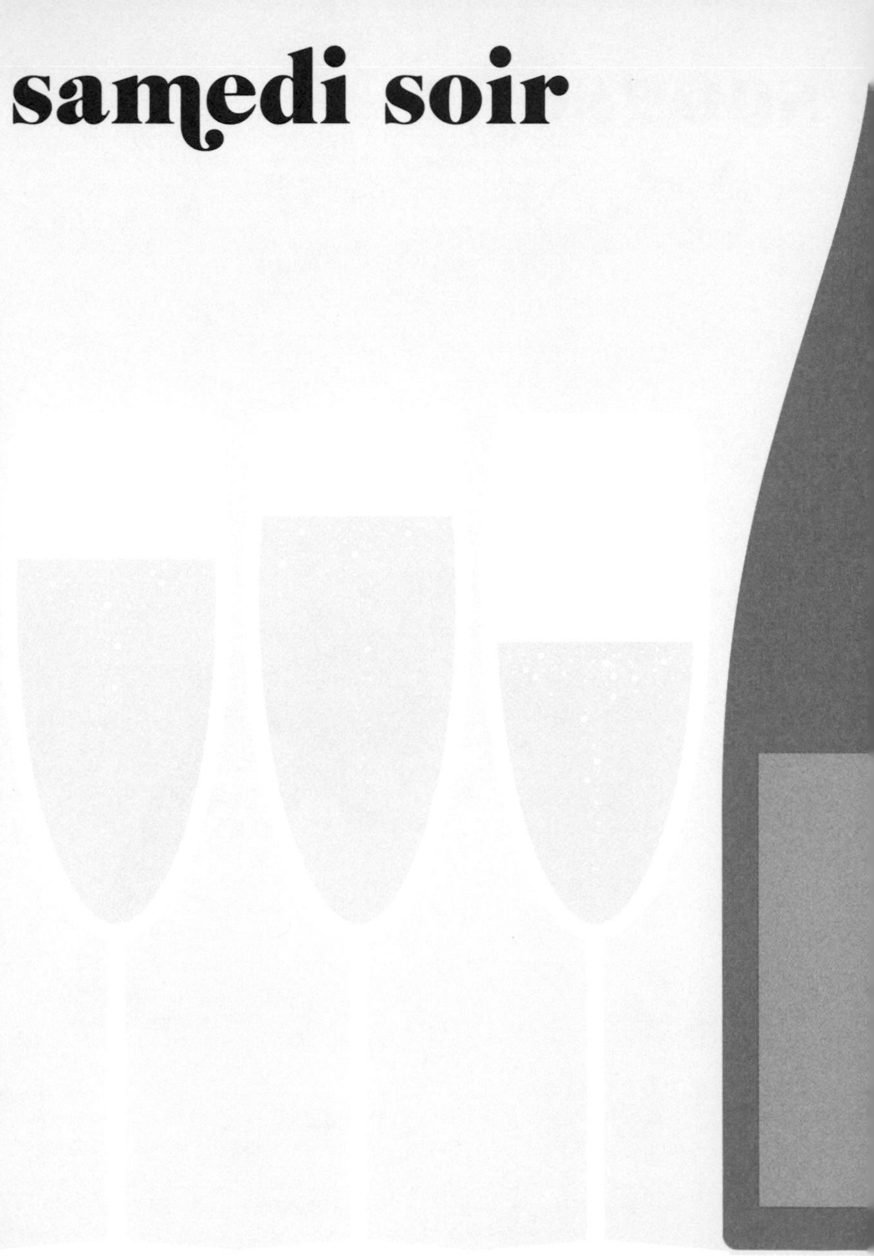

saturday night

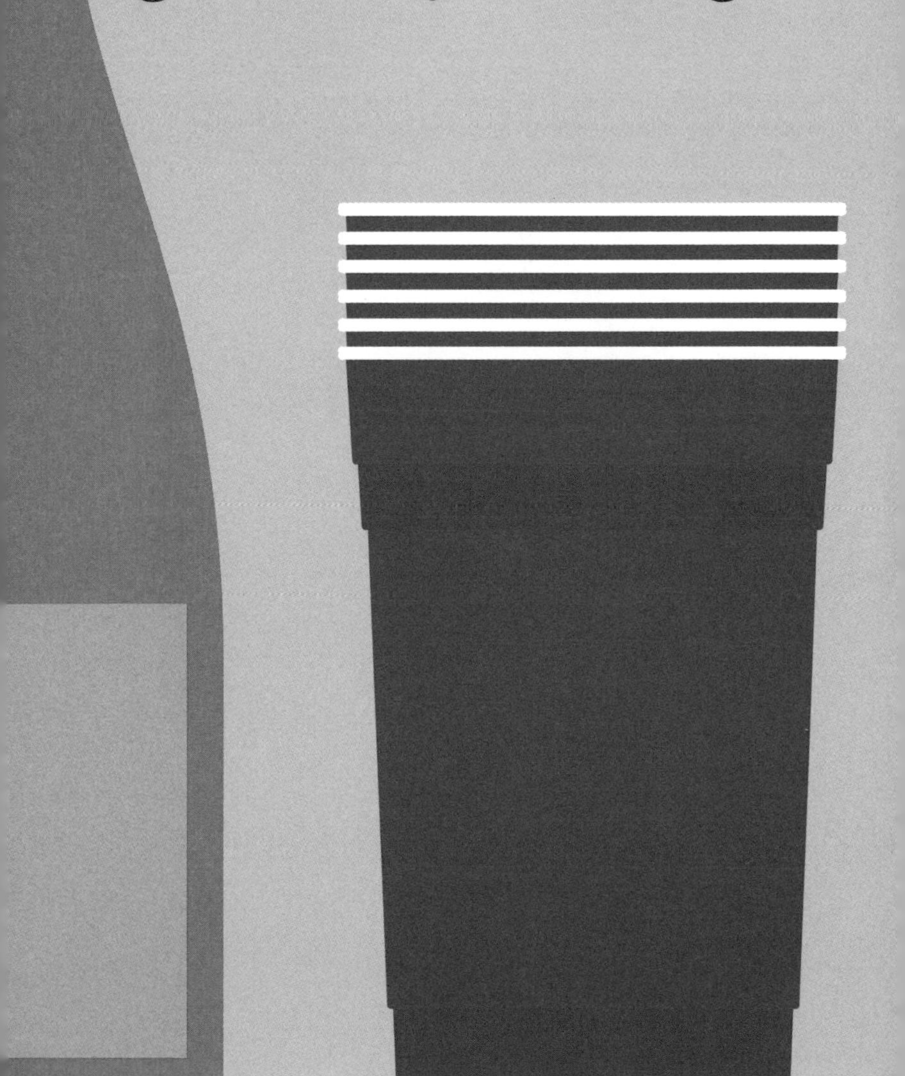

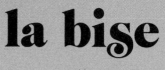

la bise

quand harry...

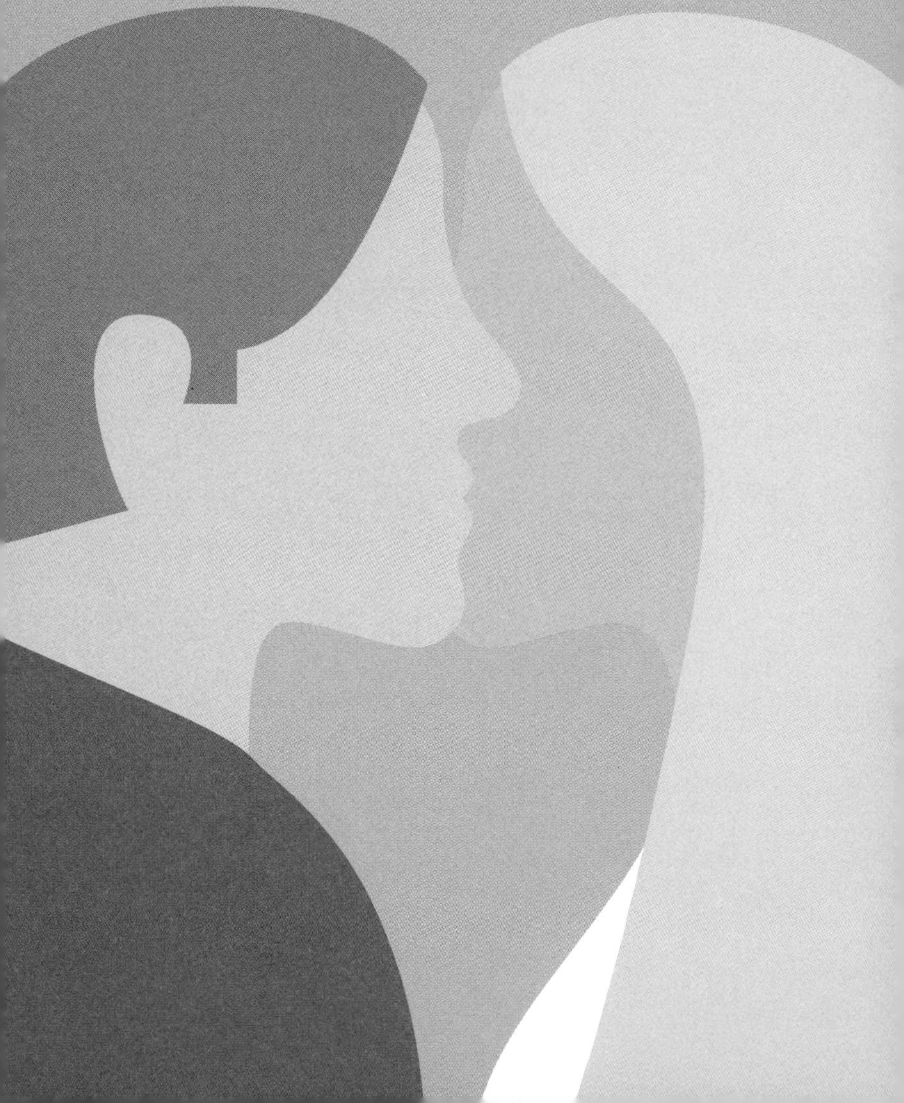

shake

...meets sally

daft punk.

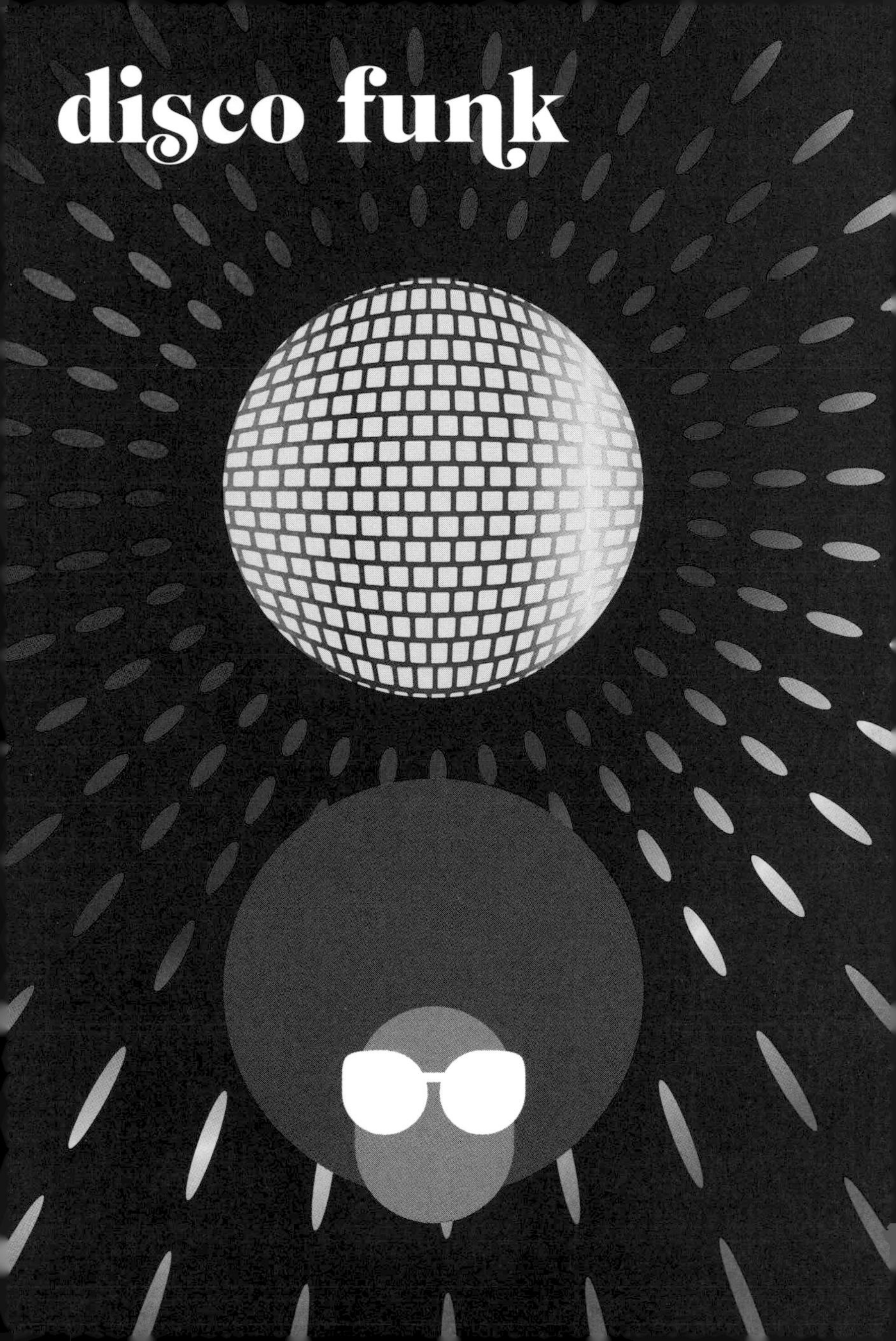
disco funk

dimanche matin

quand paris s'éveille, toutes les fêtes se terminent à la boulangerie

sunday morning

the best hangover song by the velvet underground

ventilo

lorsque la température monte au moulin rouge

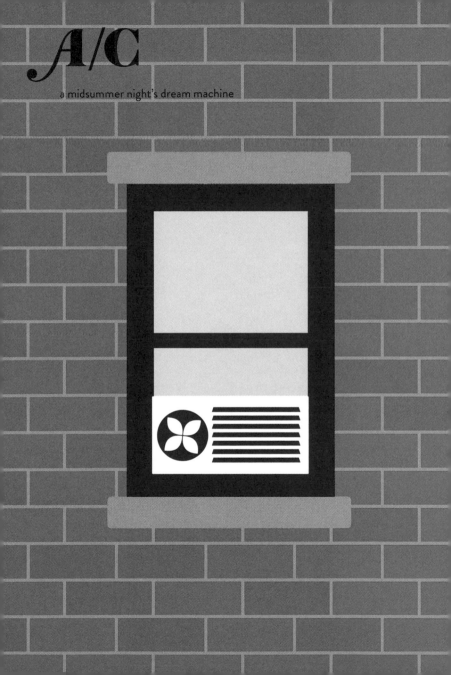

A/C

a midsummer night's dream machine

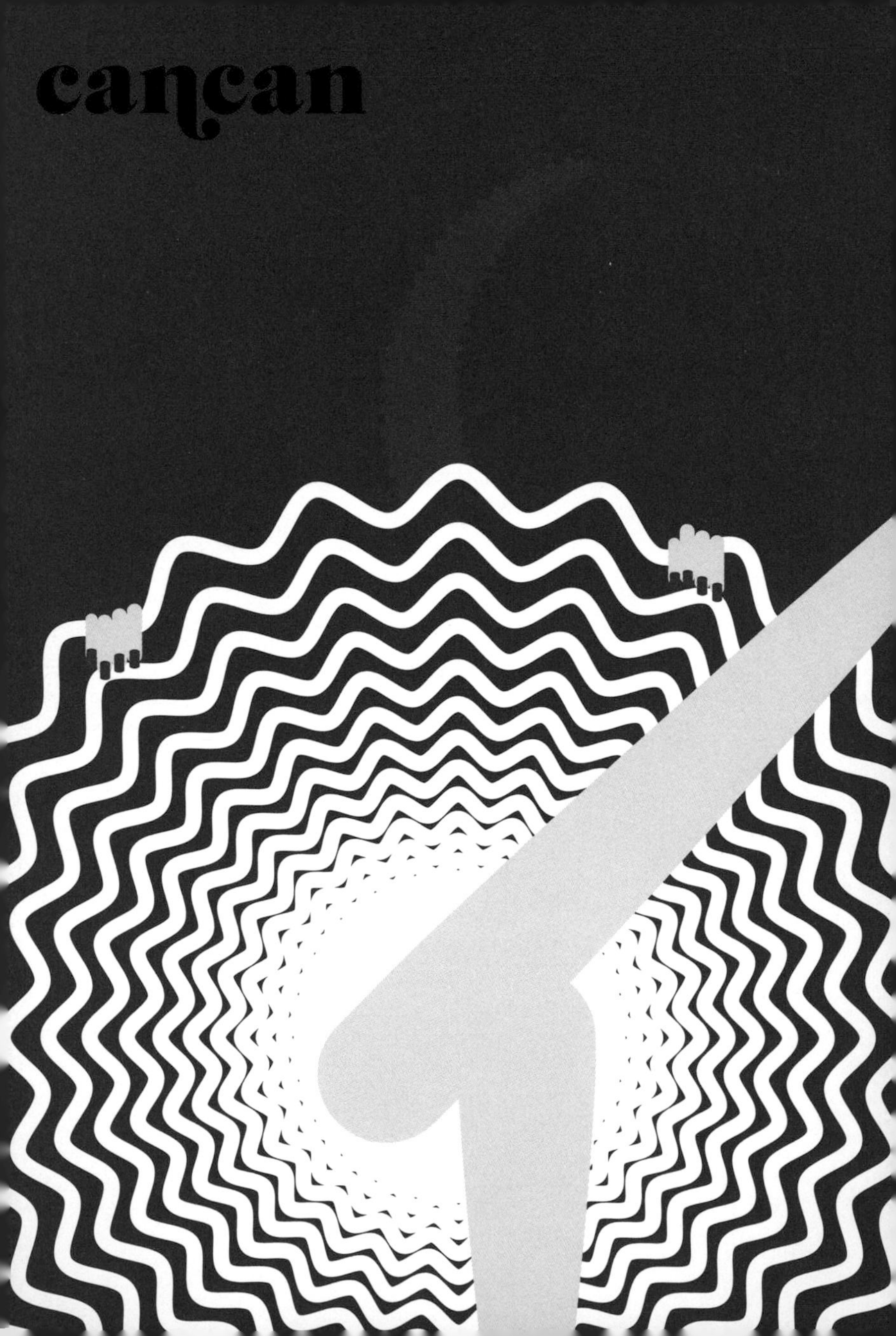
cancan

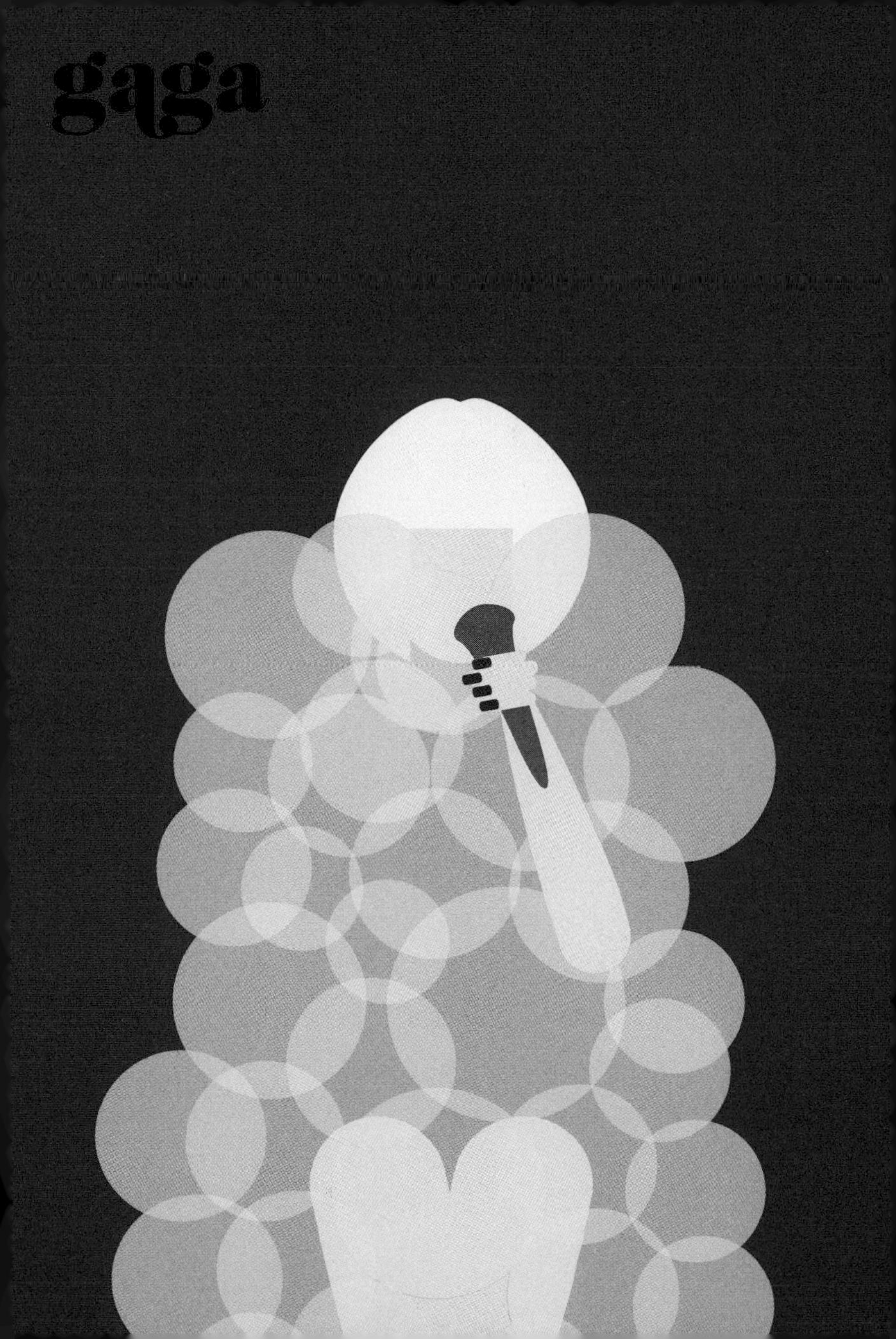
gaga

tabac

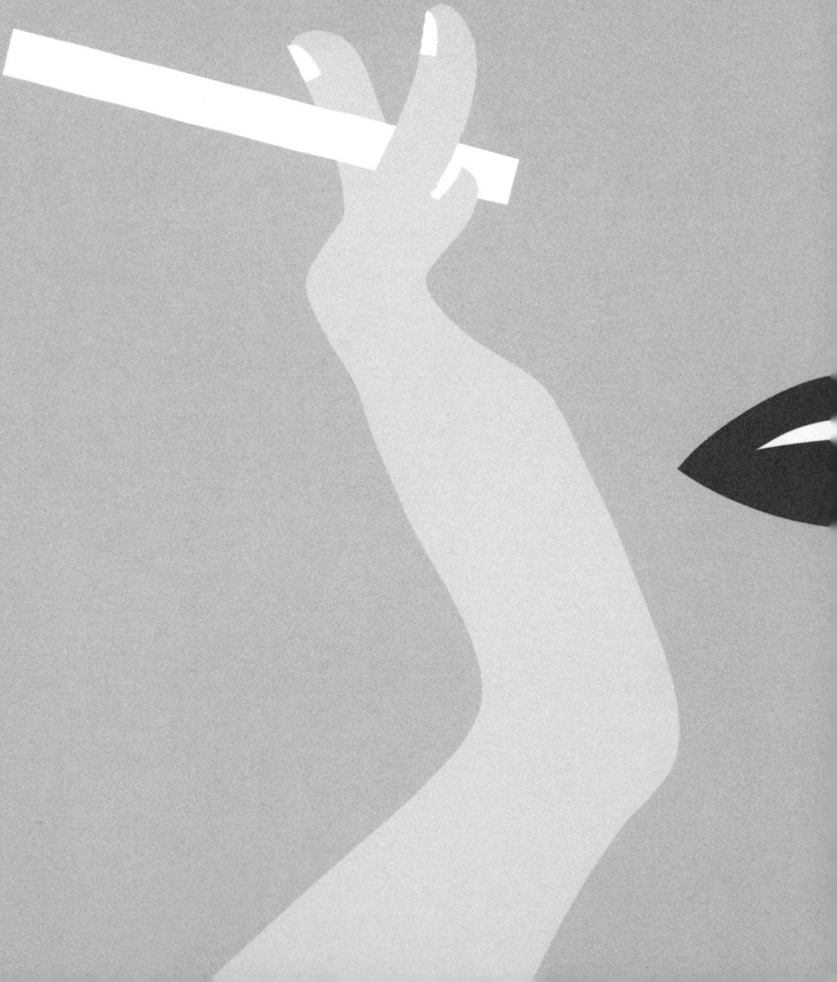

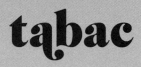

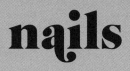

nails

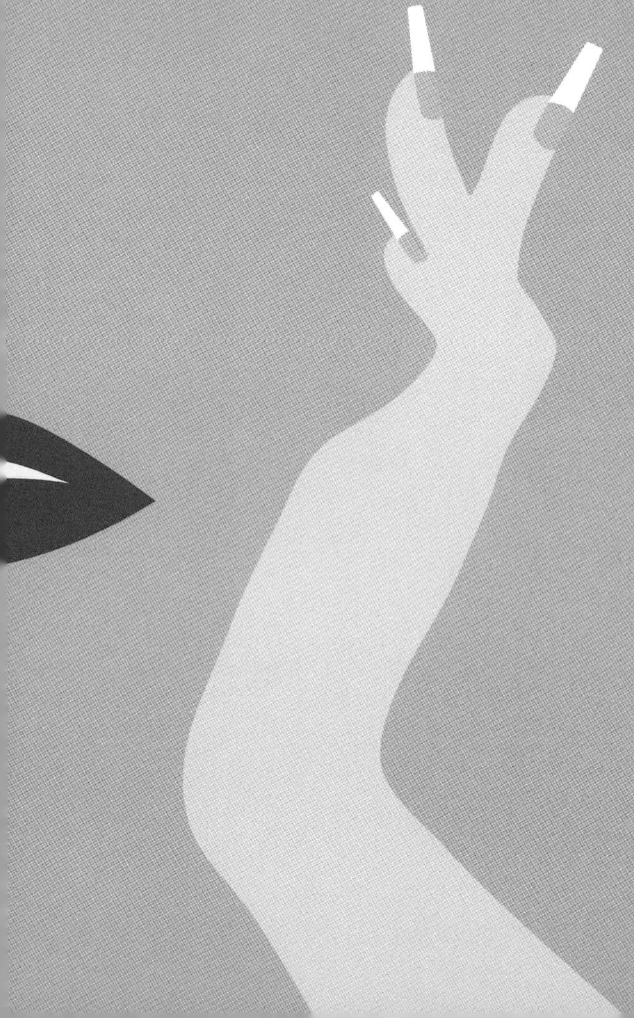

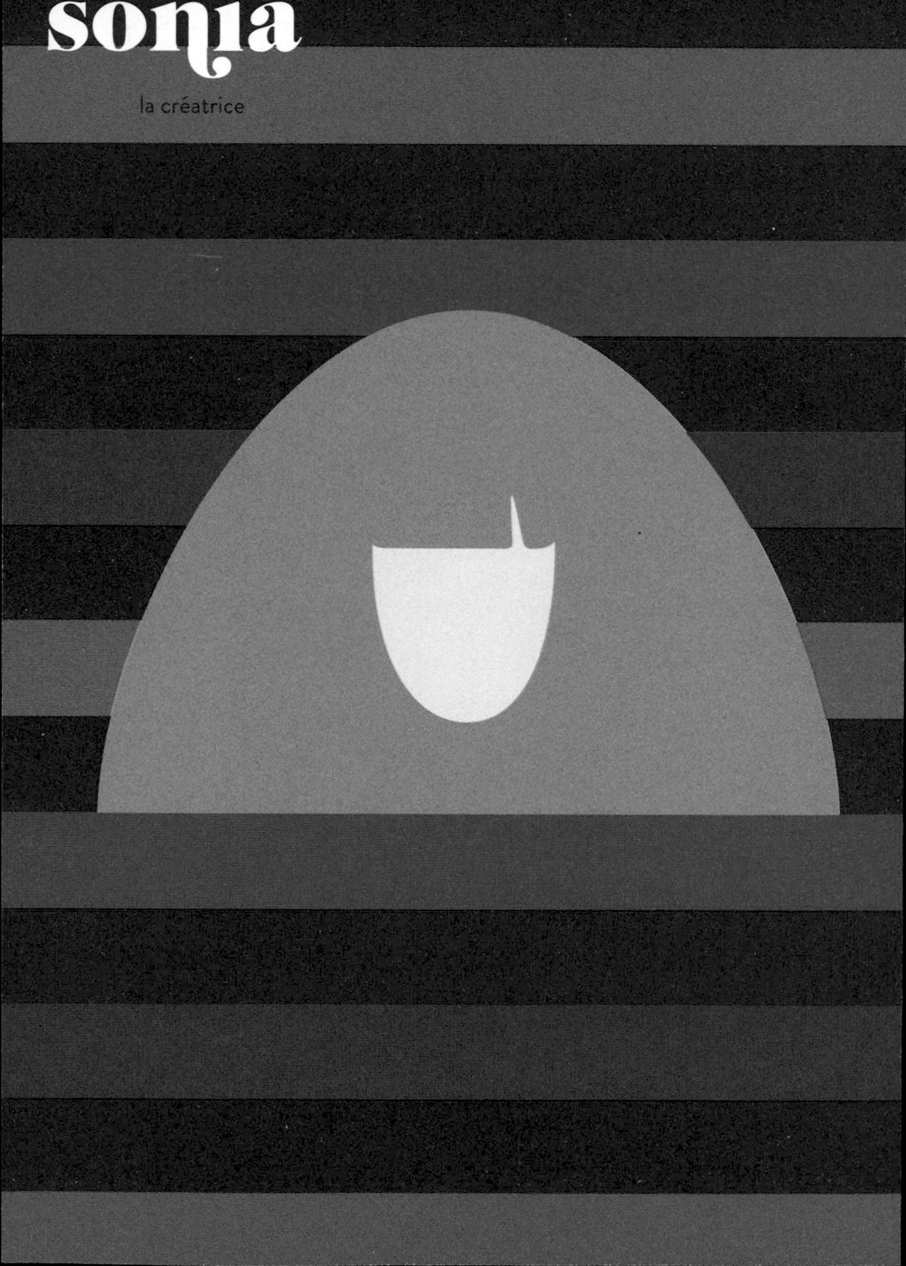
sonia
la créatrice

anna

the critic

bobo

dans l'est parisien

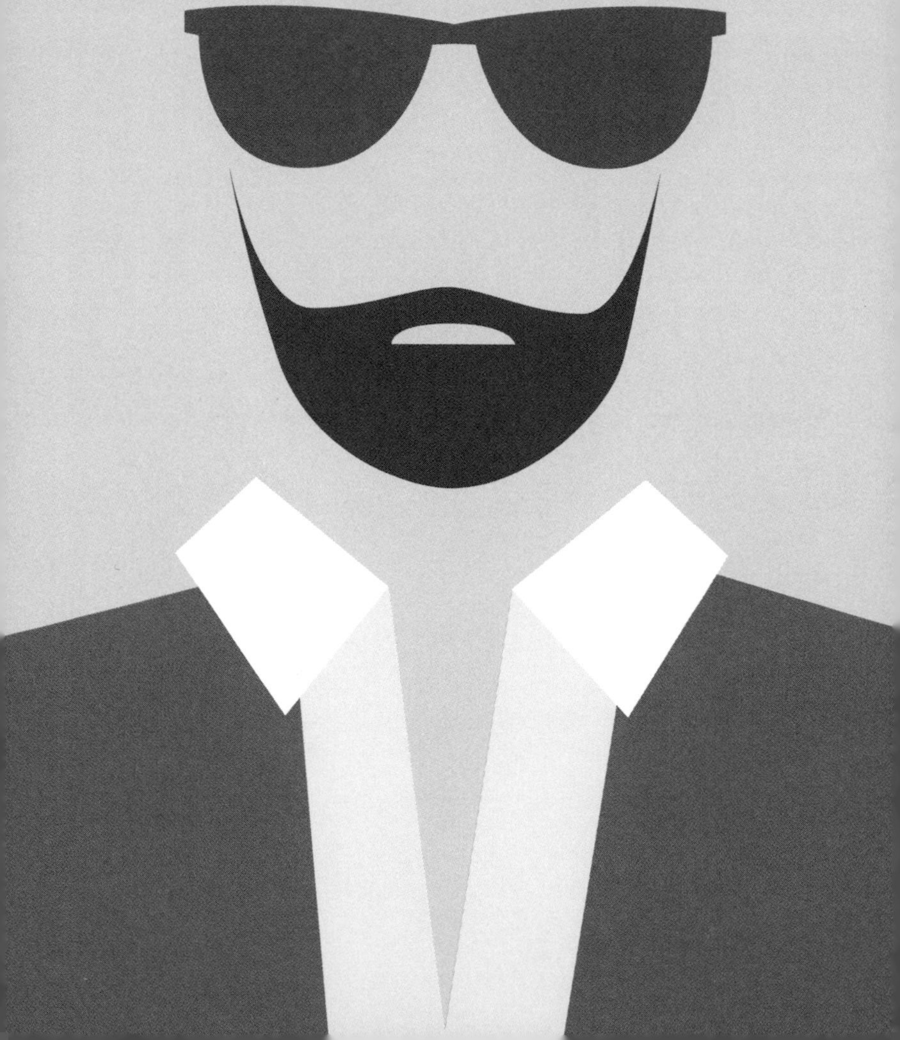

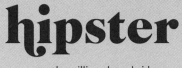

hipster

on the williamsburg bridge

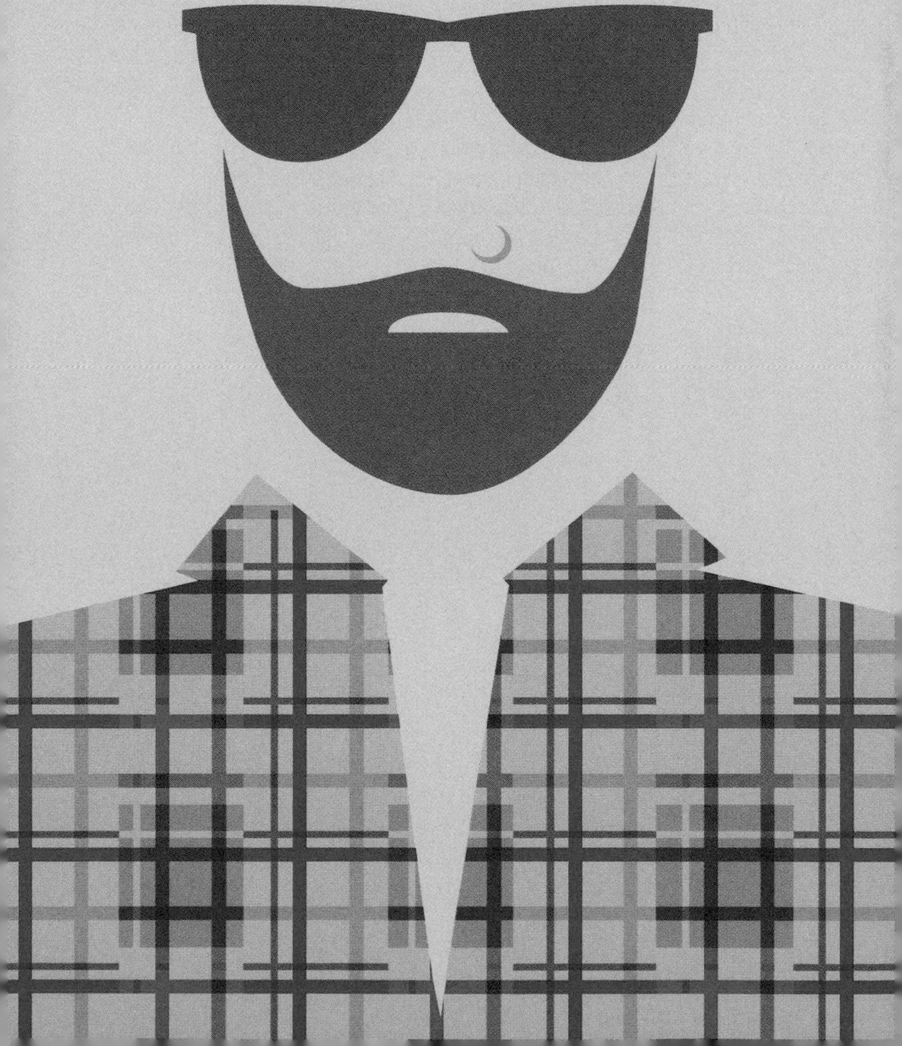

Roland-Garros

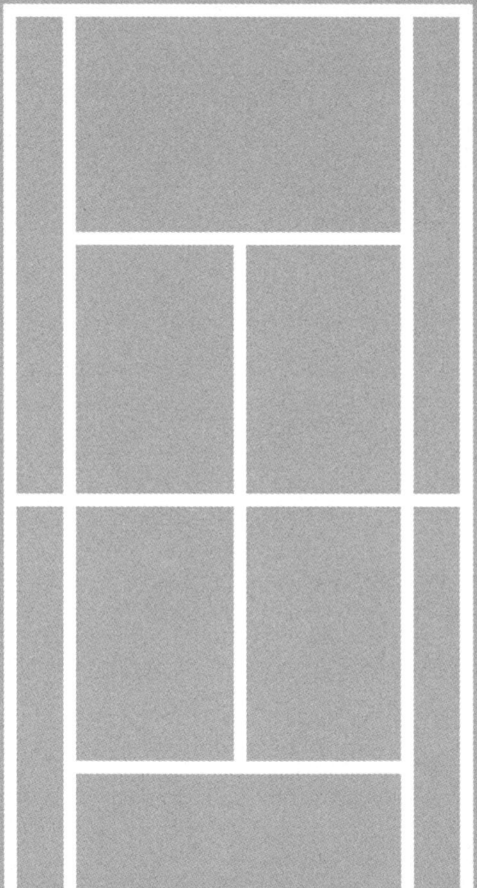

US Open

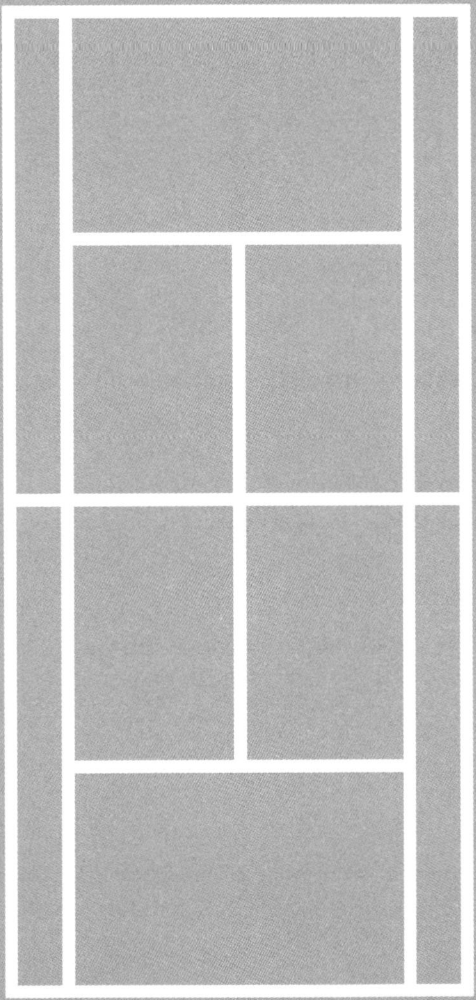

bouquins

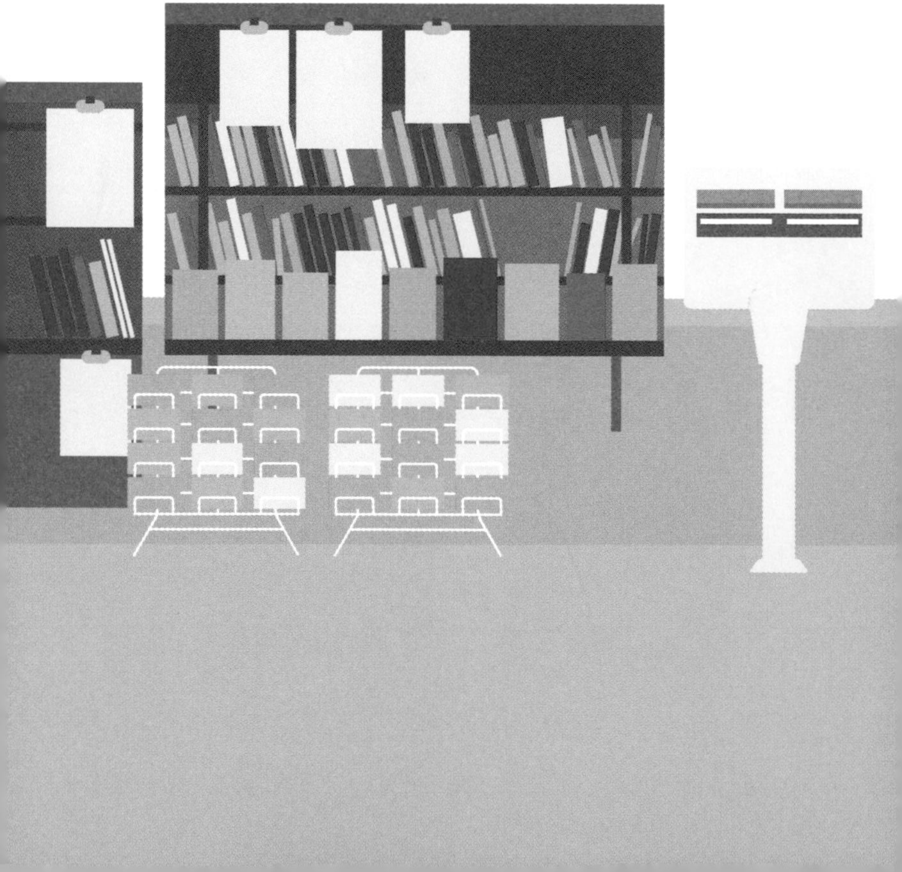

news

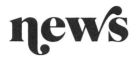

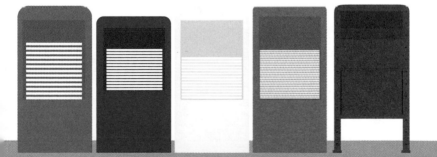

poussettes

9ᵉ – 11ᵉ – 20ᵉ arrondissements

strollers

park slope – upper west side – tribeca

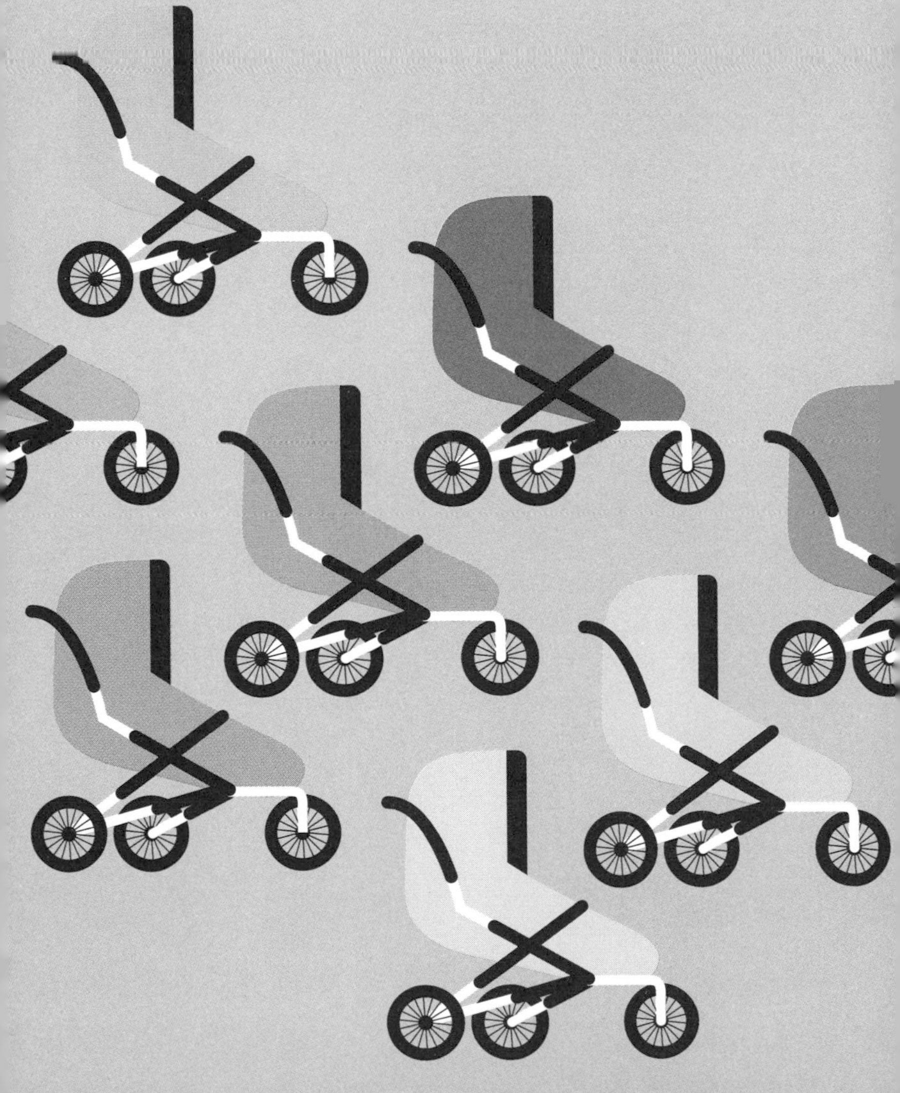

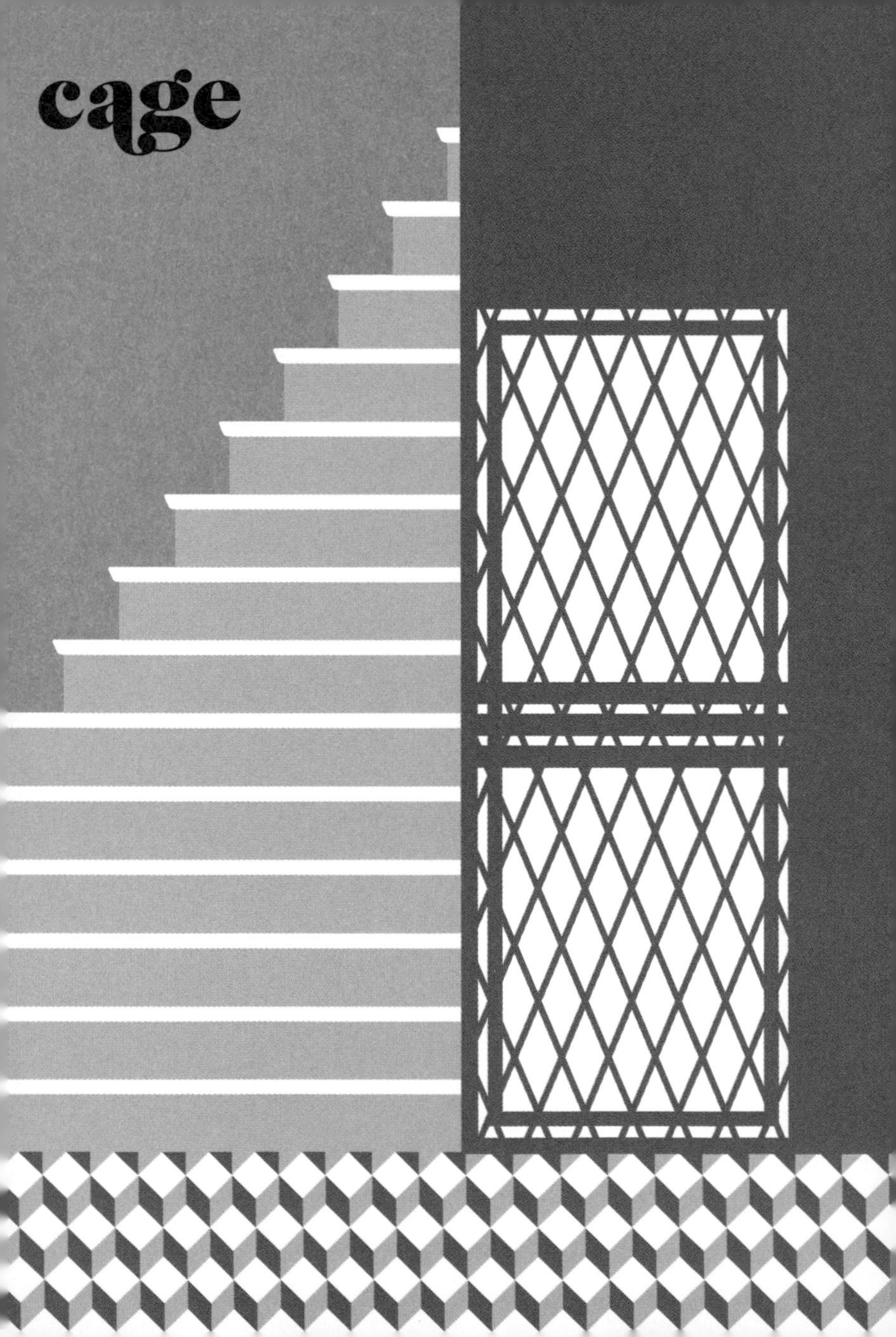
cage

elevator

23
24
PH
20
21
22
17
18
19
14
15
16
10
11
12
B
G
9

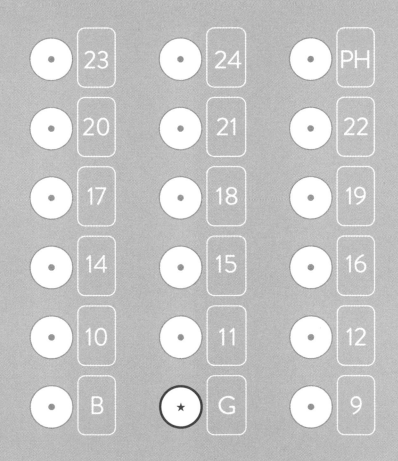

quasimodo

king kong

espaces verts

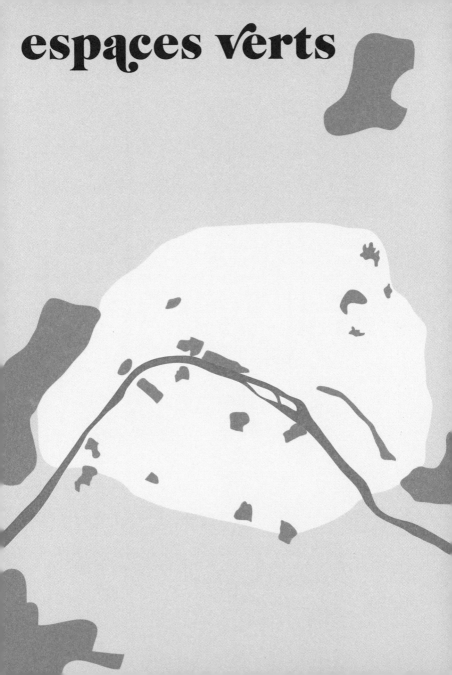

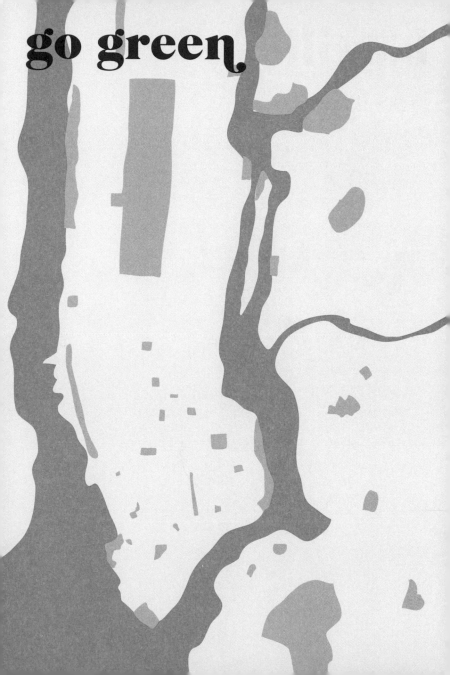

go green

bastille

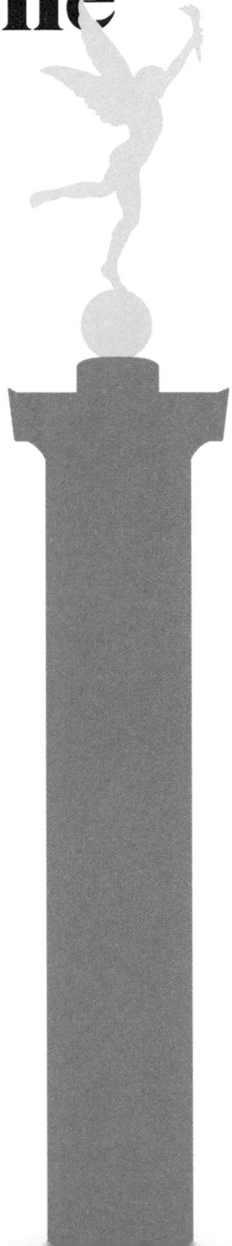

bethesda

pepé le pew

à la poursuite du grand amour dans le quartier latin

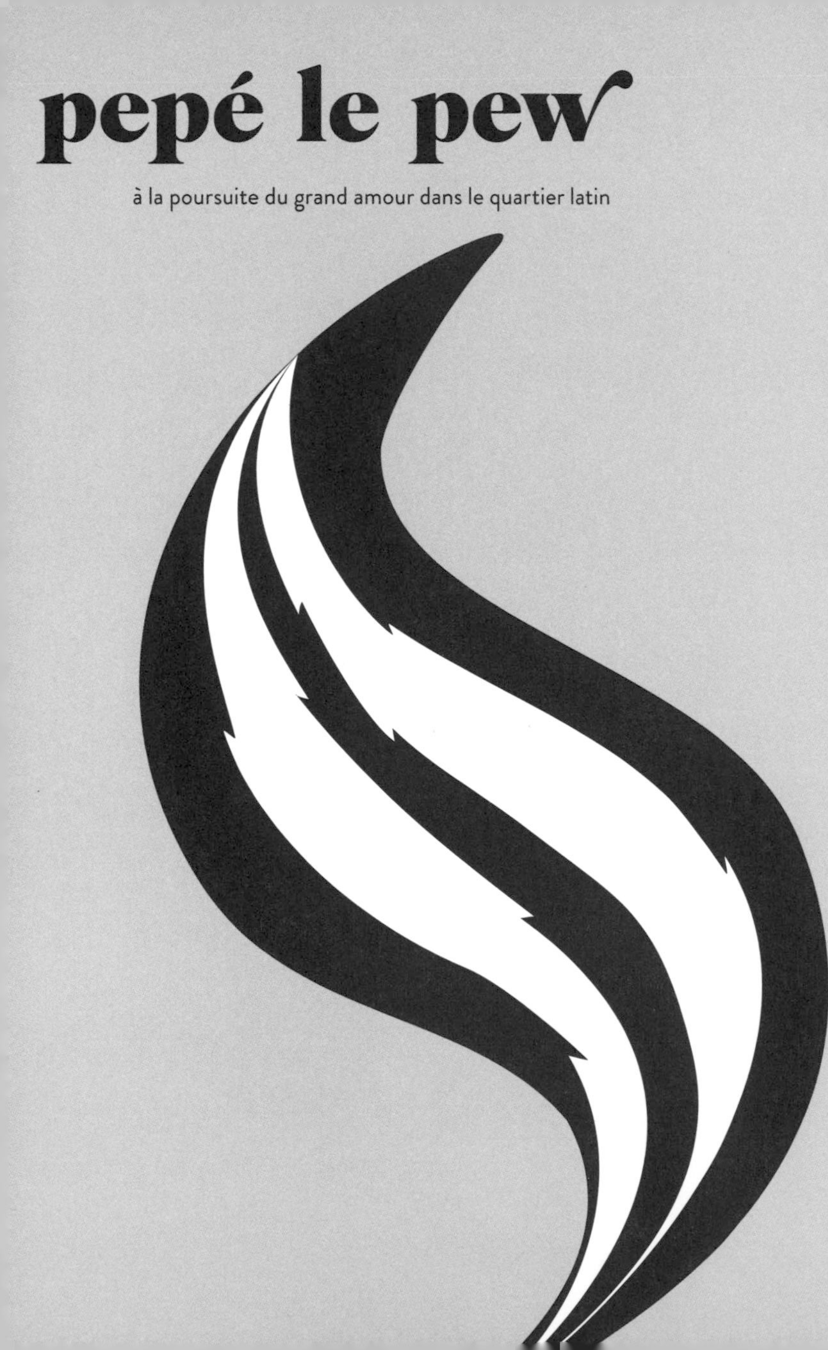

squirrel

on the hunt for hot dog buns in central park

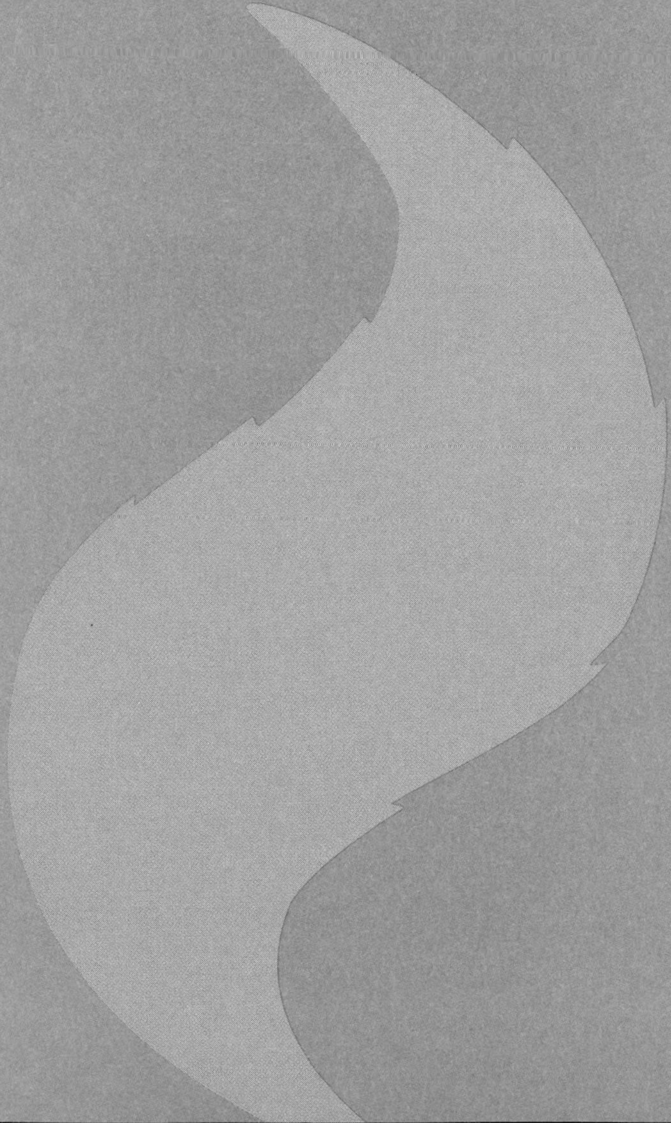

croque-monsieur

hot dog

sous le ciel de Paris

New York
october sky

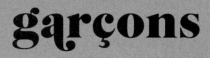

garçons

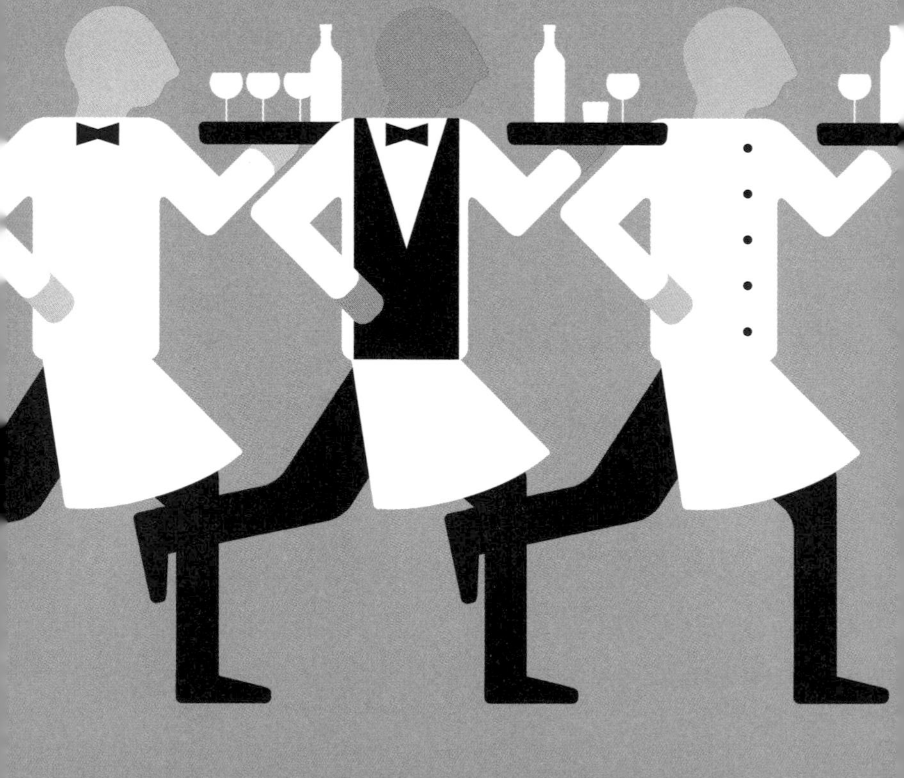

marathon

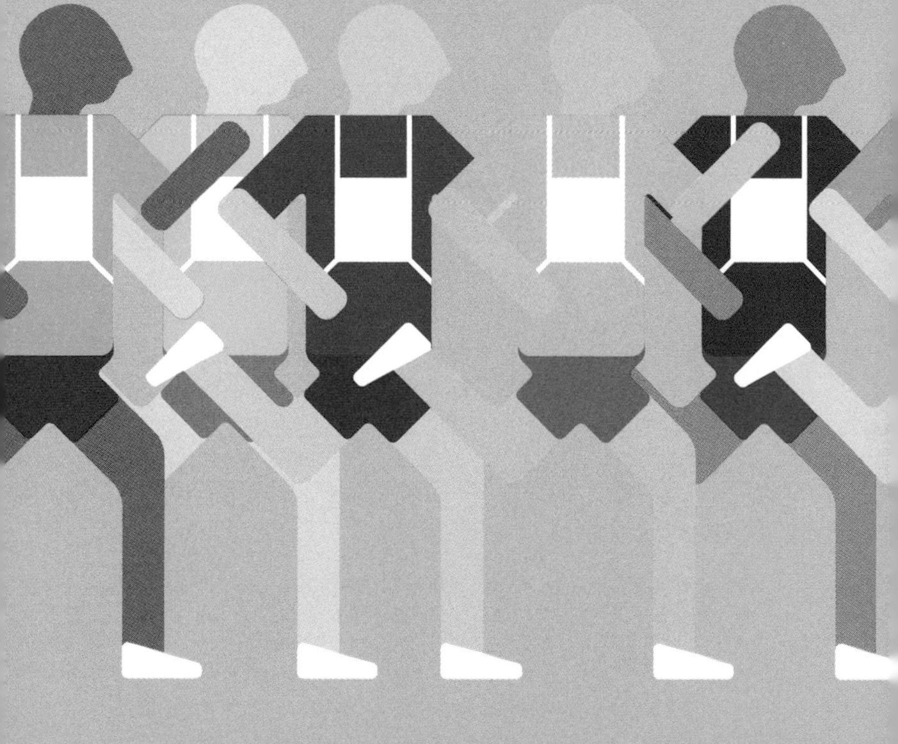

au soleil

speakeasy

boulette

entrez dans la file pour un falafel

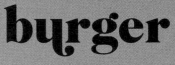

burger

get in the line for shake shack

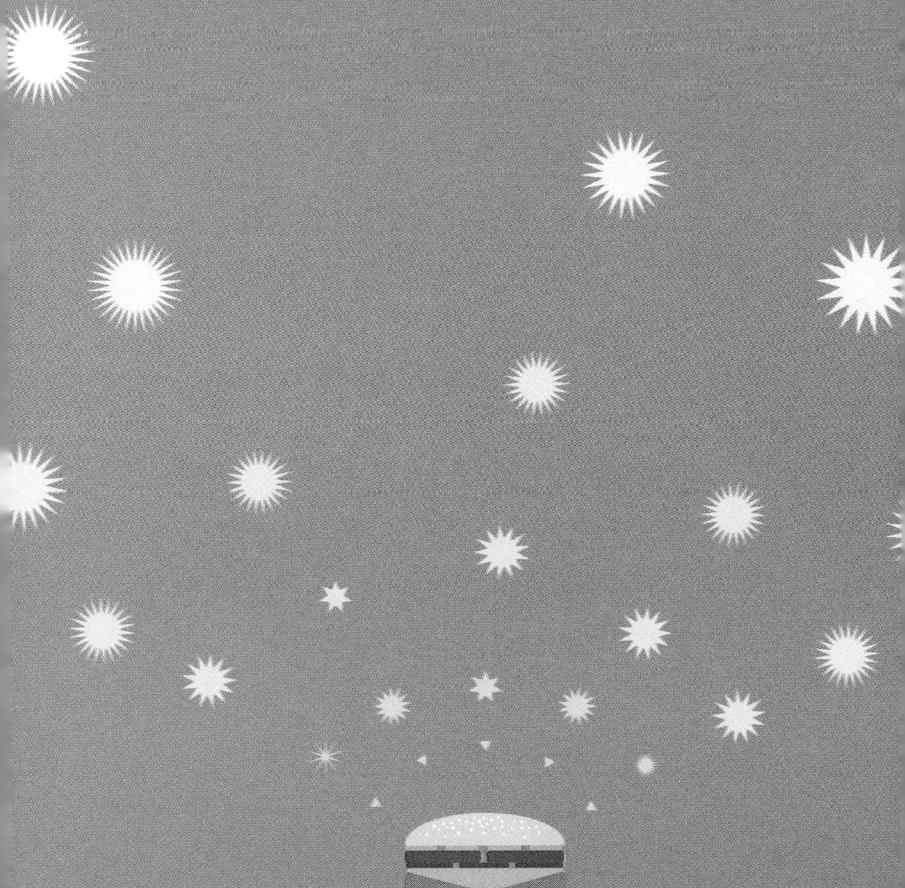

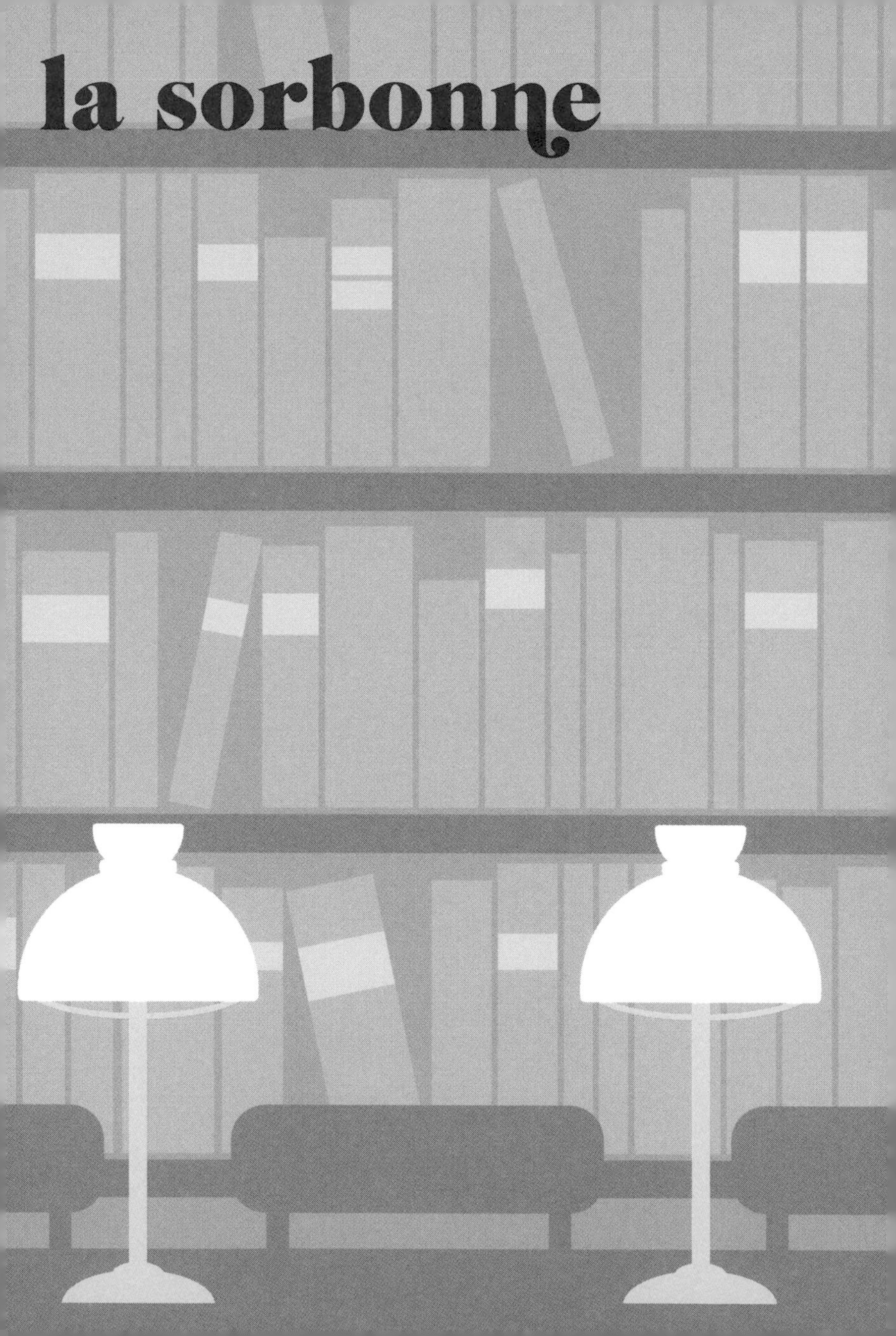
la sorbonne

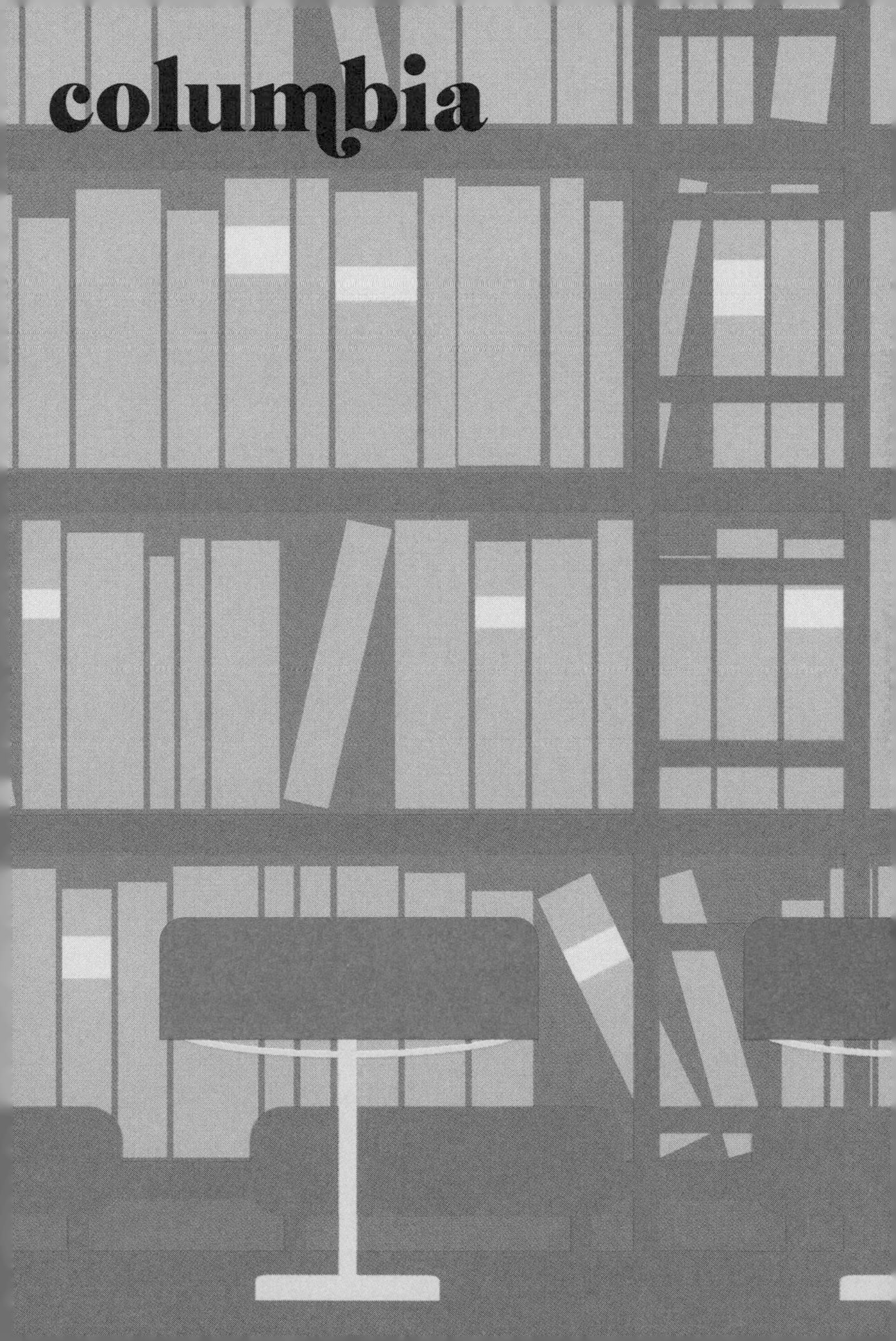
columbia

godard

nouvelle vague

woody

new yorker

proust

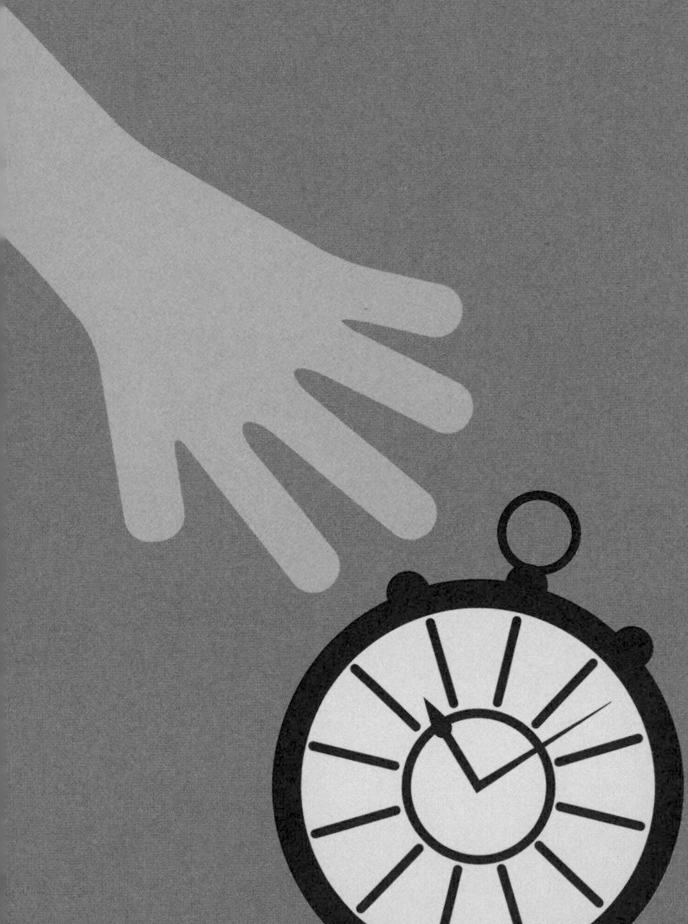

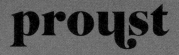

salinger

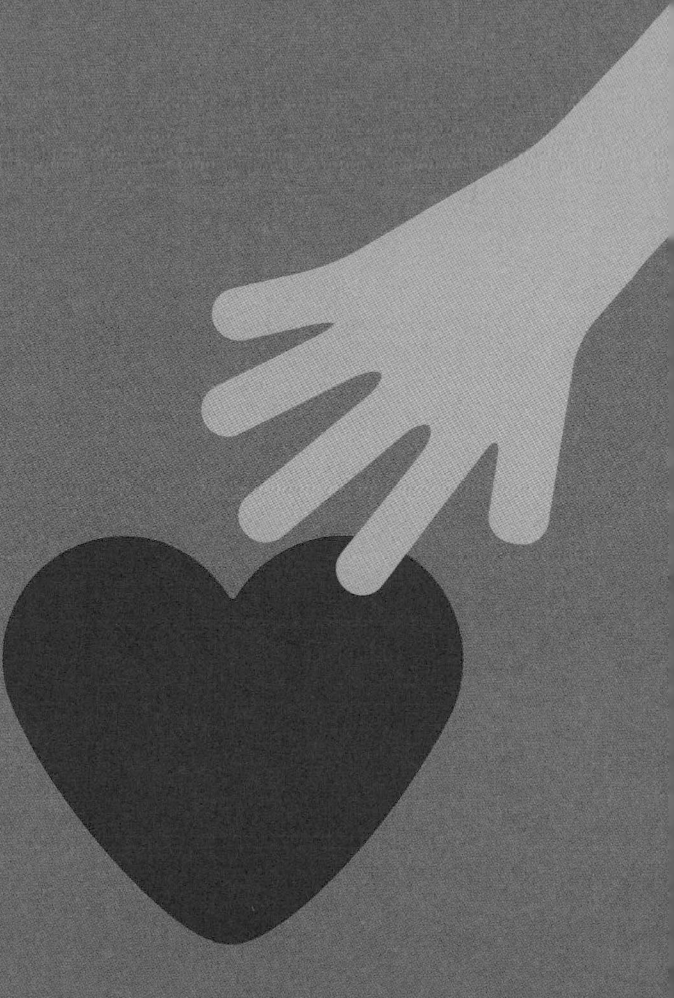

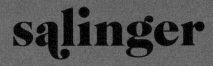

pour tous

le *vélib'*, le prêt-à-rouler

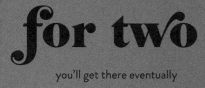

for two

you'll get there eventually

man on wire

alias philippe petit

spider-man

aka peter parker

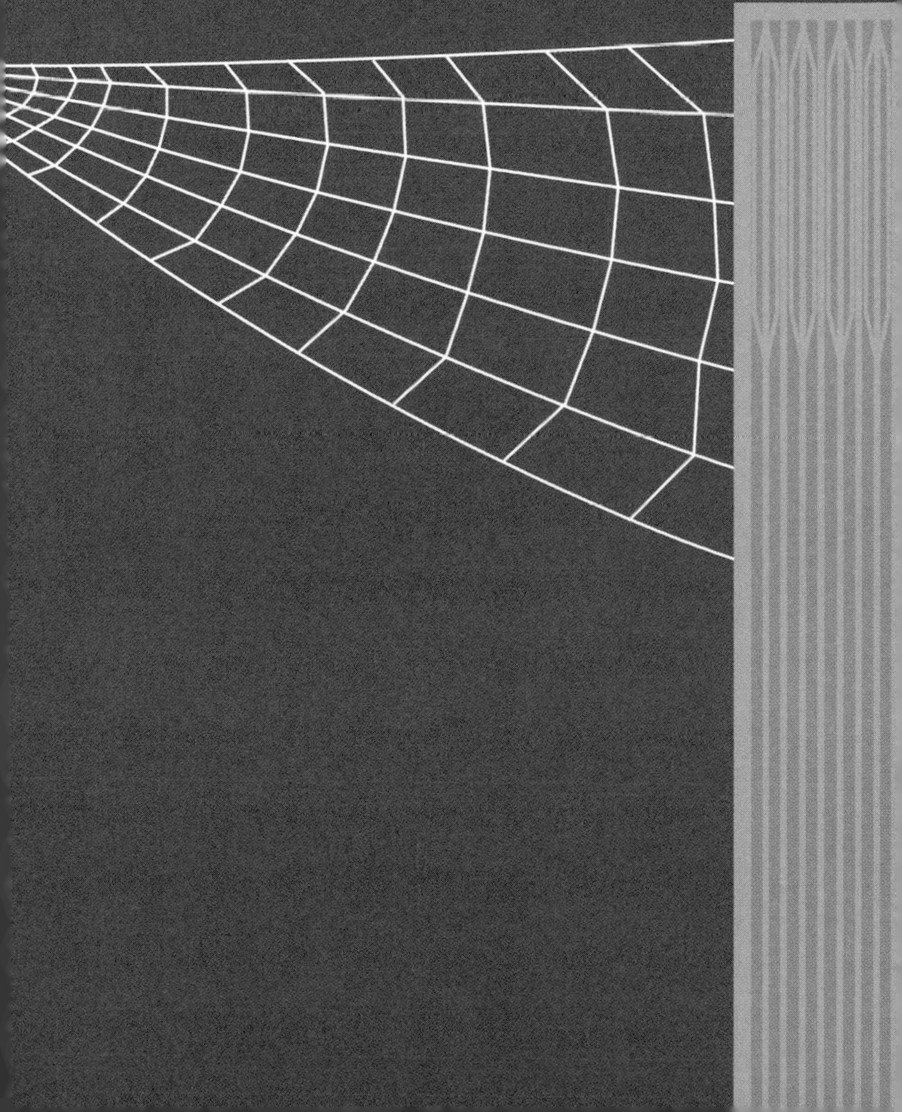

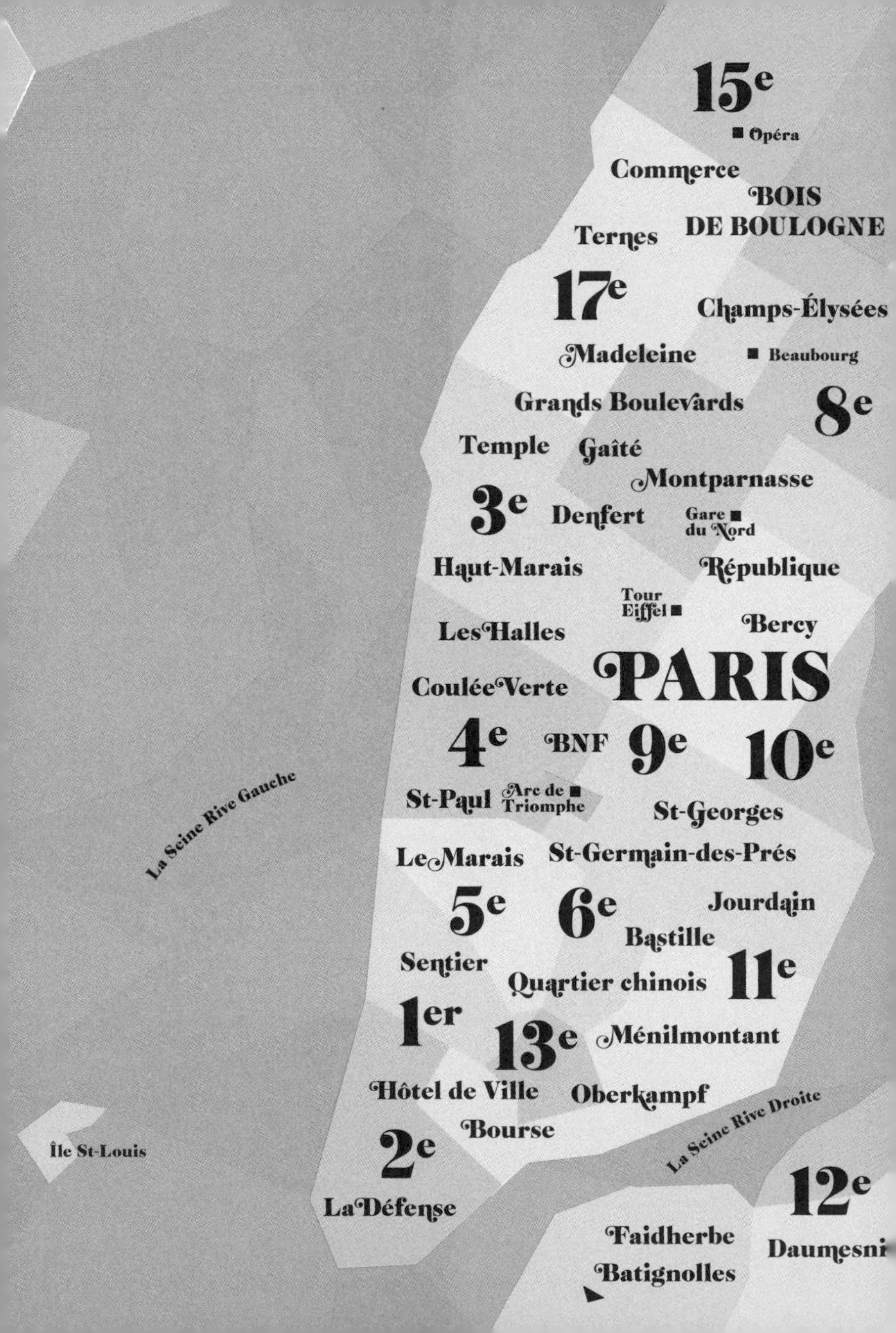

15e
Opéra
Commerce
BOIS
DE BOULOGNE
Ternes
17e
Champs-Élysées
Madeleine
Beaubourg
Grands Boulevards
8e
Temple
Gaîté
Montparnasse
3e
Denfert
Gare
du Nord
Haut-Marais
République
Tour
Eiffel
Les Halles
Bercy
PARIS
Coulée Verte
4e
BNF
9e
10e
St-Paul
Arc de
Triomphe
St-Georges
La Seine Rive Gauche
Le Marais
St-Germain-des-Prés
5e
6e
Jourdain
Bastille
Sentier
Quartier chinois
11e
1er
13e
Ménilmontant
Hôtel de Ville
Oberkampf
Bourse
La Seine Rive Droite
Île St-Louis
2e
12e
La Défense
Faidherbe
Daumesni
Batignolles

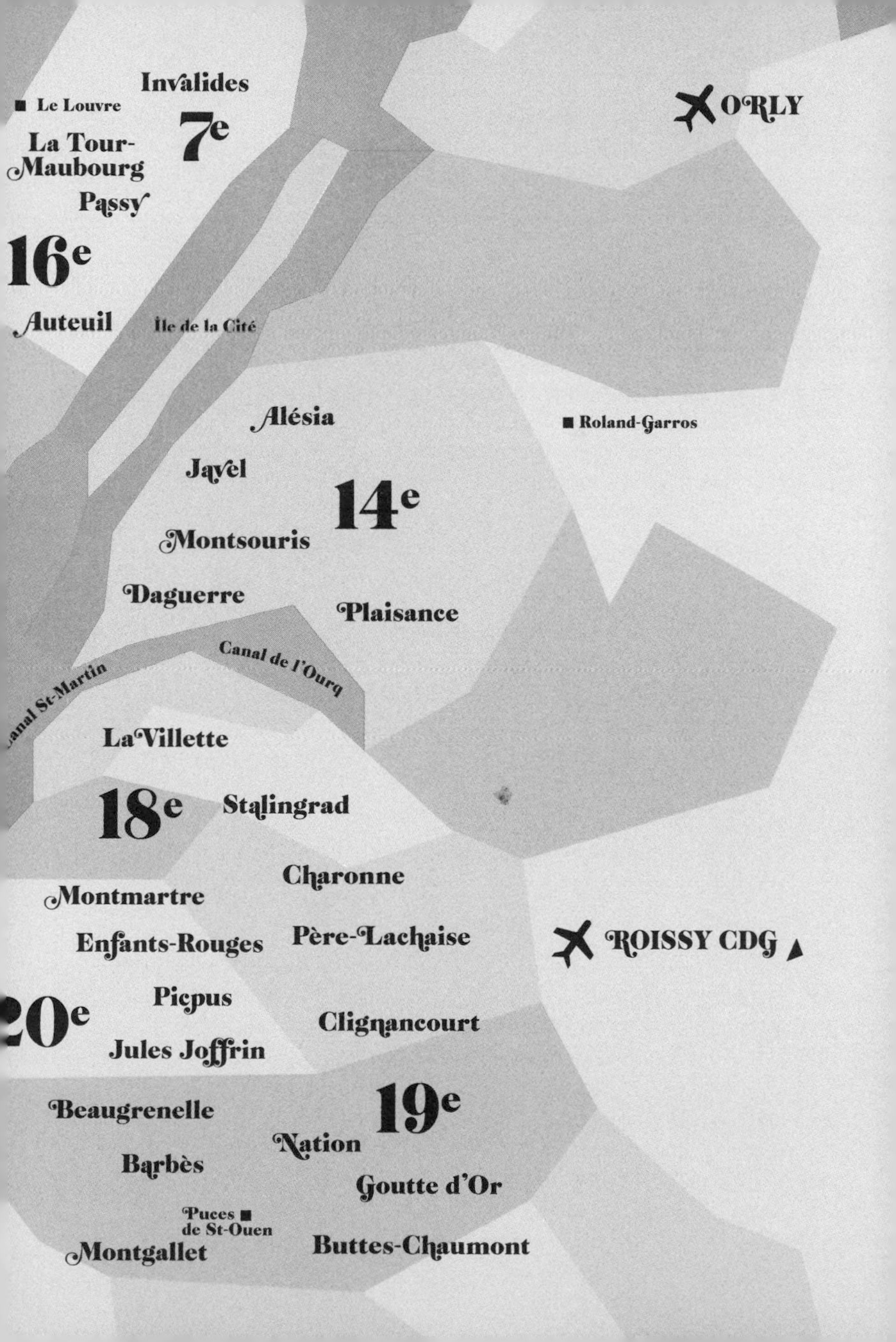
Invalides
Le Louvre
7e
ORLY
La Tour-Maubourg
Passy
16e
Auteuil
Île de la Cité
Alésia
Roland-Garros
Javel
14e
Montsouris
Daguerre
Plaisance
Canal de l'Ourq
Canal St-Martin
La Villette
18e
Stalingrad
Charonne
Montmartre
Enfants-Rouges
Père-Lachaise
ROISSY CDG
Picpus
20e
Clignancourt
Jules Joffrin
Beaugrenelle
19e
Nation
Barbès
Goutte d'Or
Puces de St-Ouen
Montgallet
Buttes-Chaumont

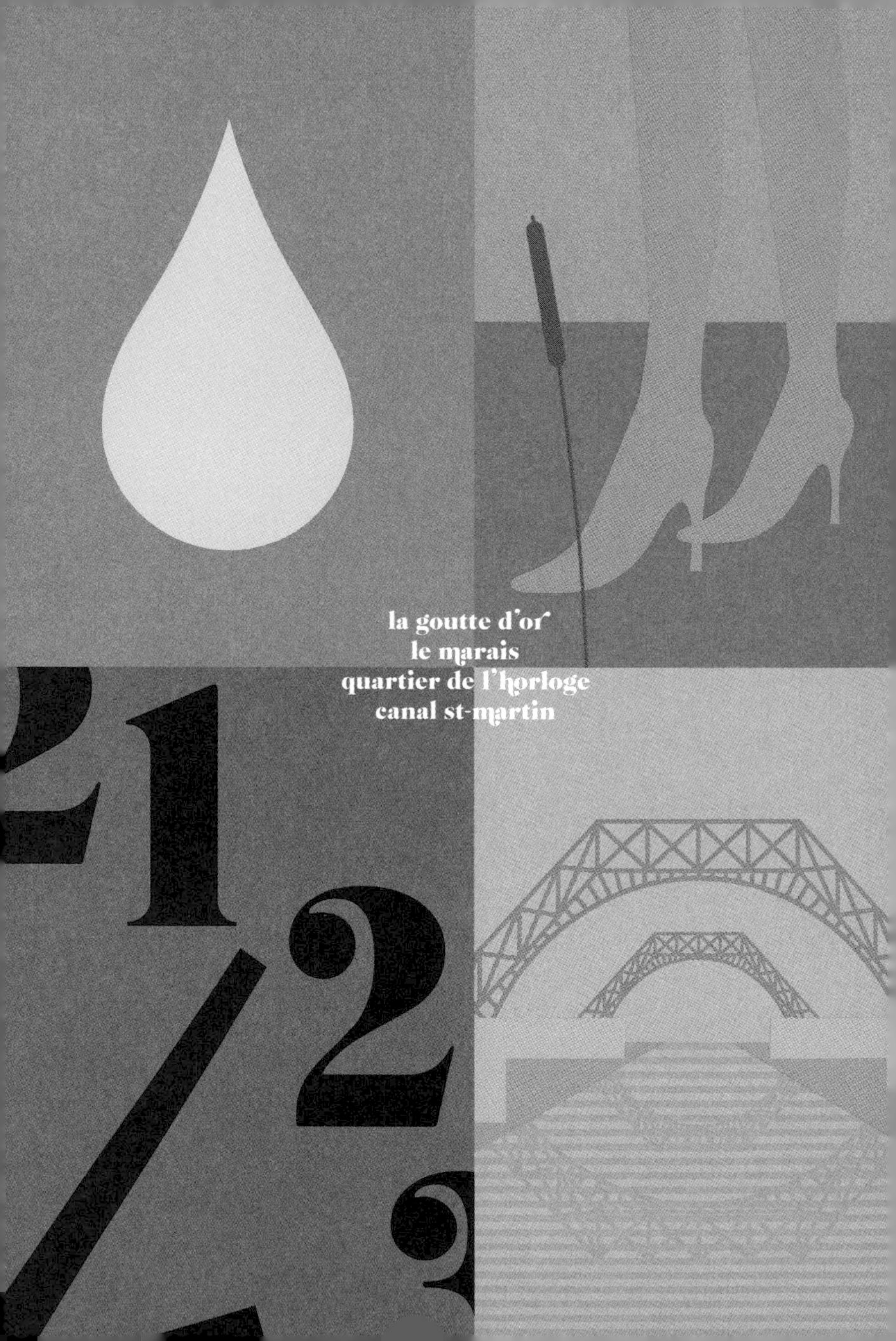
la goutte d'or
le marais
quartier de l'horloge
canal st-martin

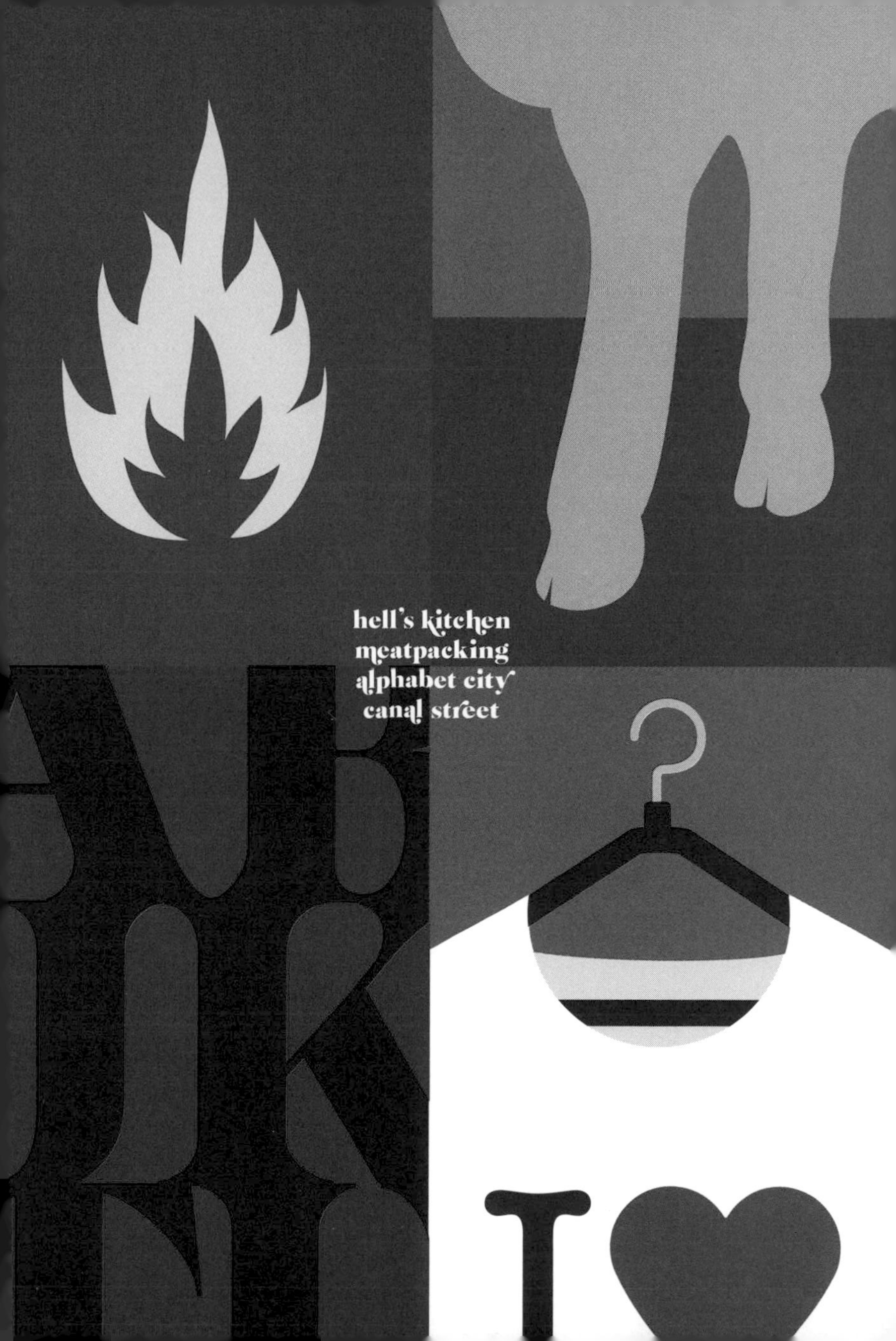
hell's kitchen
meatpacking
alphabet city
canal street

chef d'œuvre

tour st-jacques
4ᵉ arr. (1523)

bête noire

tour montparnasse
15ᵉ arr. (1973)

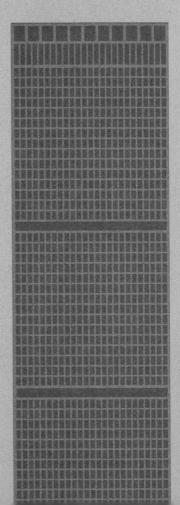

master class

flatiron building
23rd st. (1902)

the ugliest

verizon building
financial district (1975)

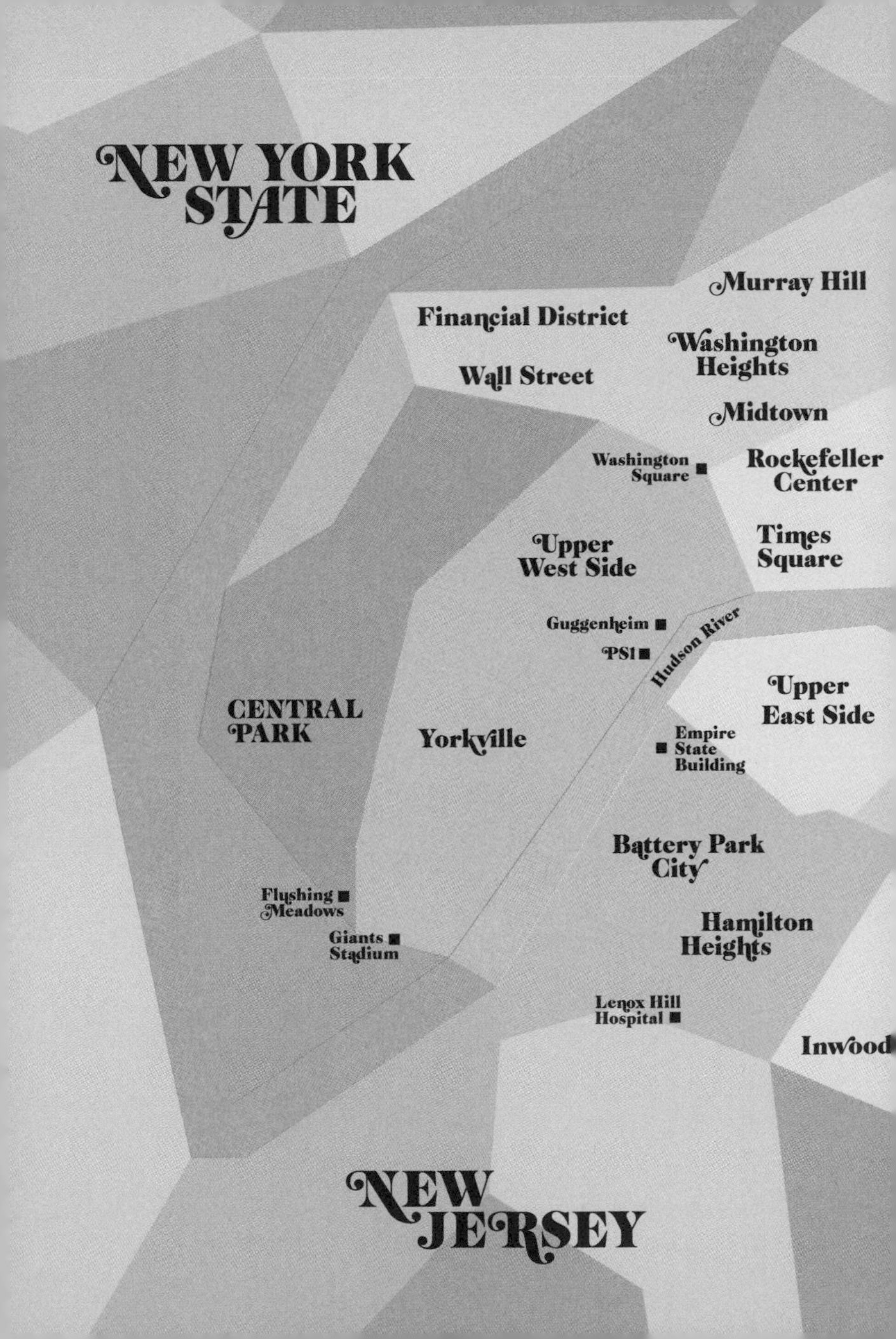

NEW YORK STATE
Murray Hill
Financial District
Washington Heights
Wall Street
Midtown
Washington Square
Rockefeller Center
Upper West Side
Times Square
Guggenheim
PS1
Hudson River
Upper East Side
CENTRAL PARK
Yorkville
Empire State Building
Battery Park City
Flushing Meadows
Hamilton Heights
Giants Stadium
Lenox Hill Hospital
Inwood
NEW JERSEY

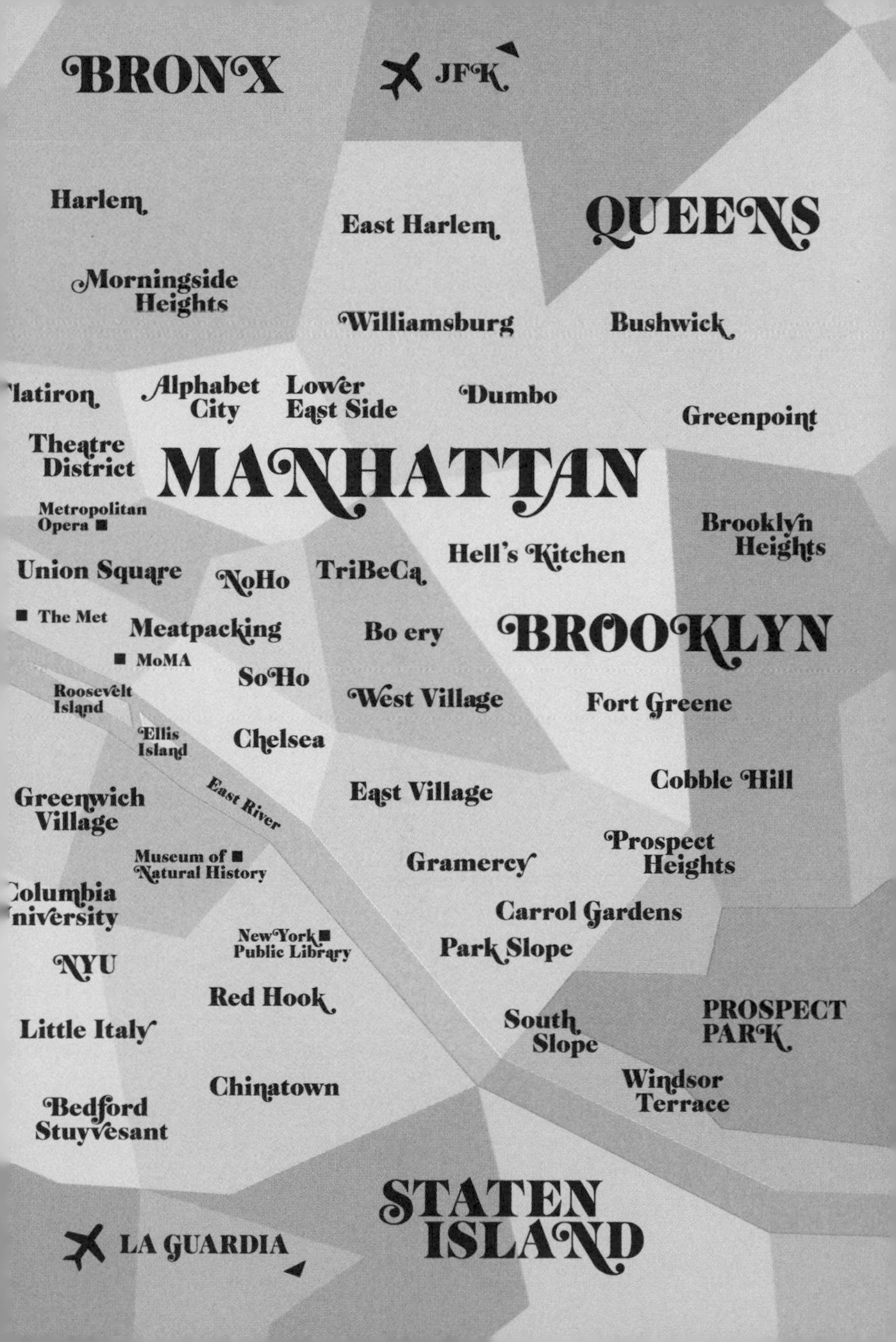
BRONX
JFK
Harlem
East Harlem
QUEENS
Morningside Heights
Williamsburg
Bushwick
latiron
Alphabet City
Lower East Side
Dumbo
Greenpoint
Theatre District
MANHATTAN
Metropolitan Opera
Brooklyn Heights
Hell's Kitchen
Union Square
NoHo
TriBeCa
The Met
Meatpacking
Bo ery
BROOKLYN
MoMA
SoHo
Roosevelt Island
West Village
Fort Greene
Ellis Island
Chelsea
Cobble Hill
Greenwich Village
East River
East Village
Prospect Heights
Museum of Natural History
Gramercy
olumbia niversity
Carrol Gardens
New York Public Library
Park Slope
NYU
Red Hook
Little Italy
South Slope
PROSPECT PARK
Windsor Terrace
Chinatown
Bedford Stuyvesant
STATEN ISLAND
LA GUARDIA

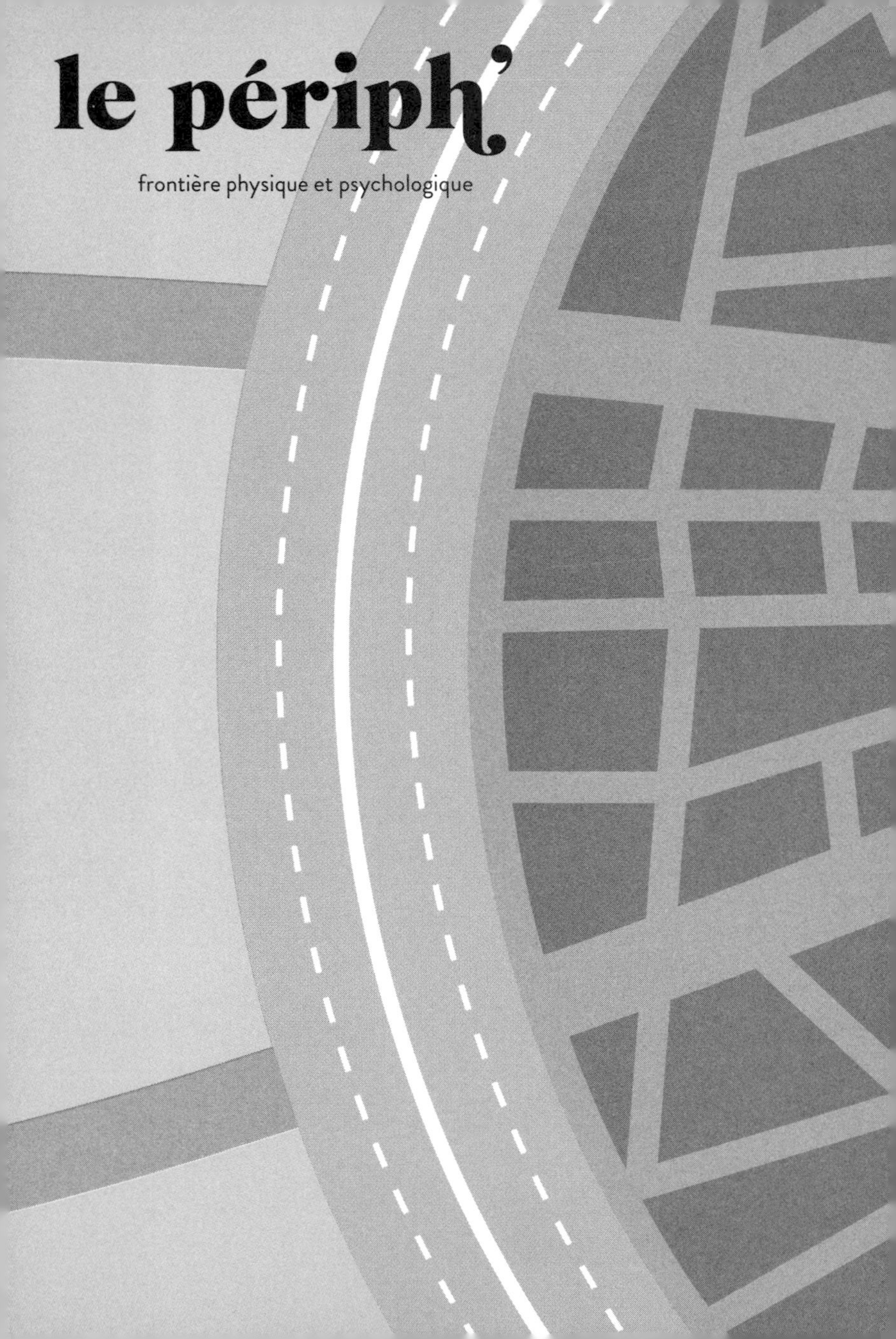
le périph'
frontière physique et psychologique

bridge & tunnel

the difference between “in and out”

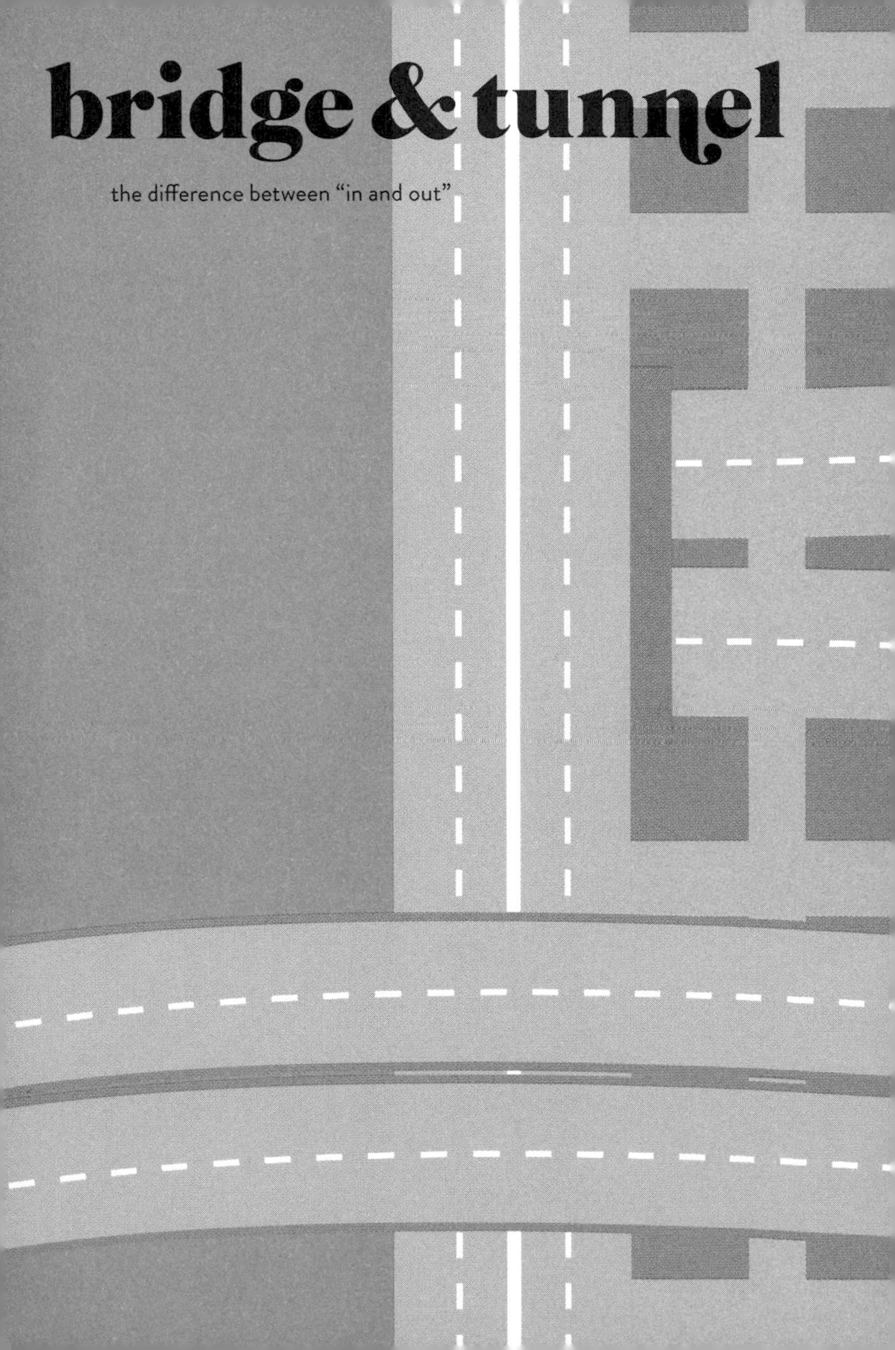

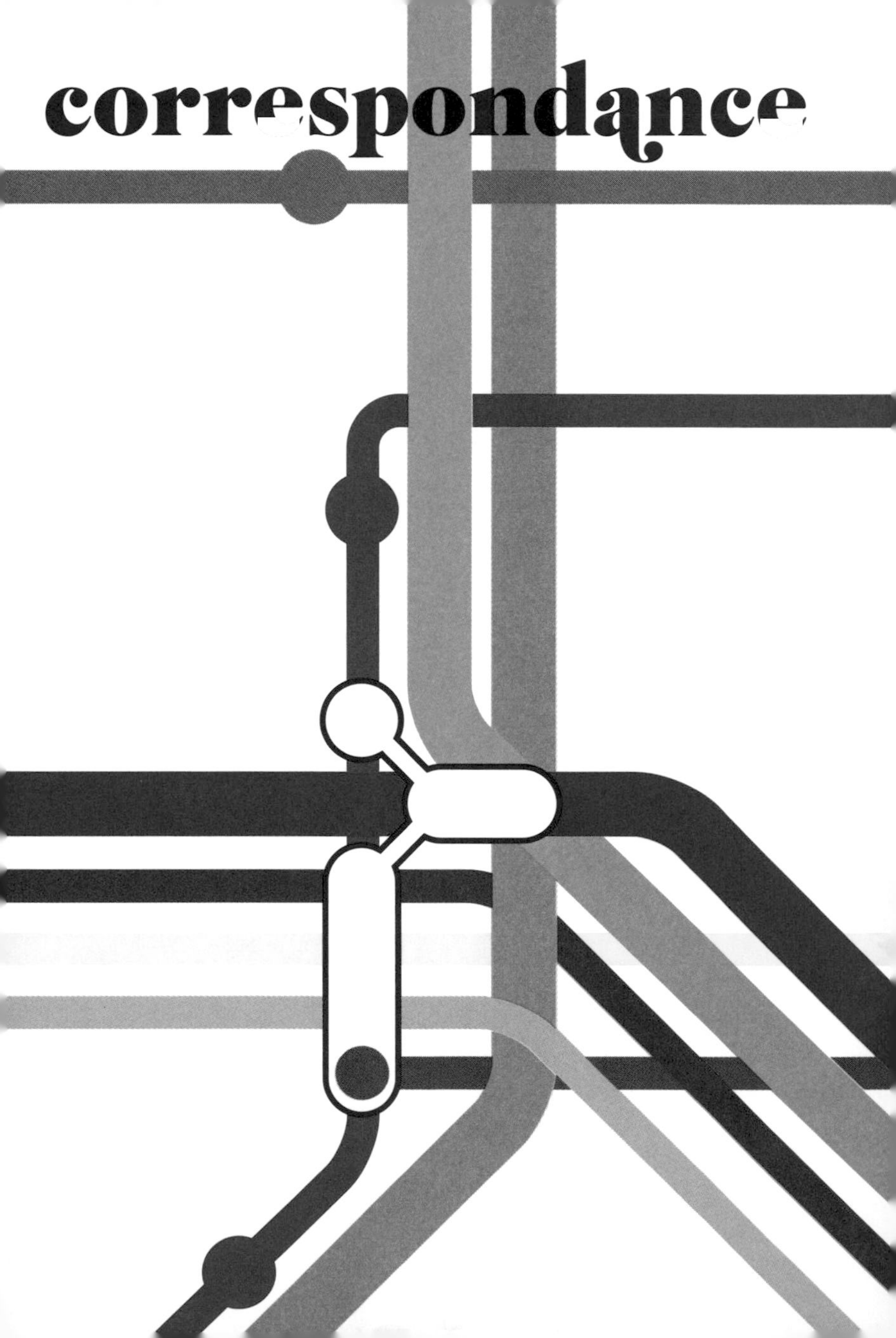
correspondance

commuting

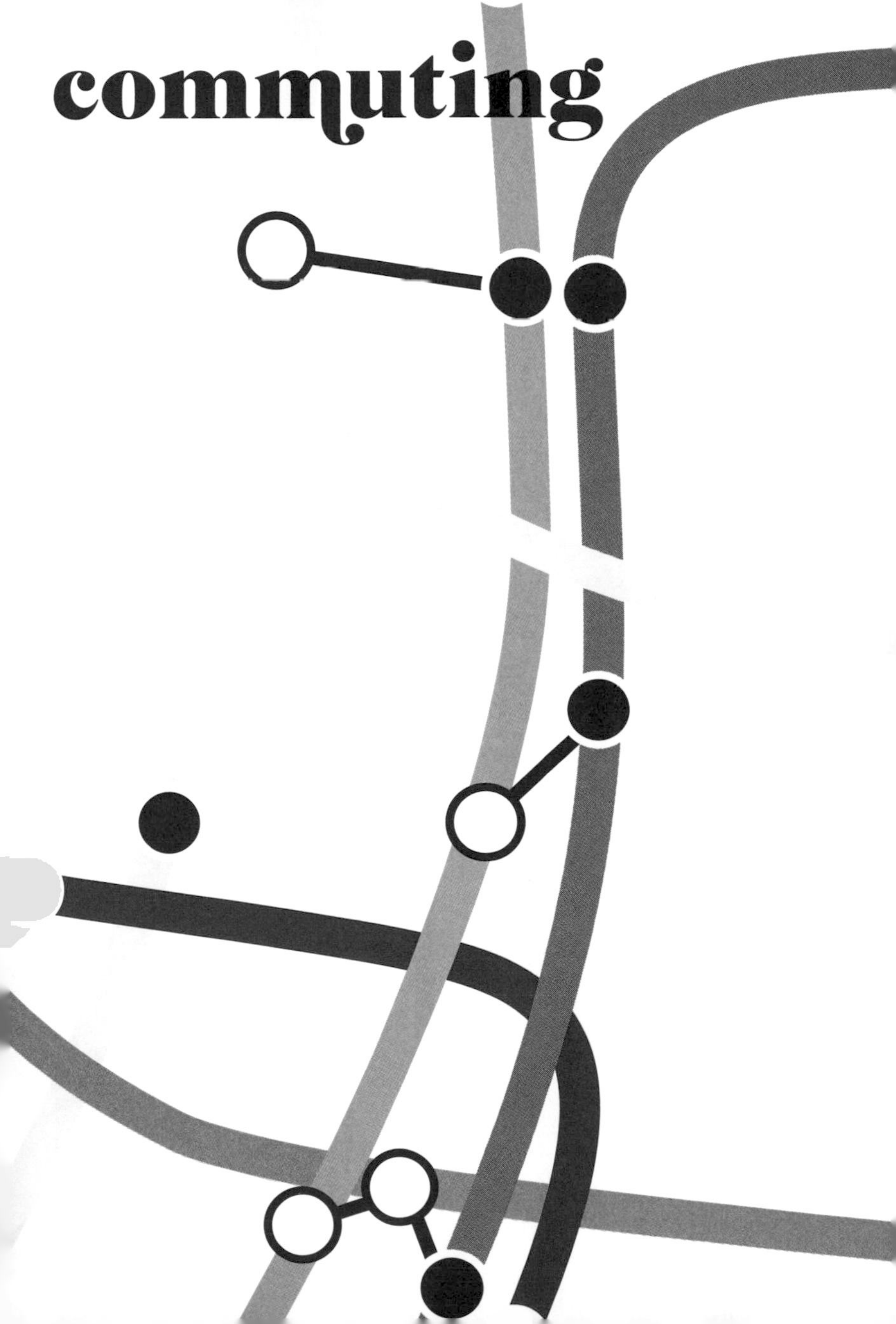

la bouche

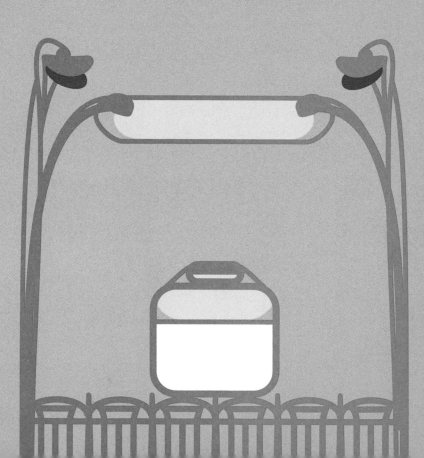

the globes

vous êtes ici

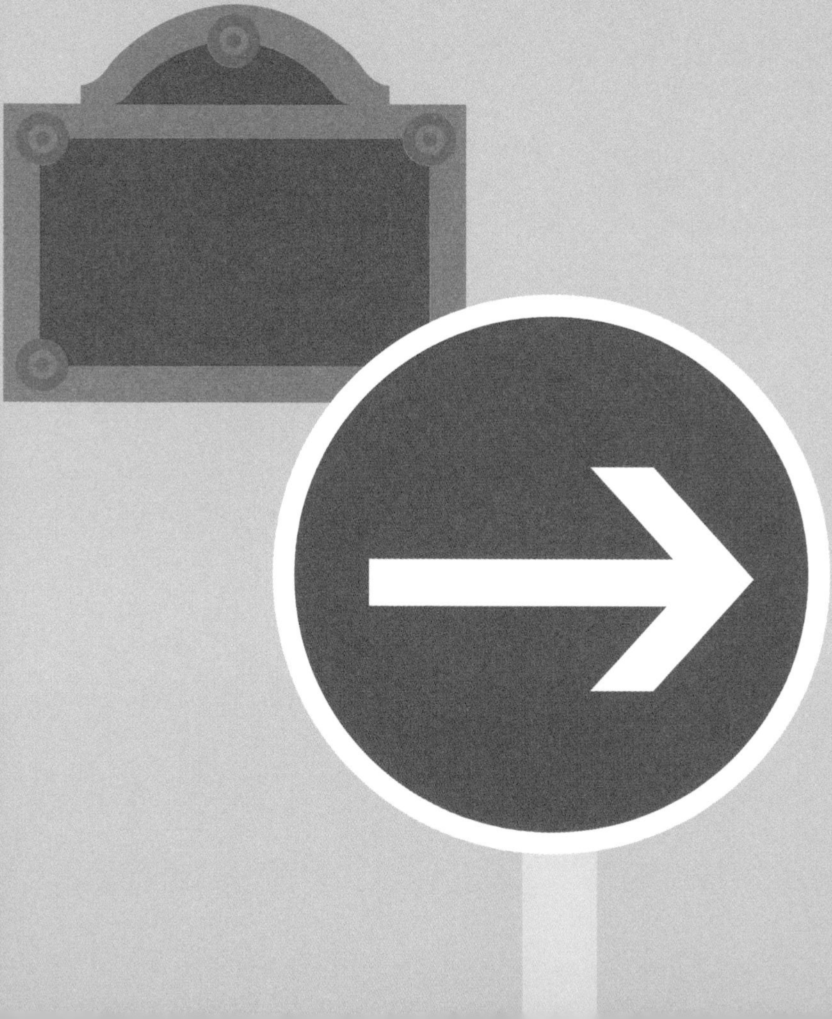

you are here

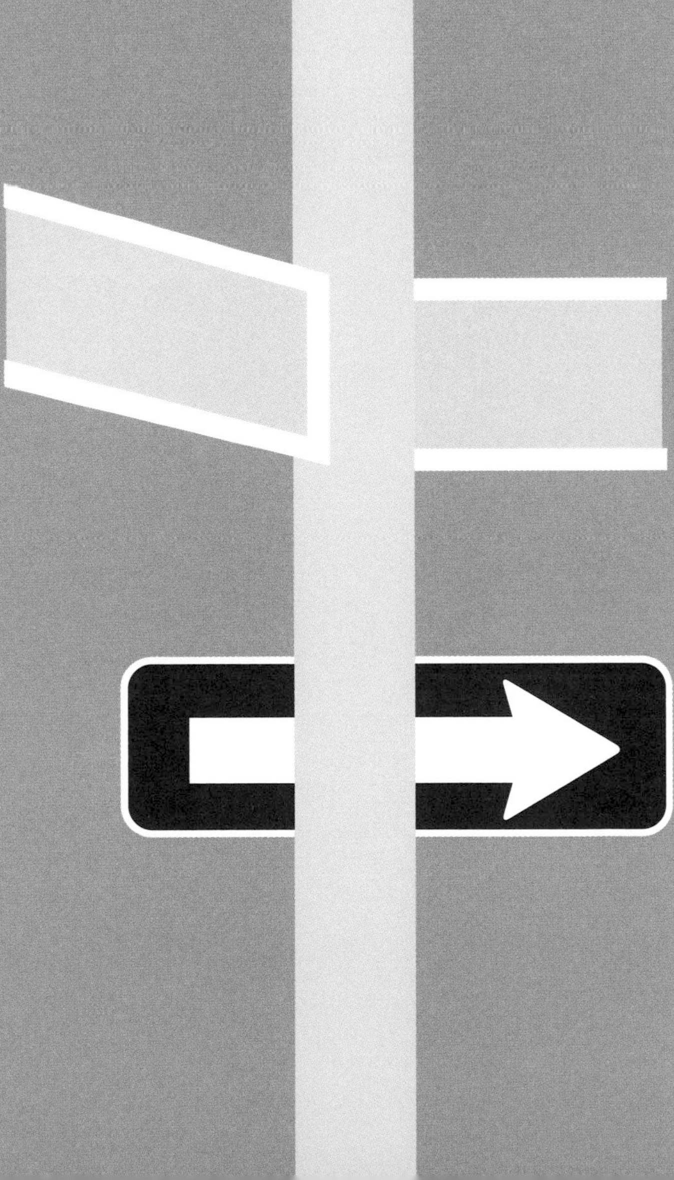

pyramide

entrée pour les arts

cube

entrance for the geeks

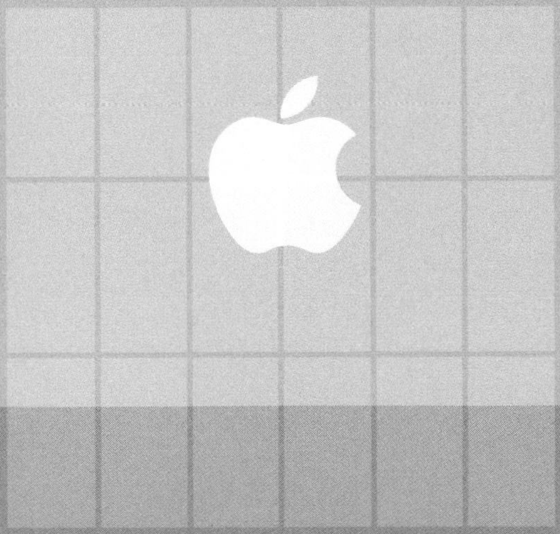

mona lisa

au musée du louvre

les demoiselles

at the moma

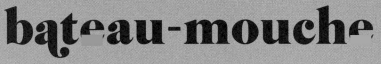

bateau-mouche

mise en seine parisienne pour touristes de tout bord

circle line

a full island three-hour cruise that keeps tourists at sea

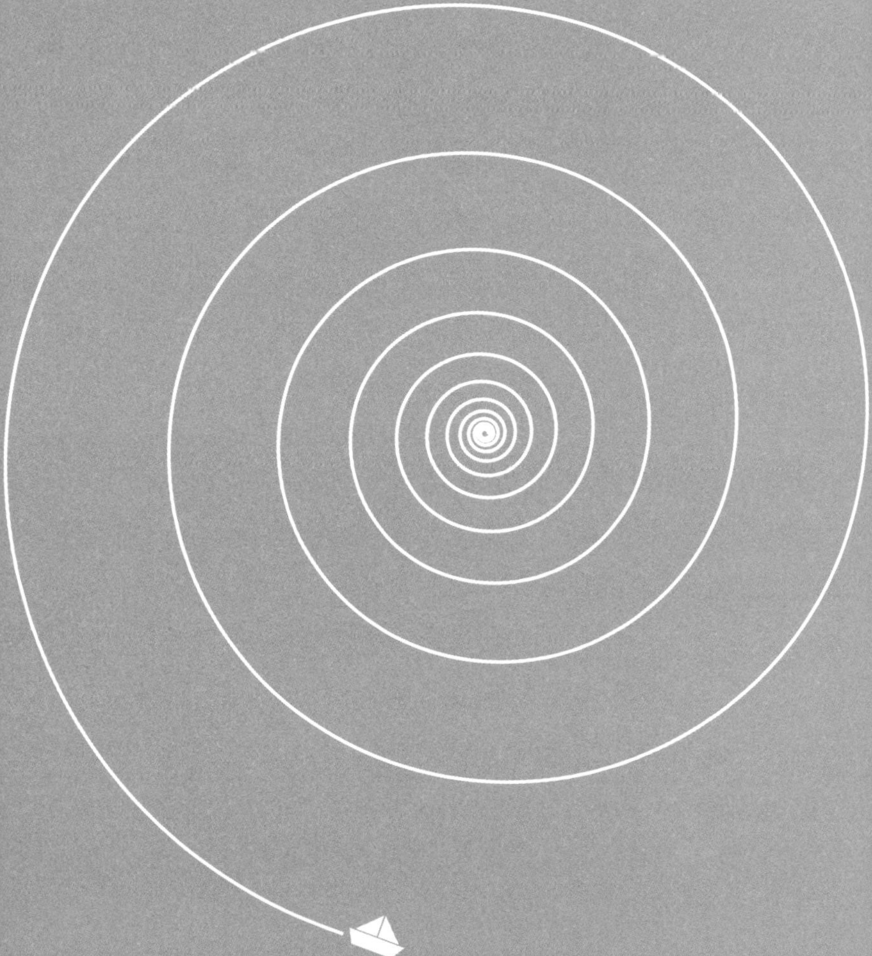

1889

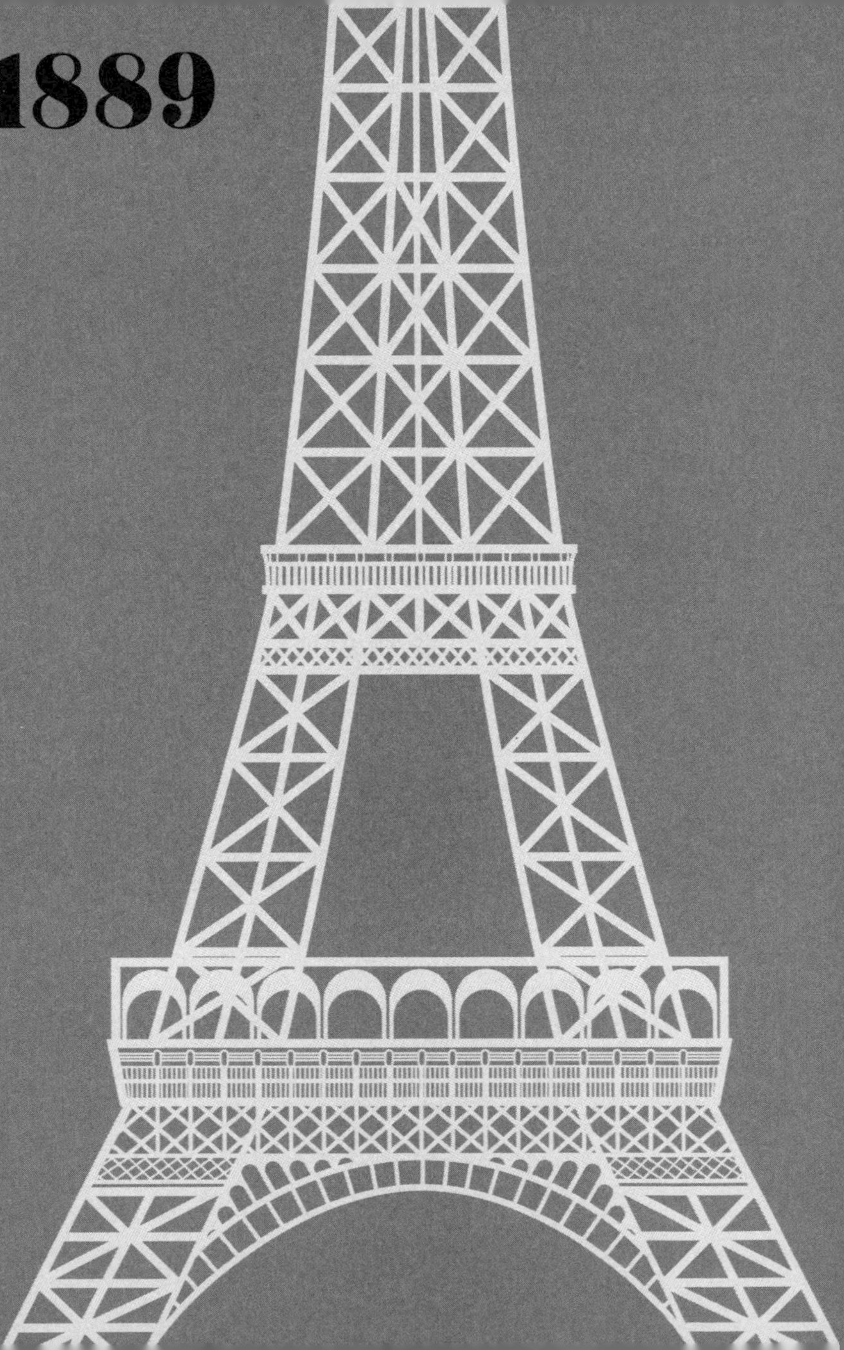

1886

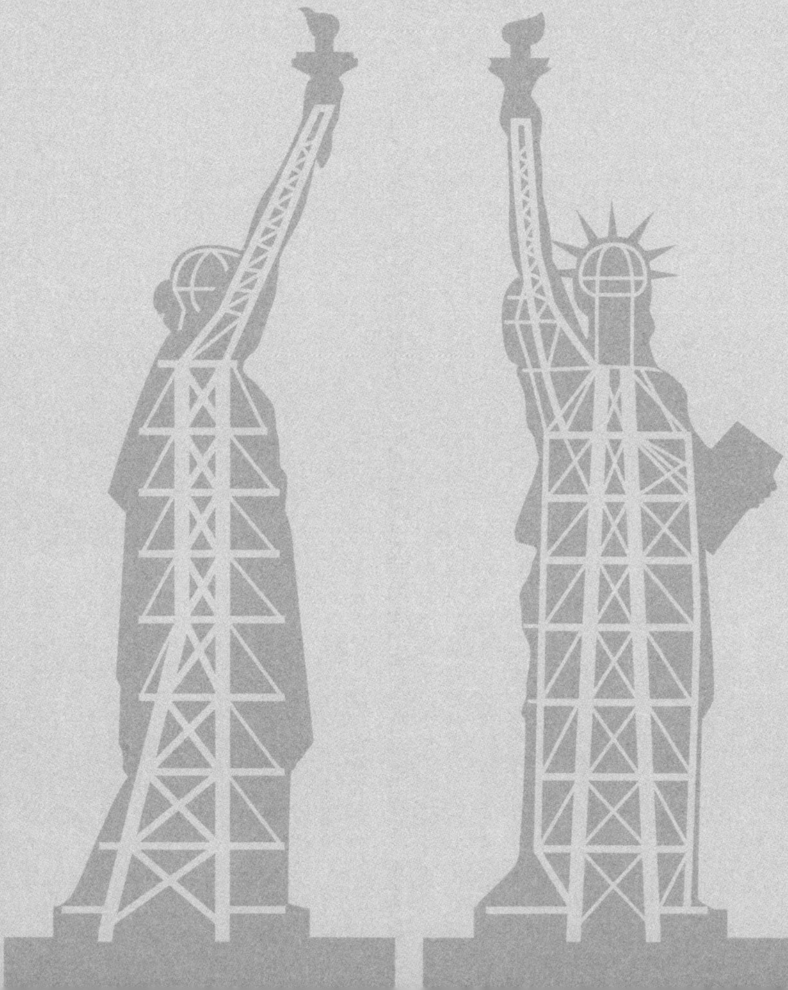

UNESCO

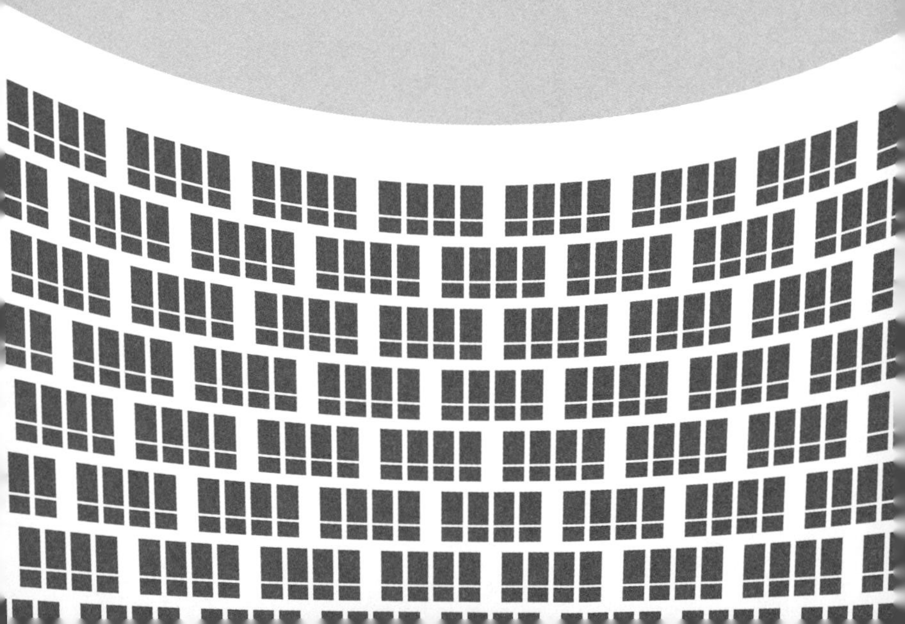

UN

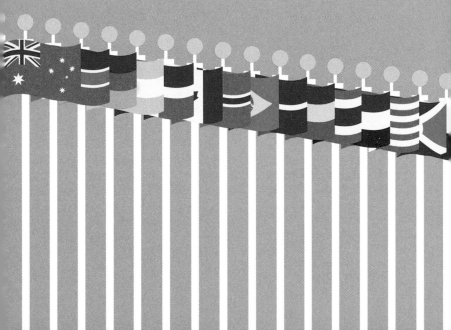

c'est magnifique

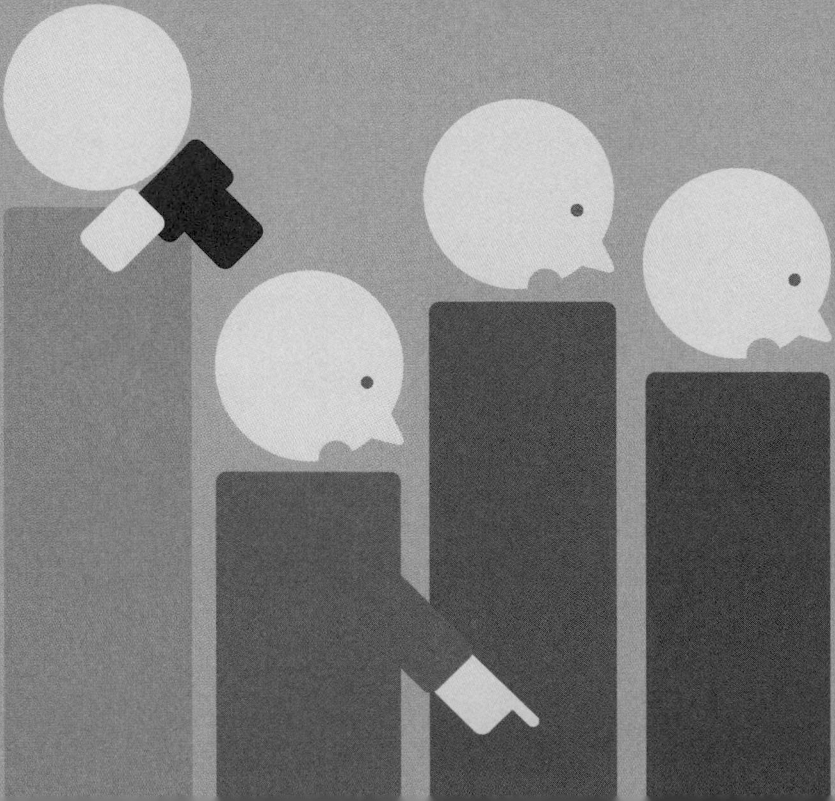

look!

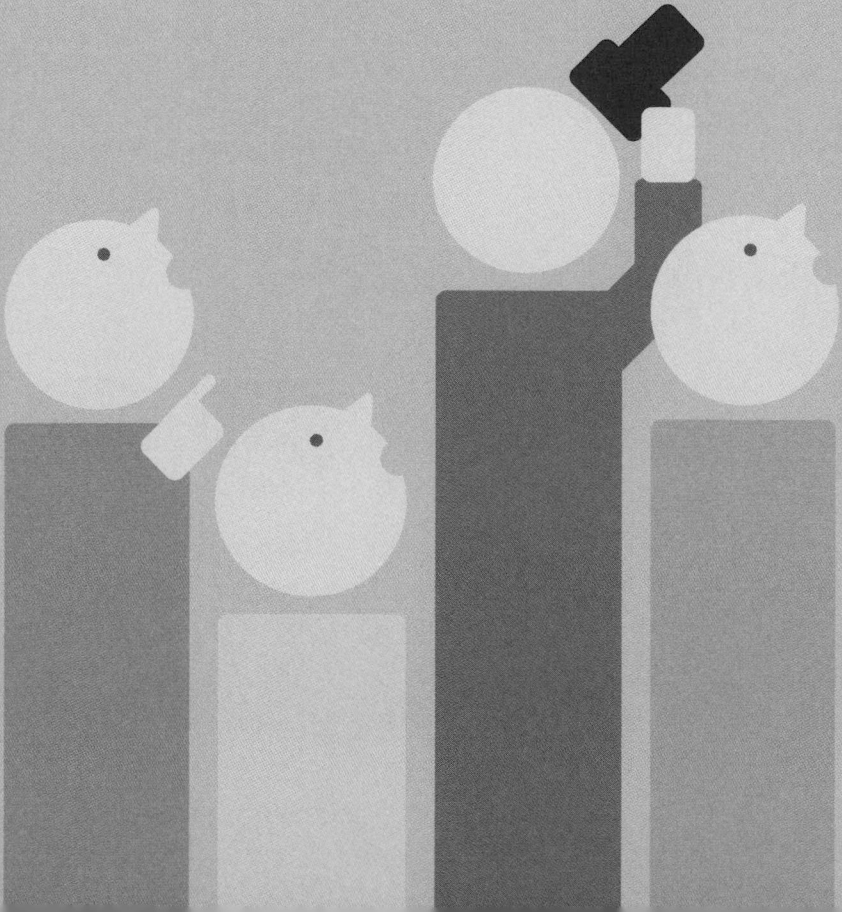

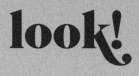

a sunday in Paris

tour eiffel
café de flore
le marais
père-lachaise

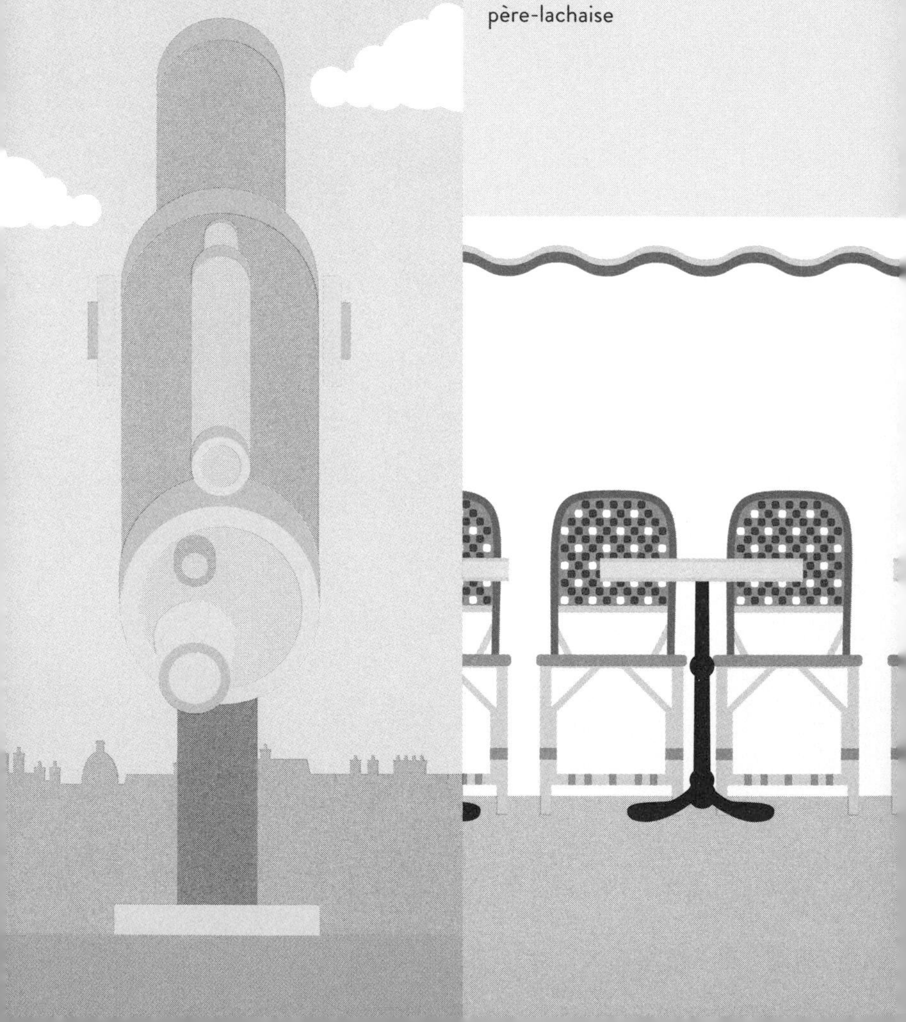

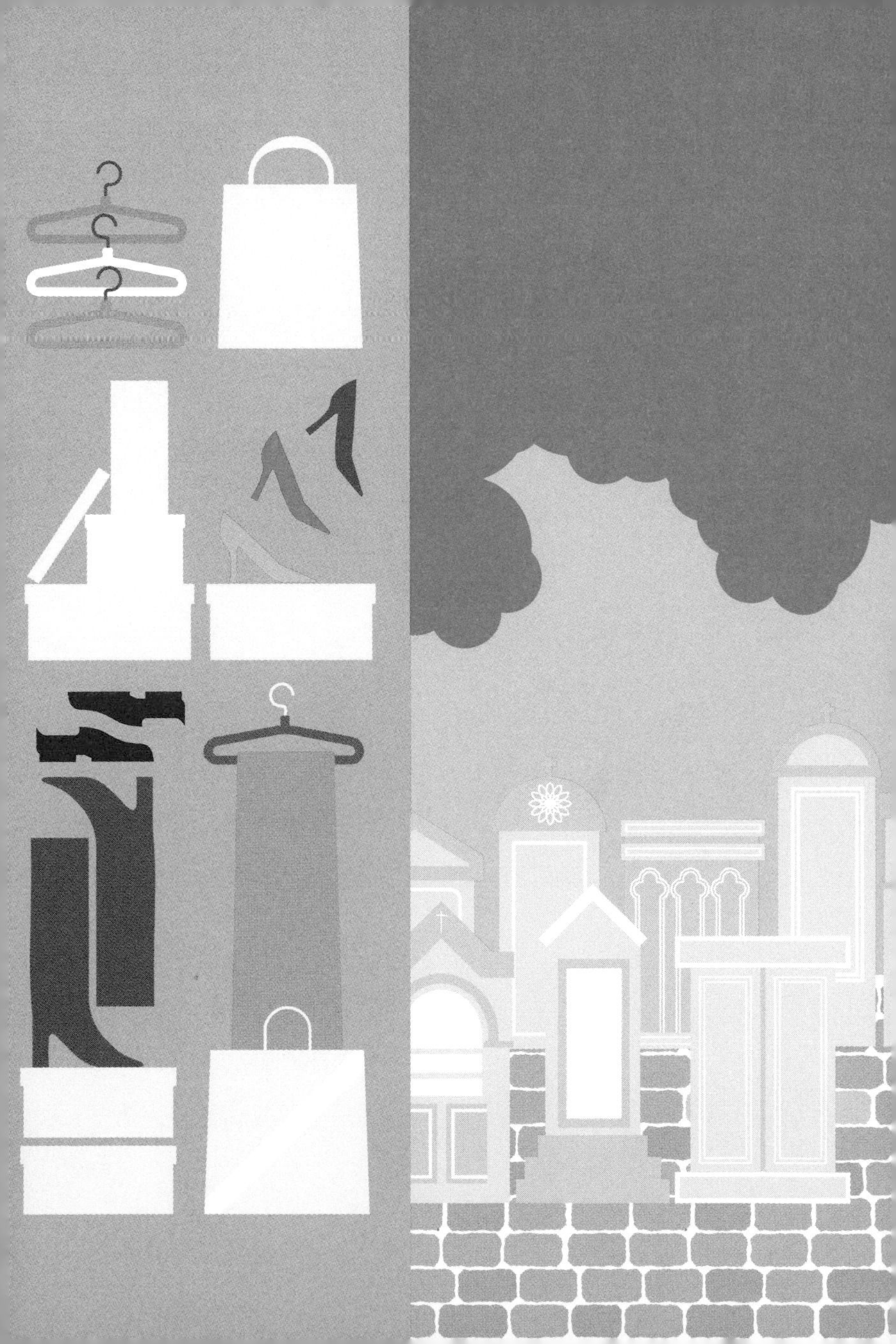

un dimanche à Manhattan

gospel in harlem
brunch
shopping on fifth ave.
central park

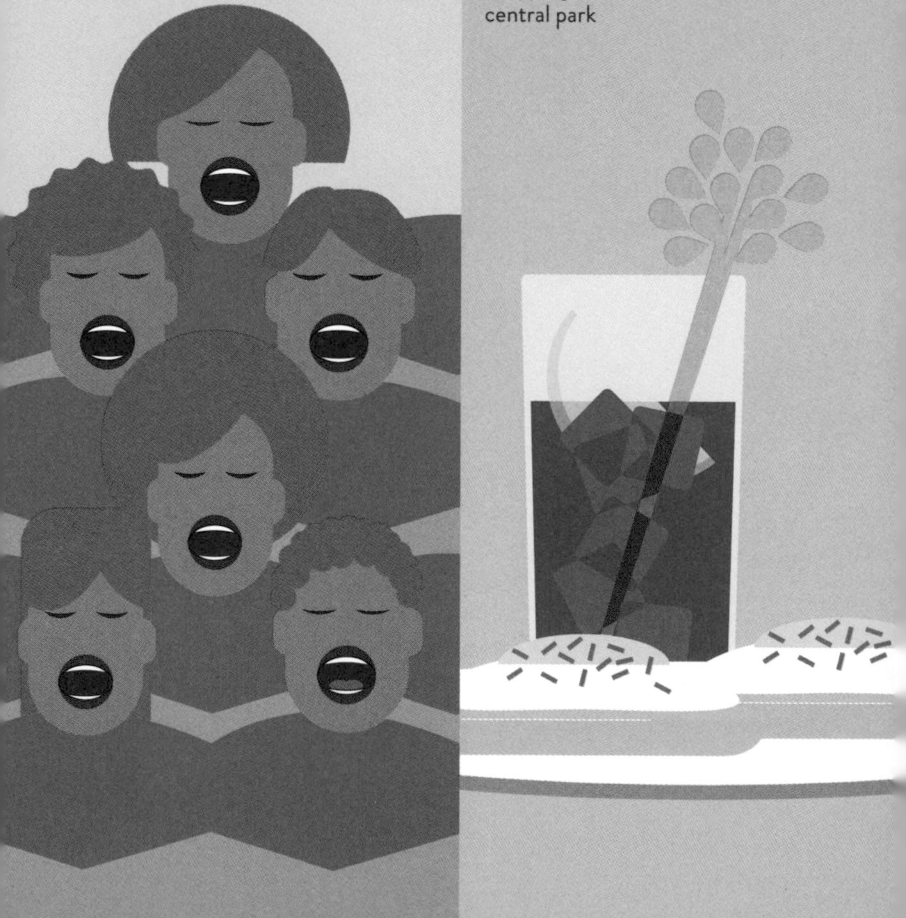

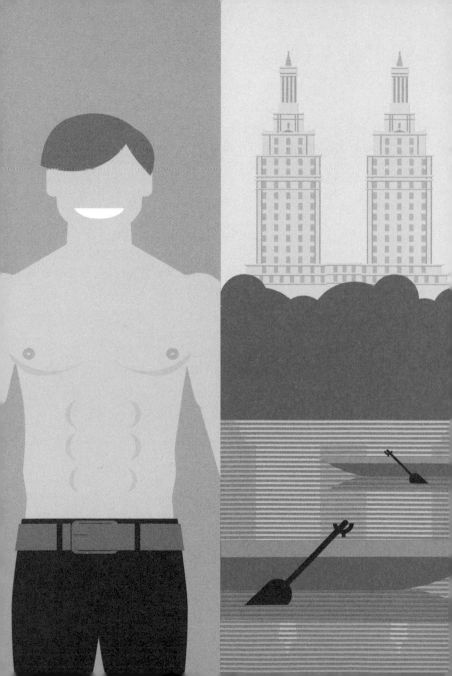

jardin

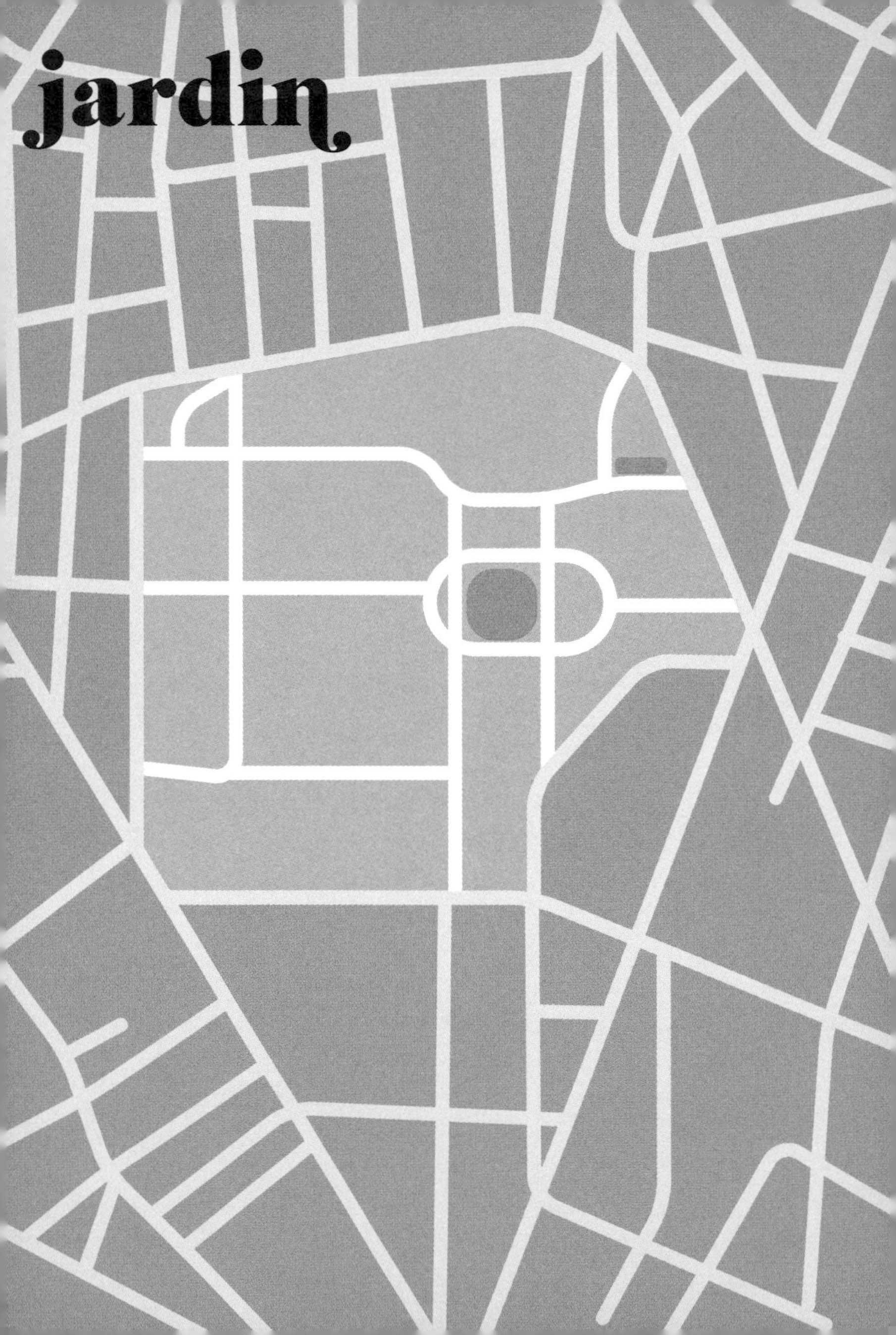

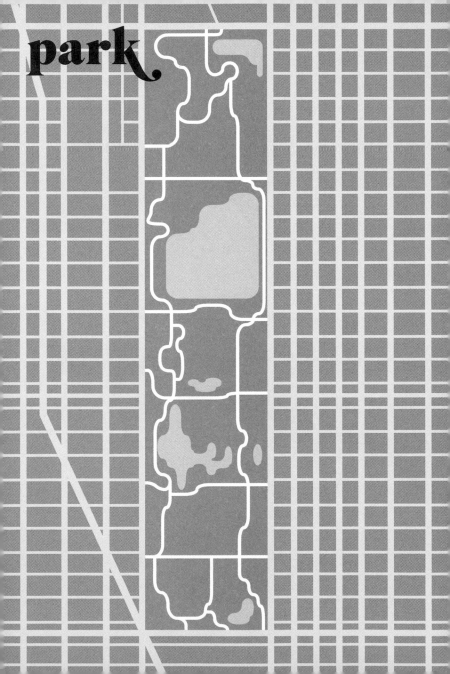

park.

pompidou

guggenheim

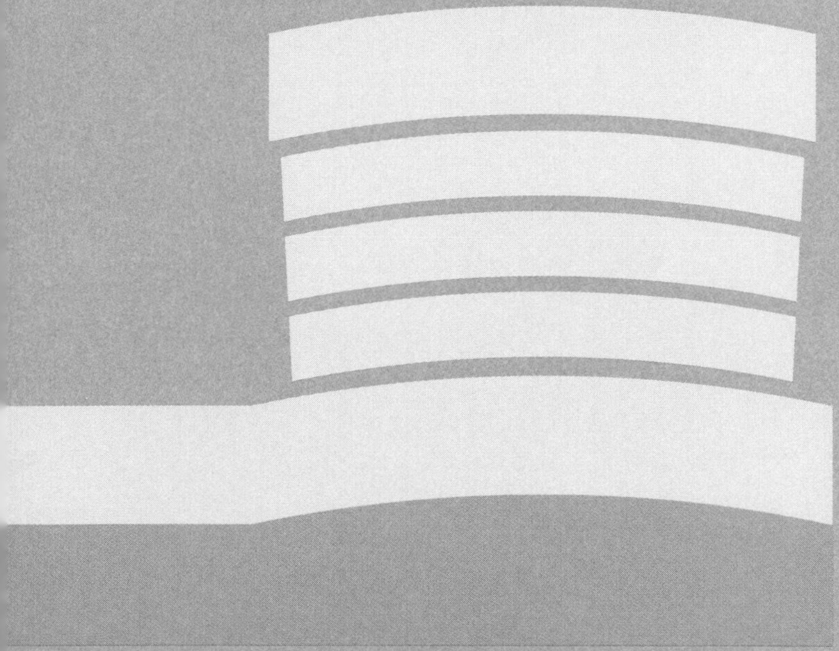

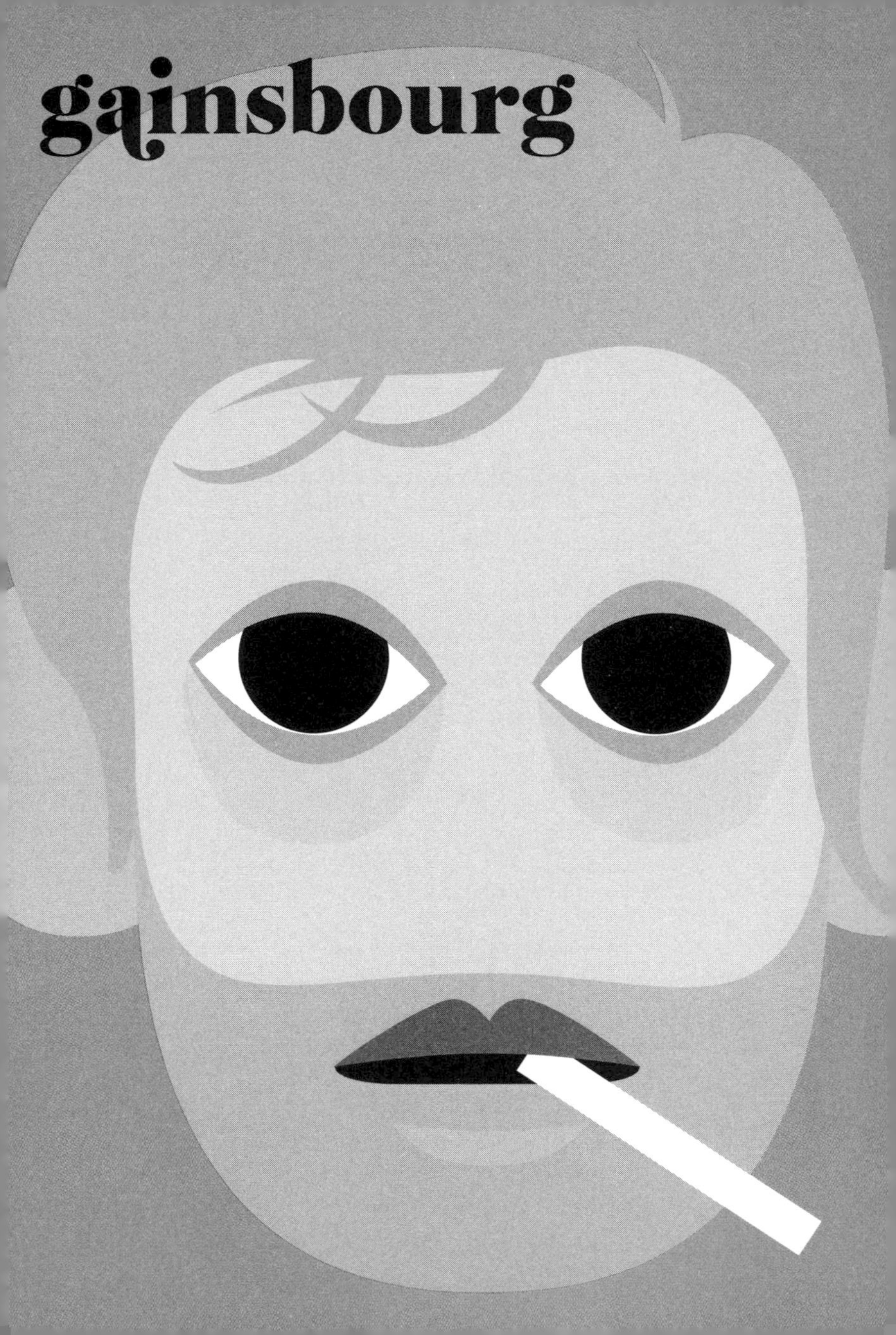
gainsbourg

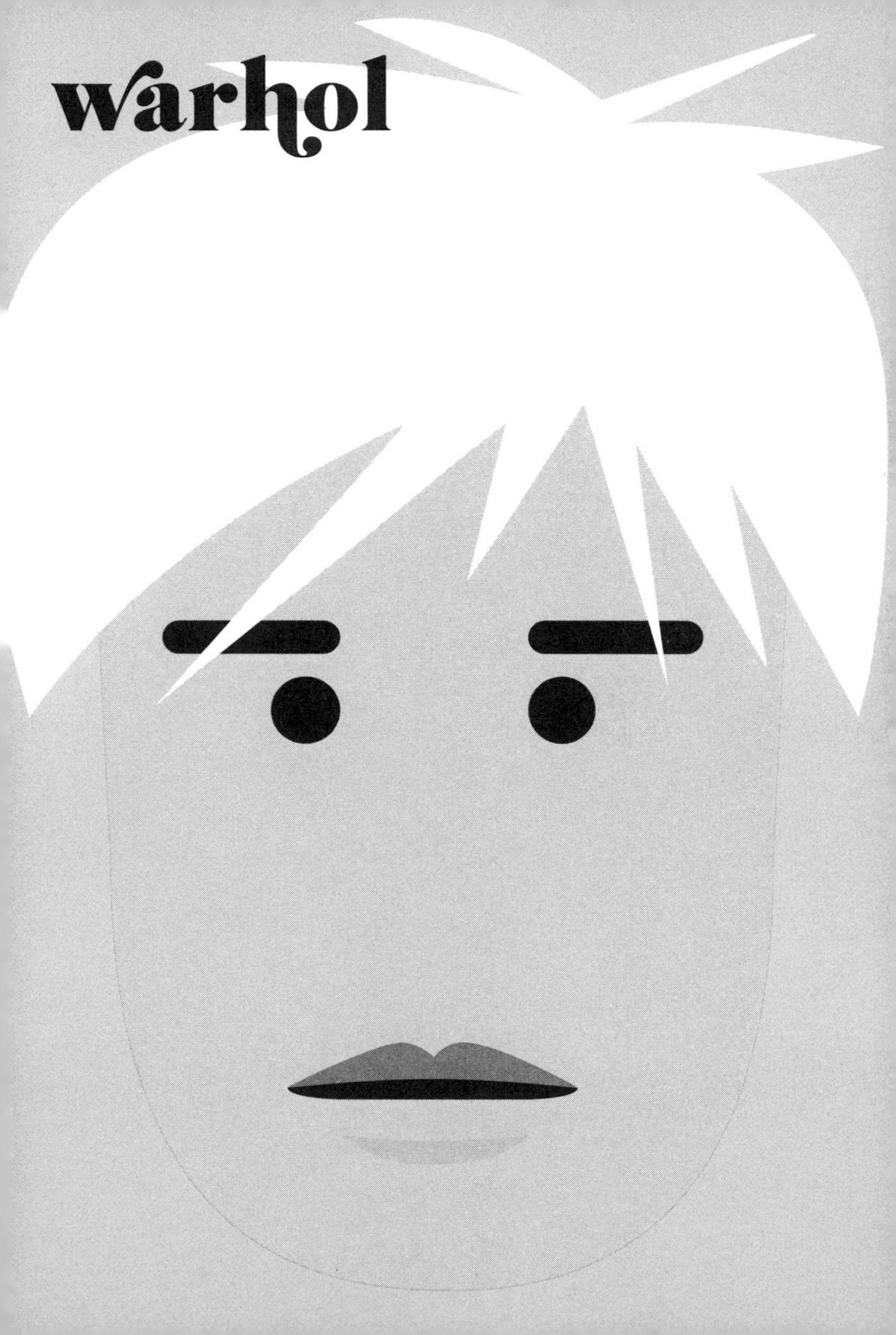
warhol

en avril

quand l'air plus doux berce une jeune romance

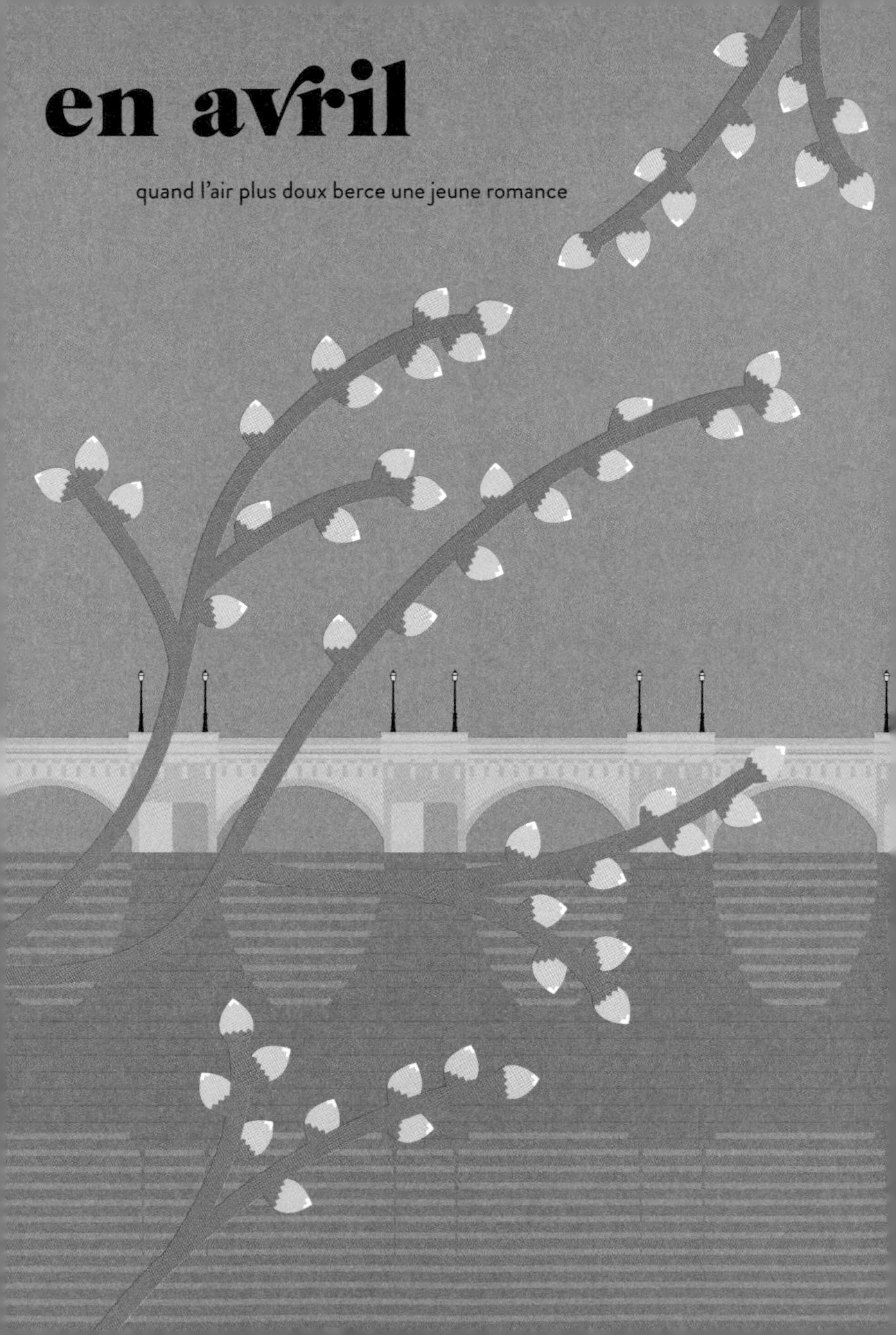

in september

experiencing indian summer

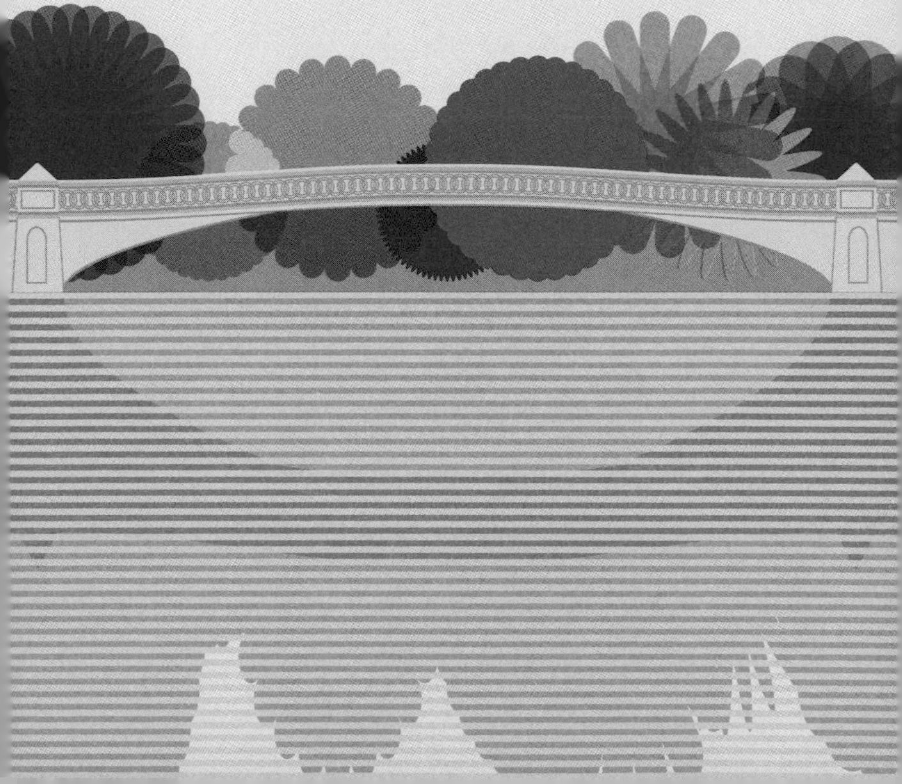

pigeon

rat volant

rat

wingless pigeon

tri sélectif

déchets — papier — verre

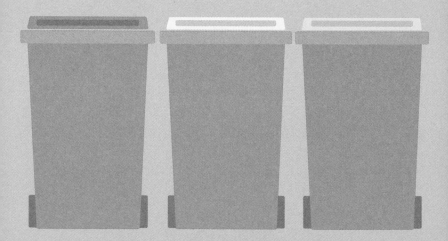

recycling

trash — paper — glass

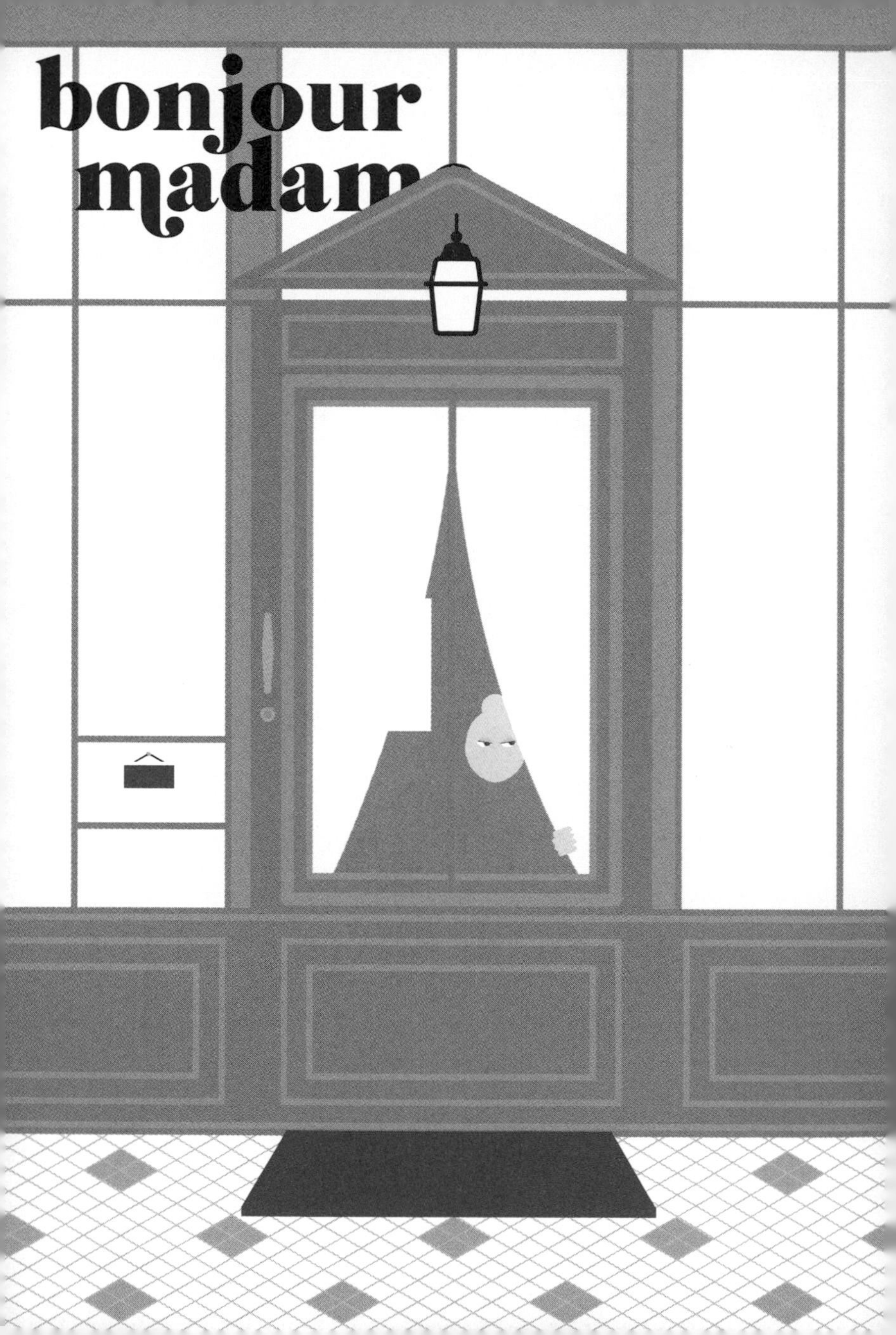
bonjour
madam

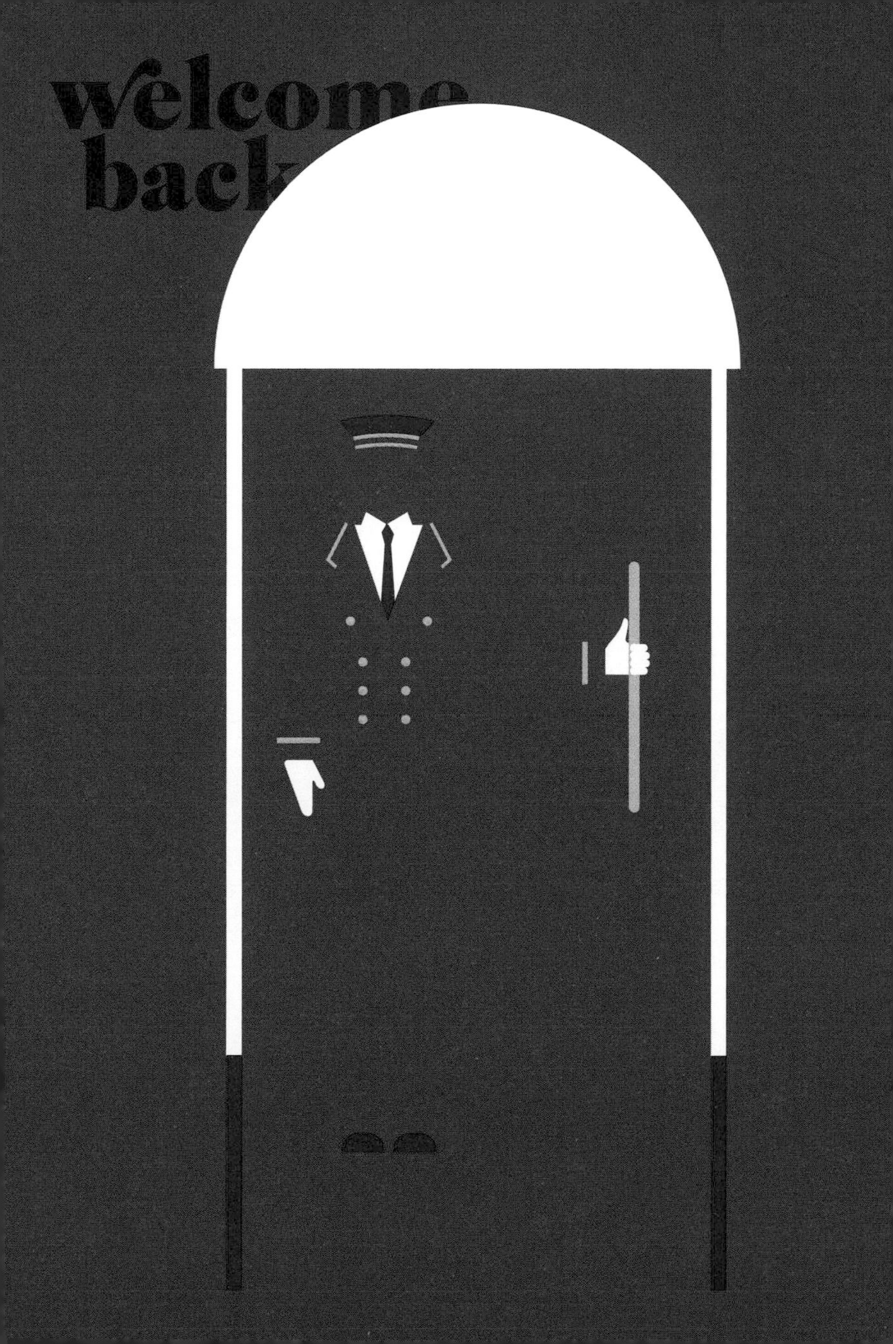
welcome
back

la crotte

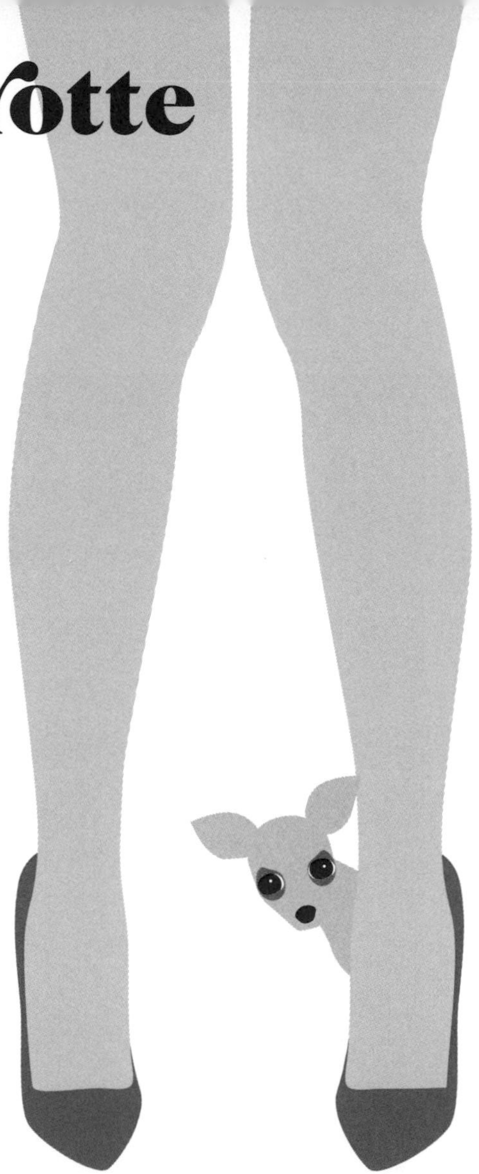

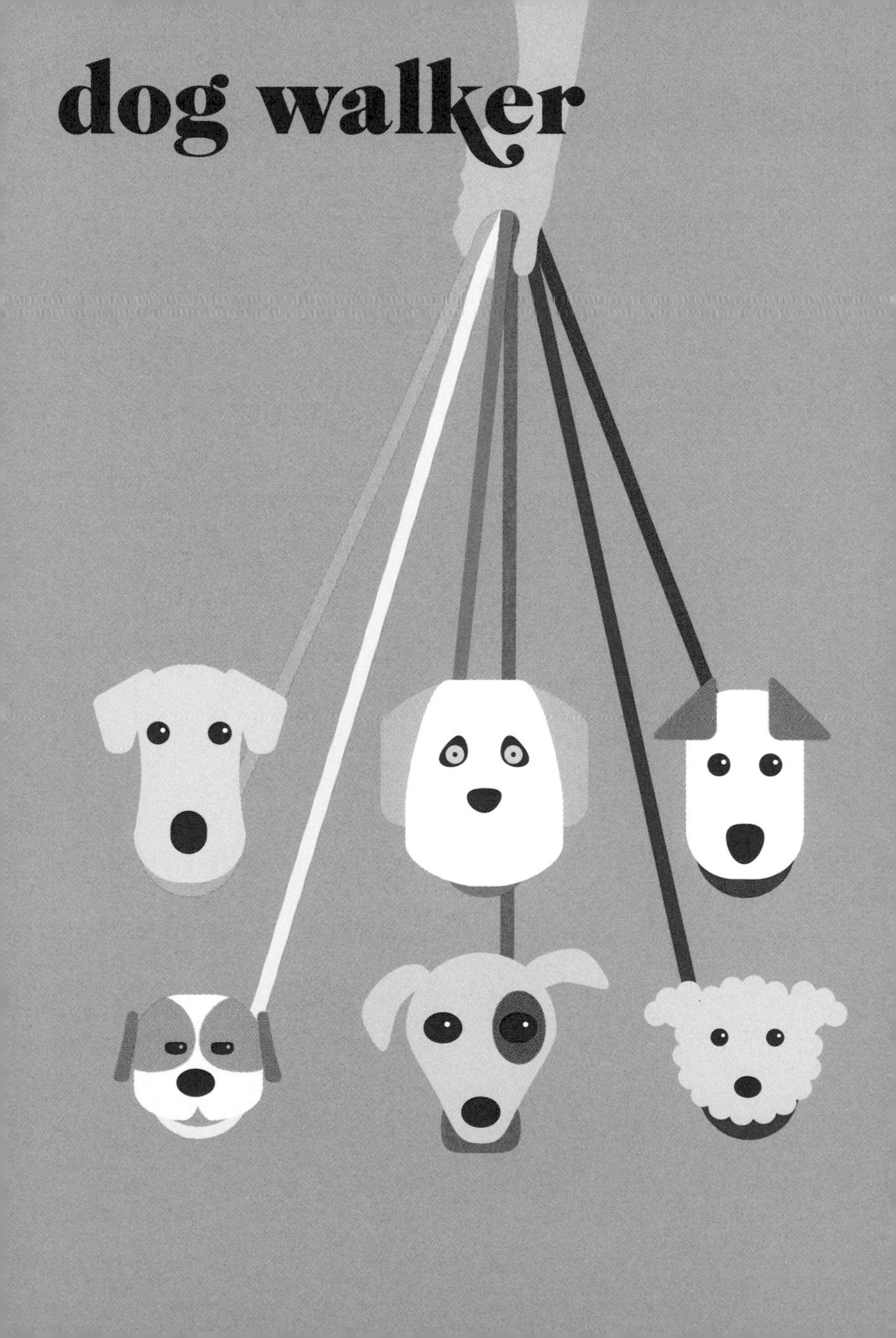
dog walker

porte-bonheur

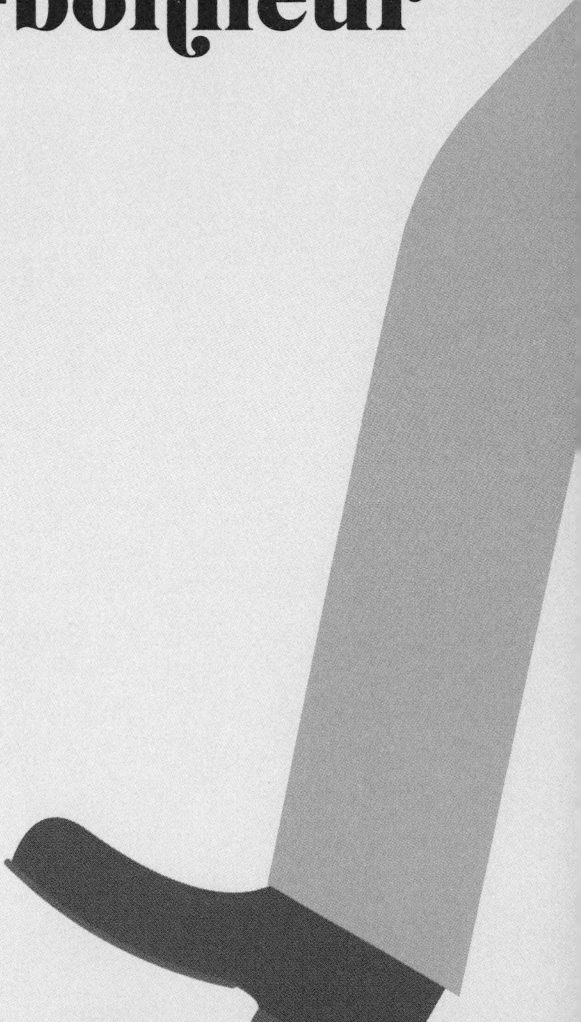

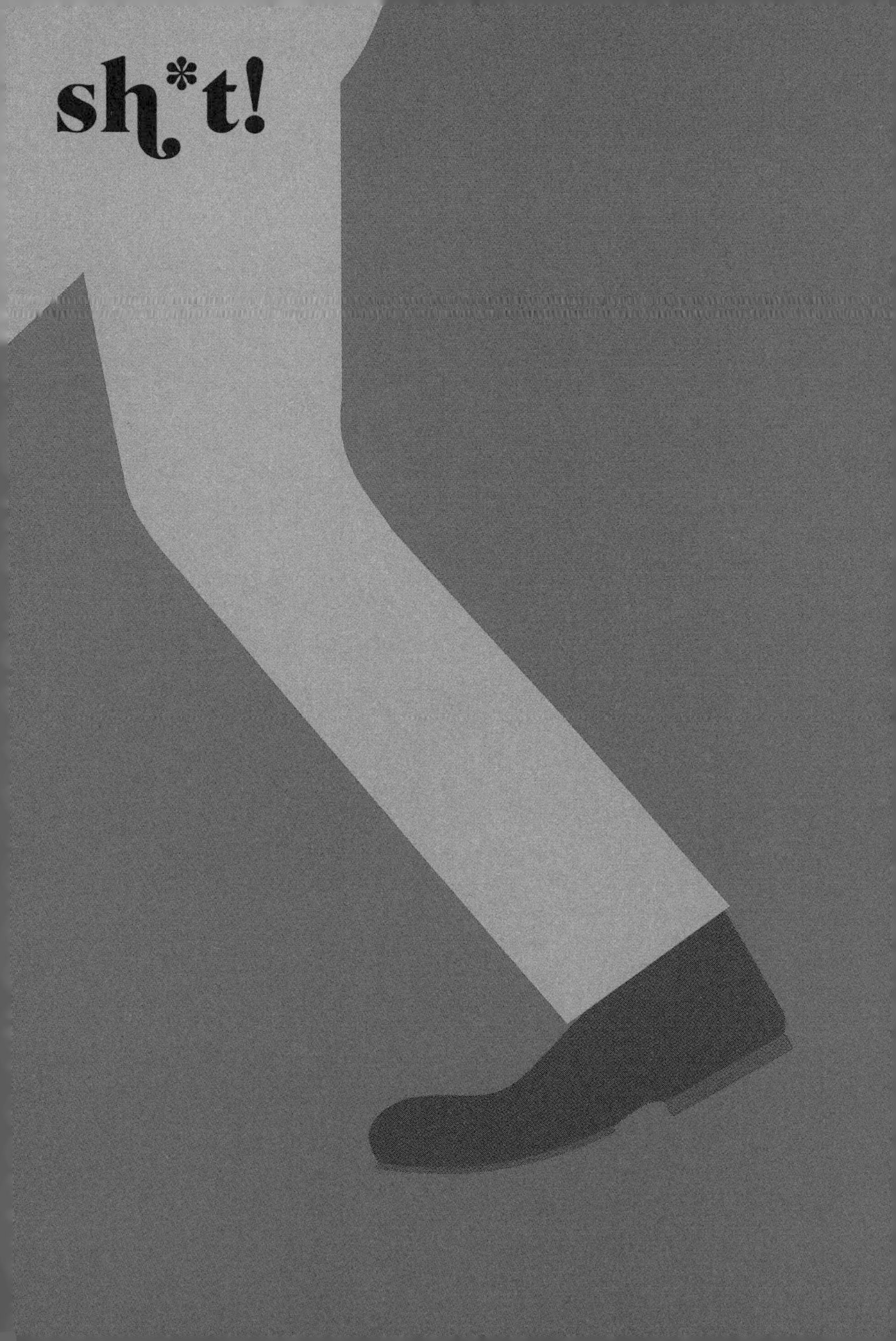
sh*t!

butte

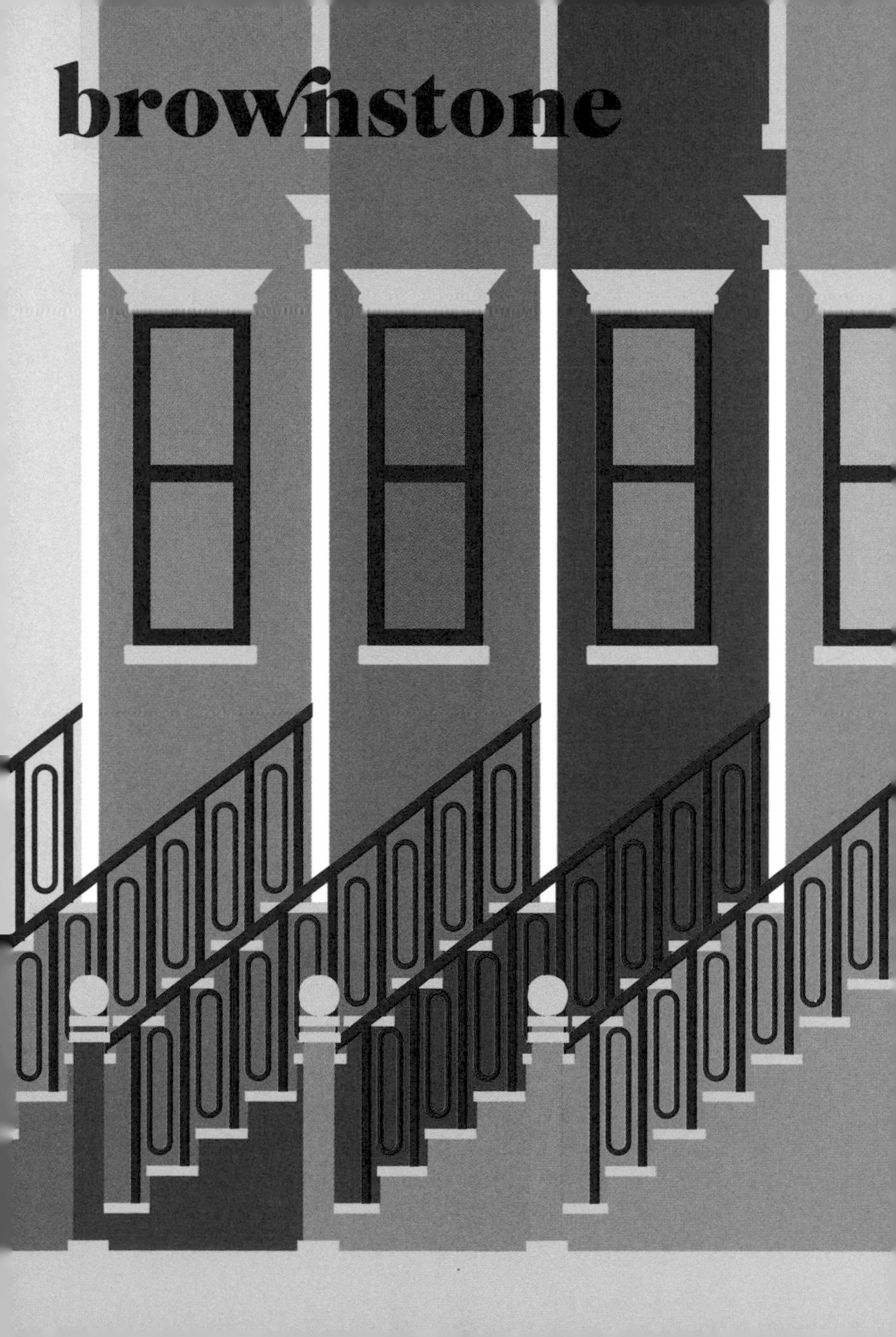
brownstone

funiculaire

pour monter au sacré-cœur

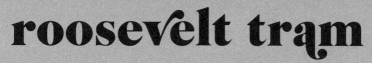

roosevelt tram

to cross the east river

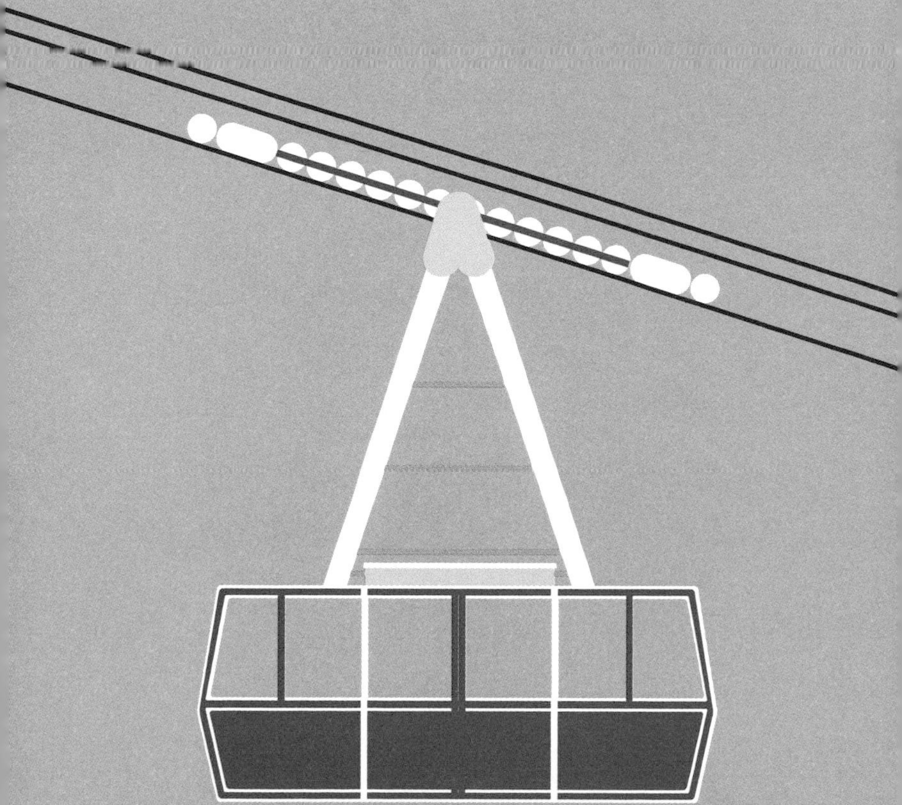

pont des arts

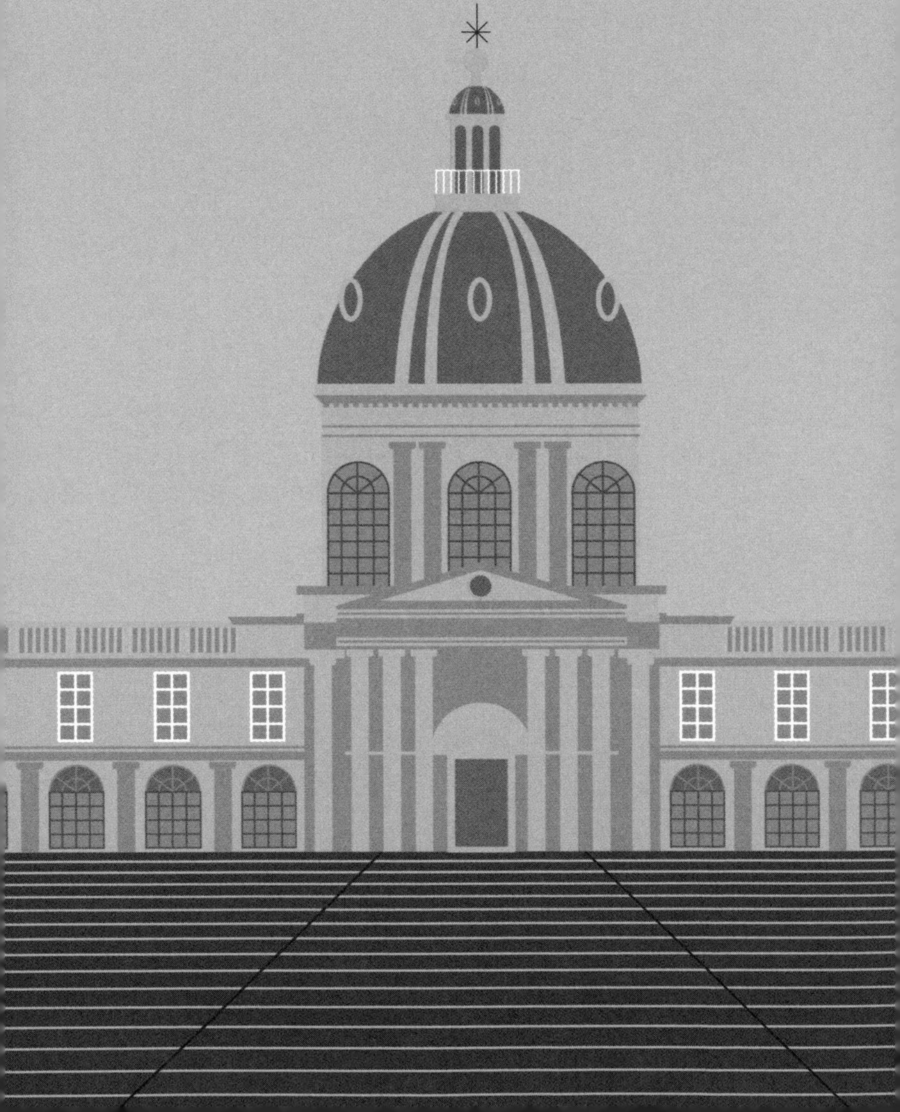

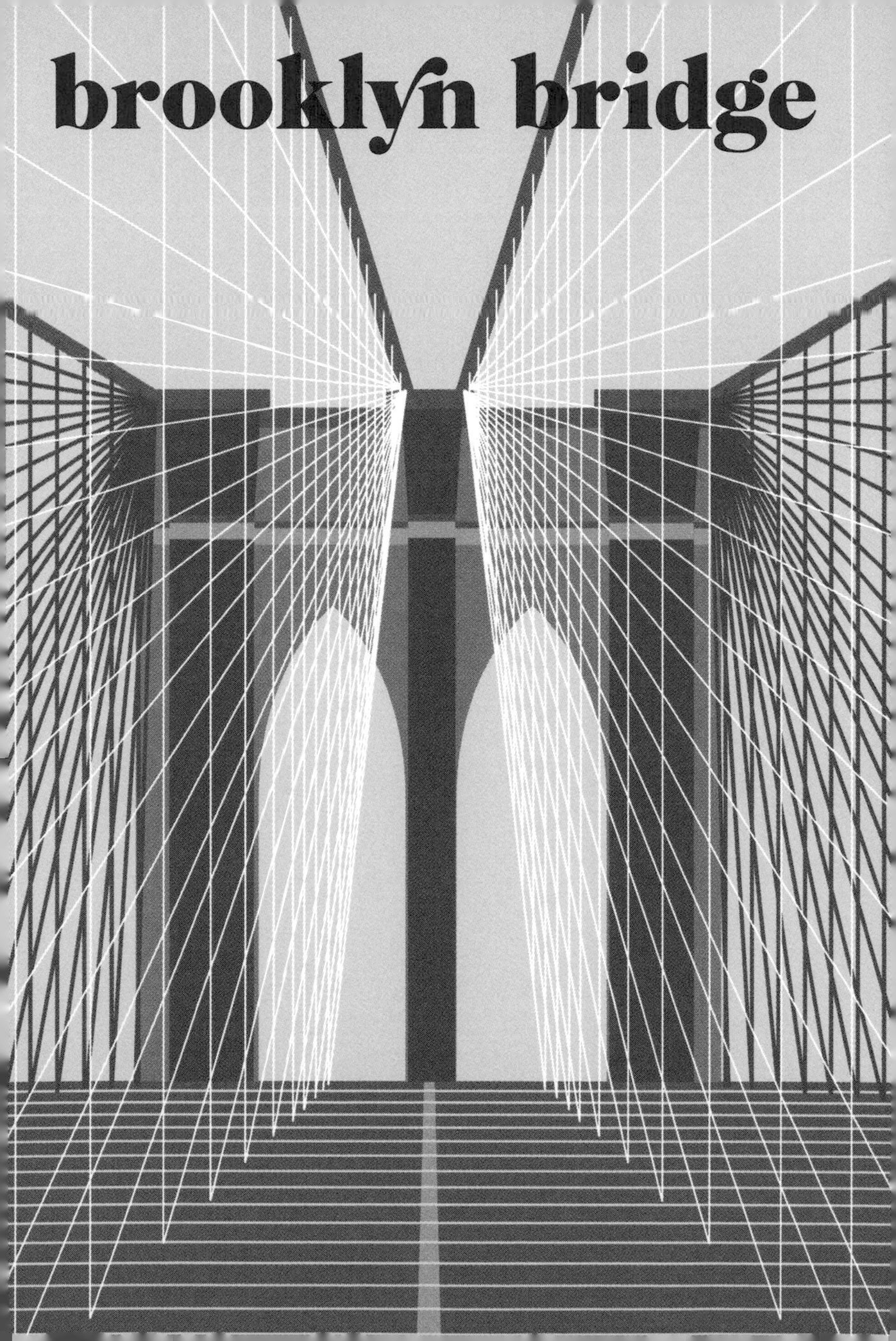
brooklyn bridge

parc des princes

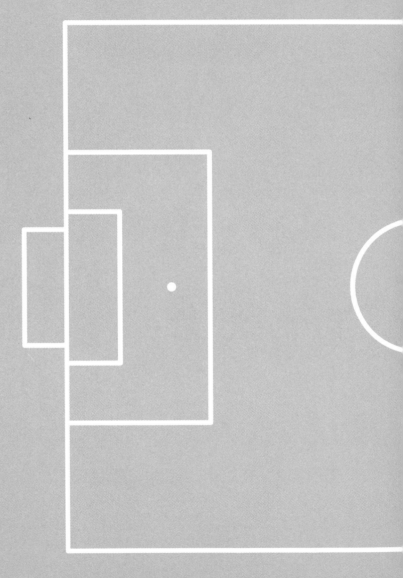

giants stadium

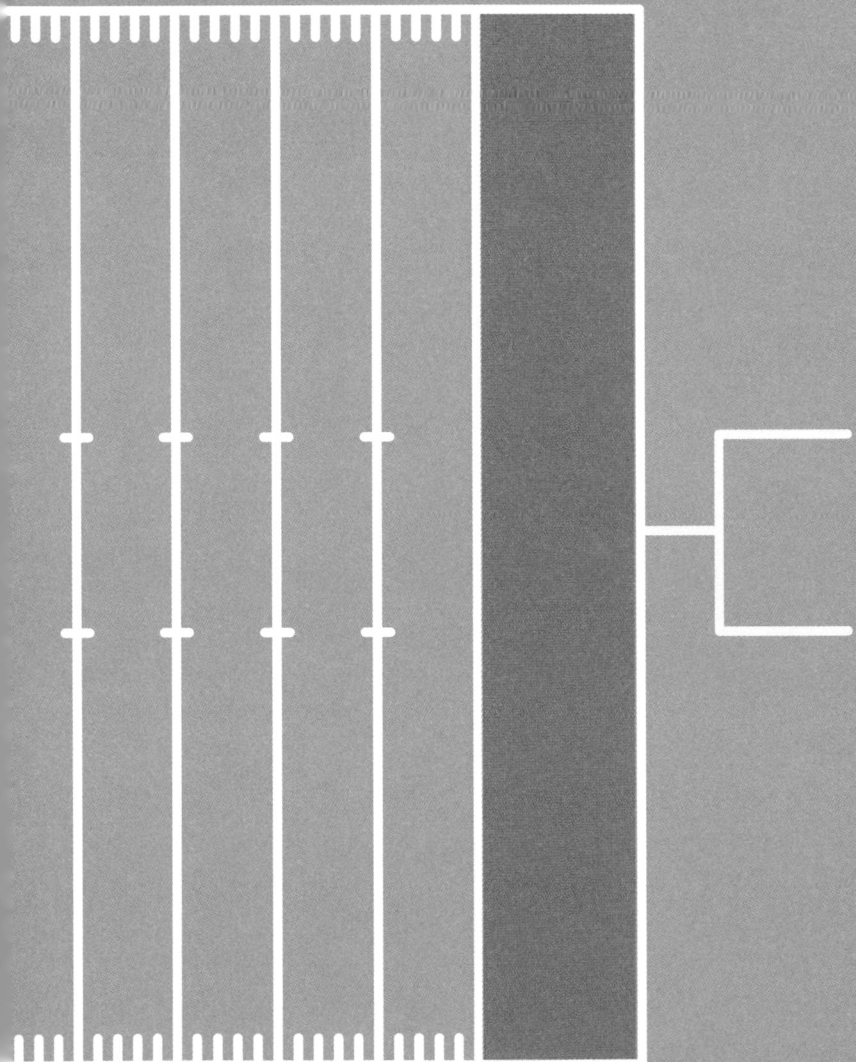

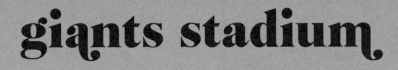

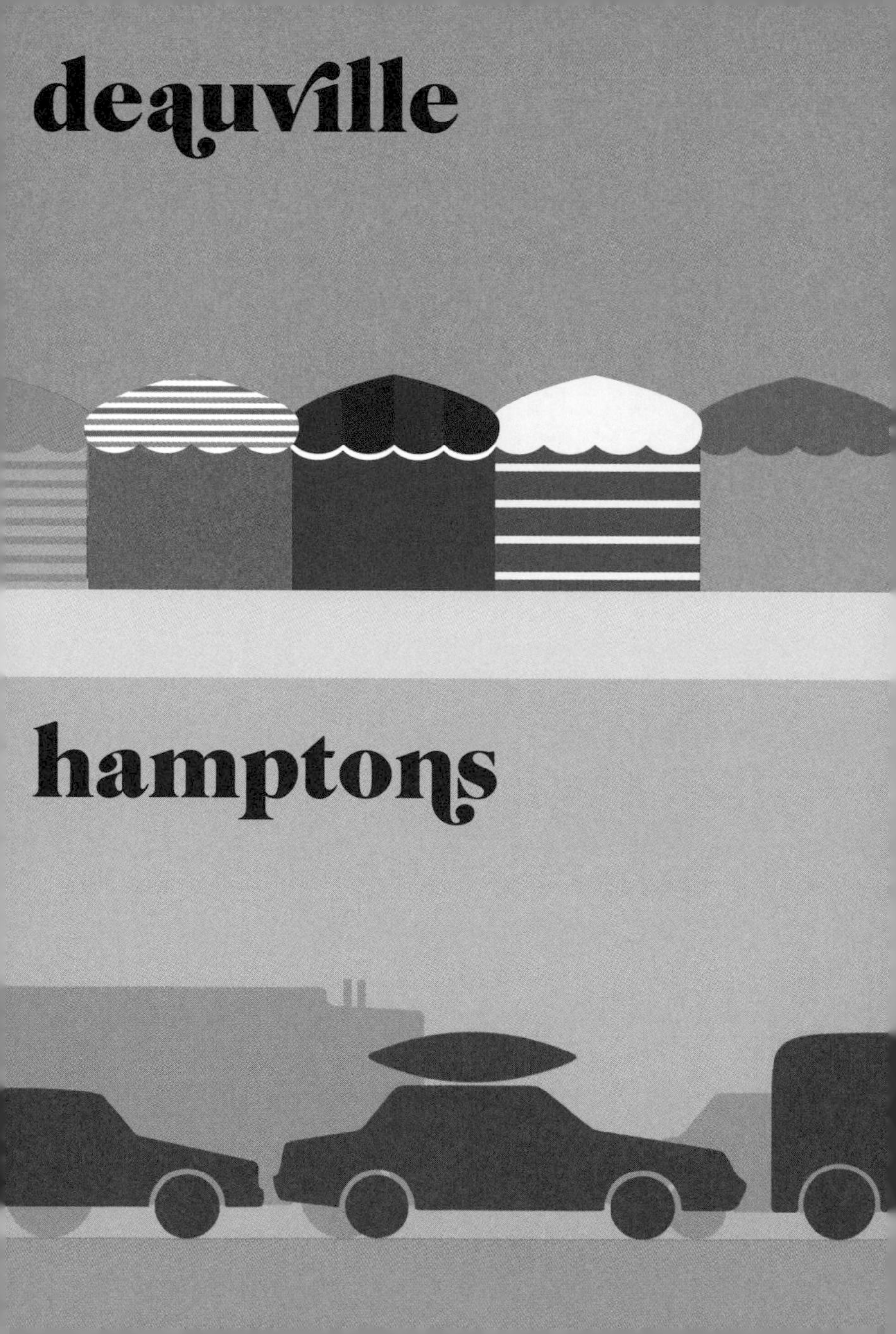
deauville
hamptons

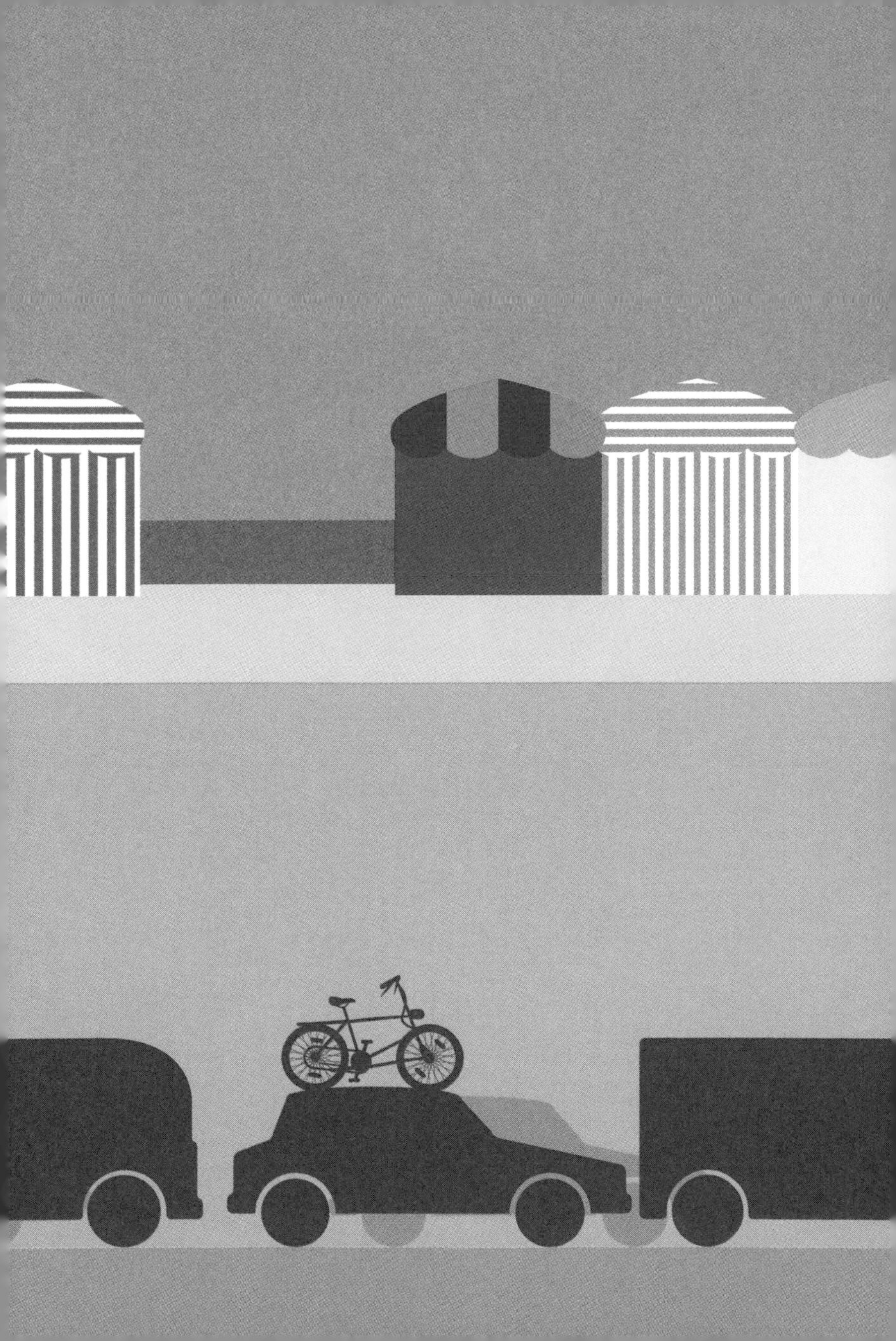

paris plages

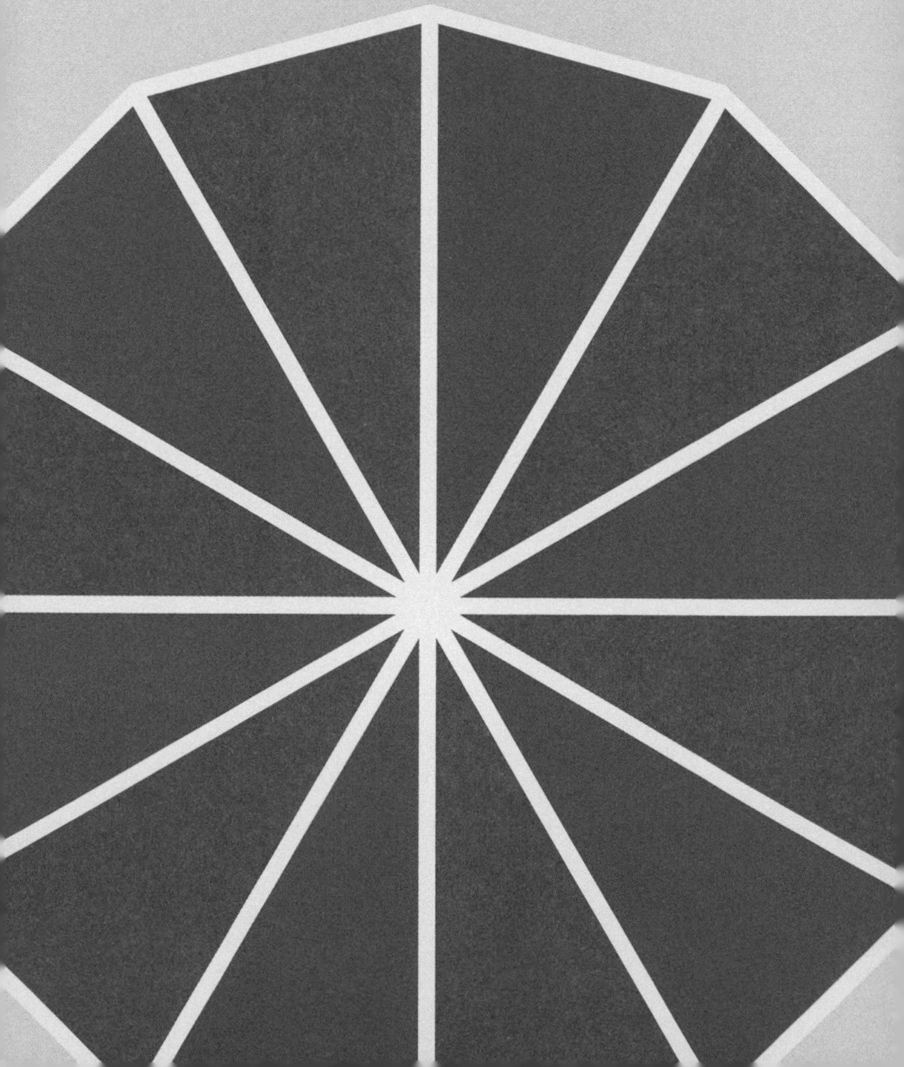

coney island

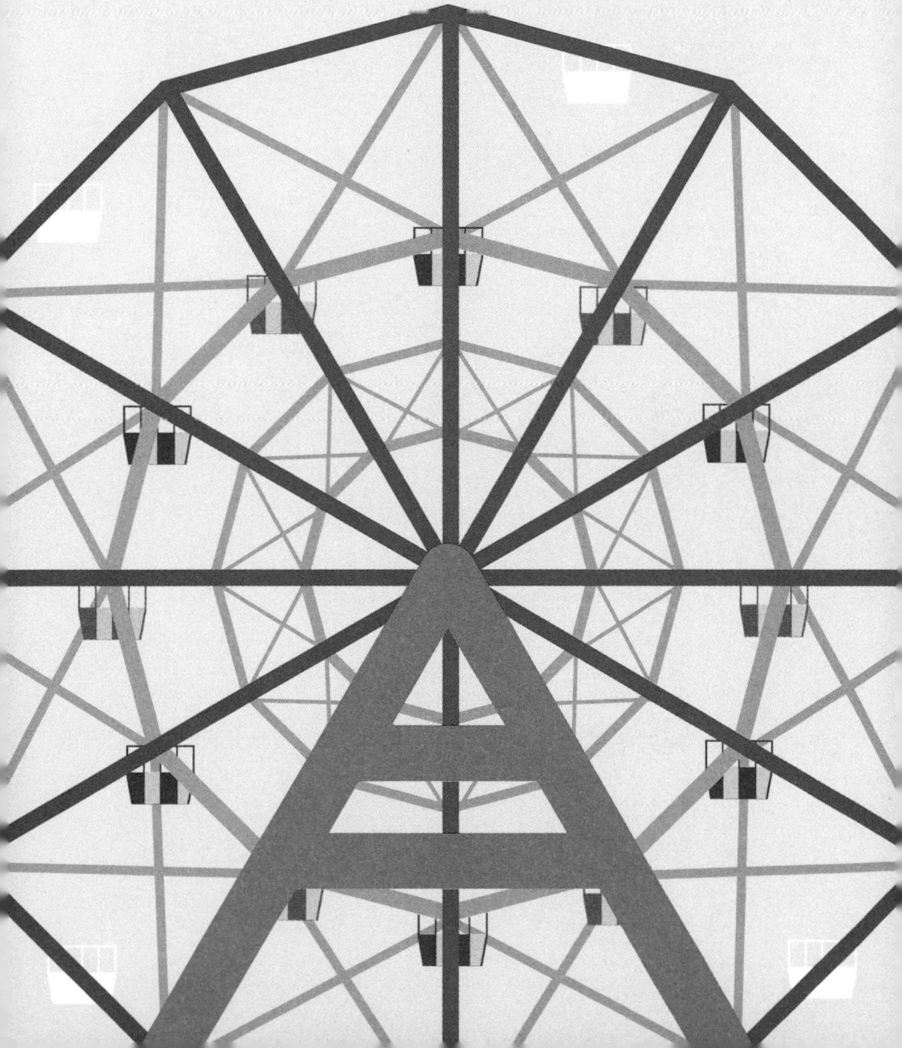

cartier

tiffany

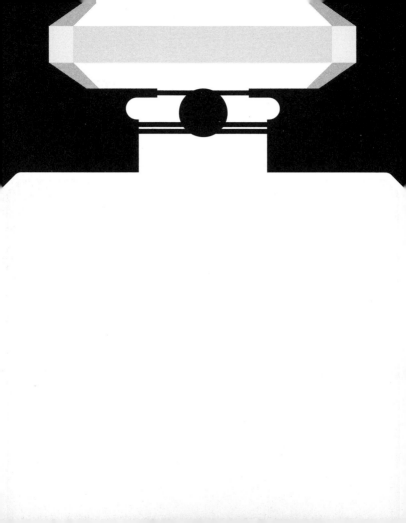

calvin

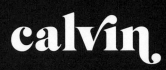

champs-élysées

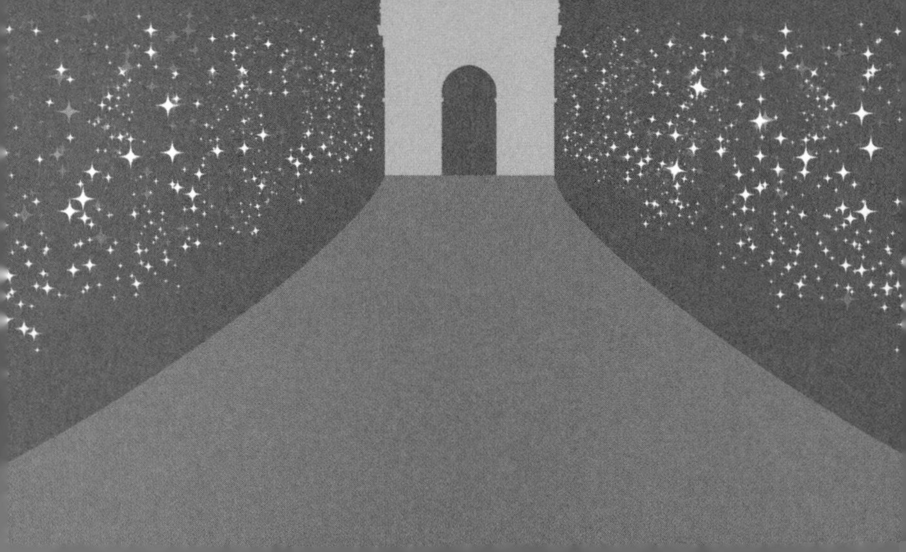

fifth avenue

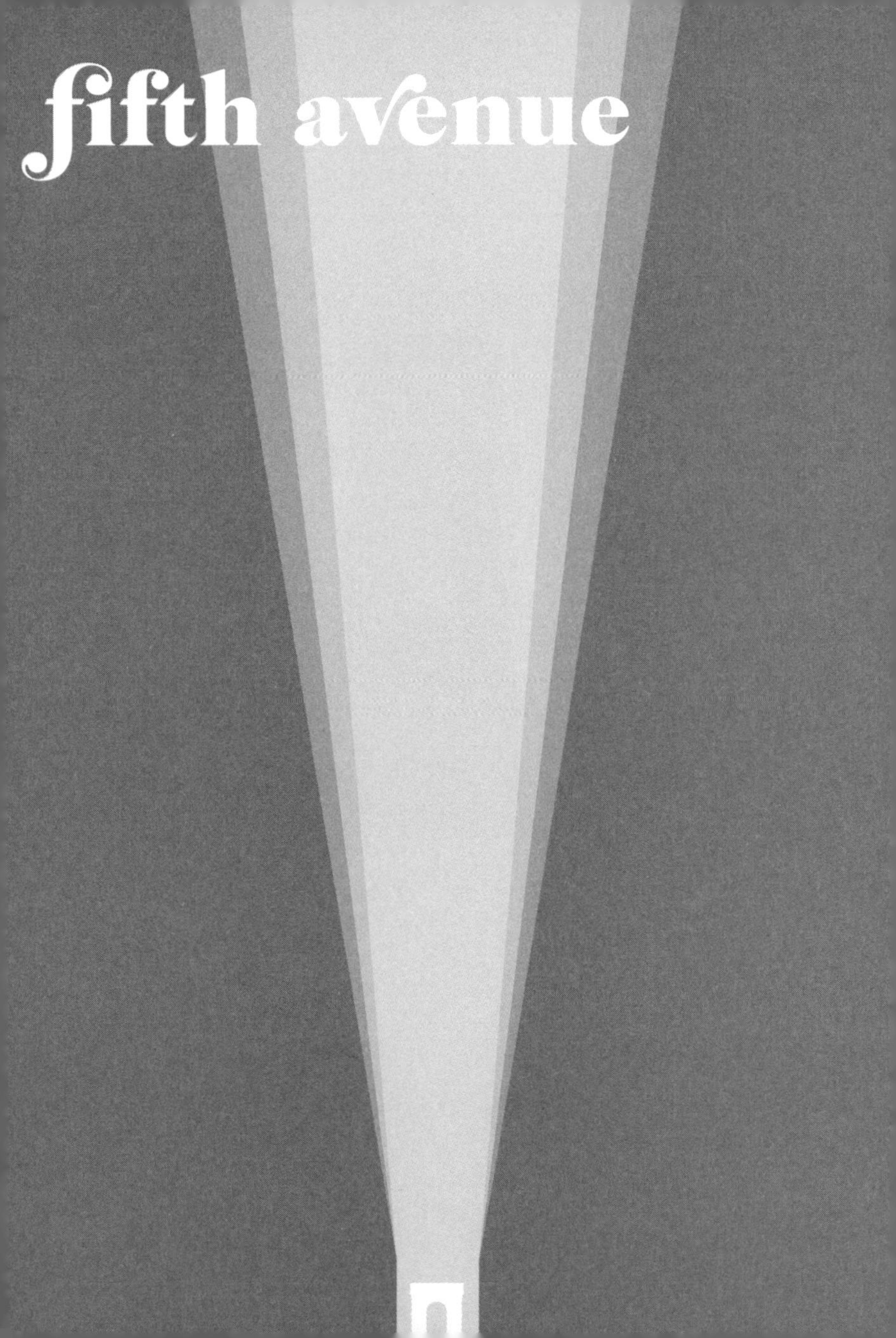

parisienne

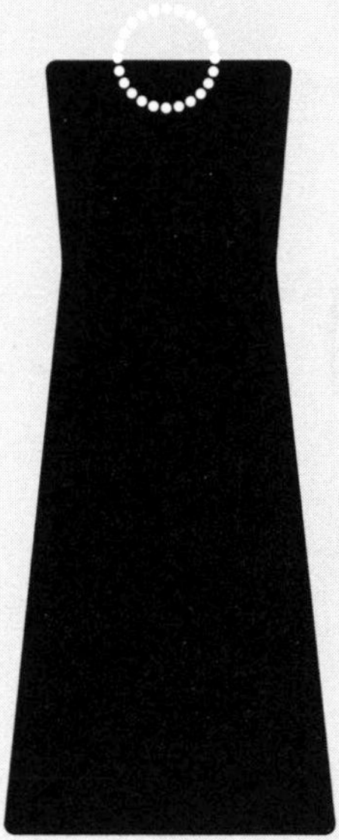

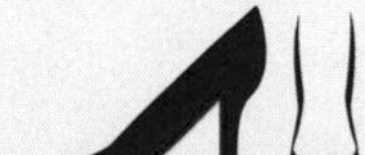

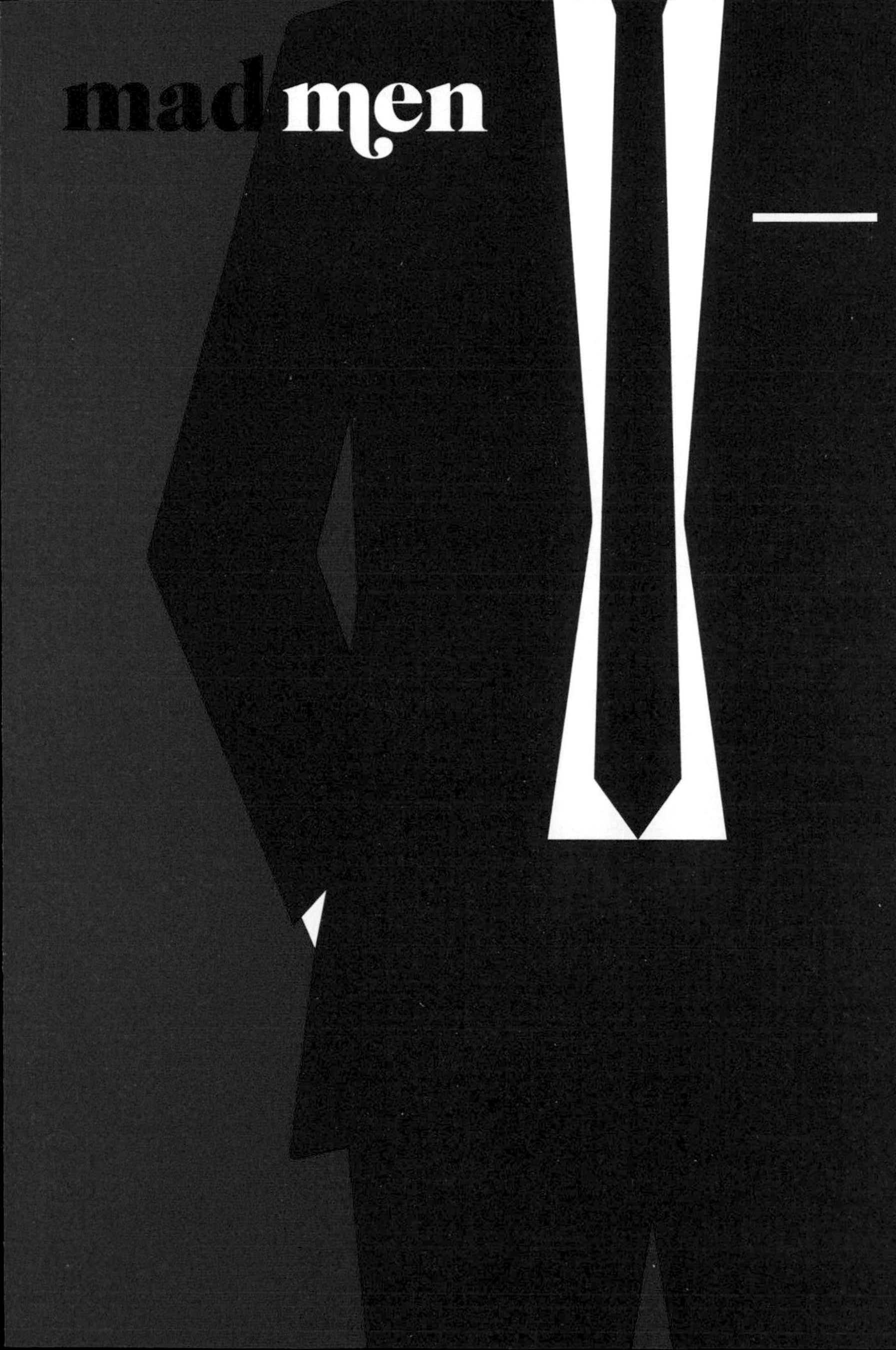
mad men

jean paul

ralph

promotion

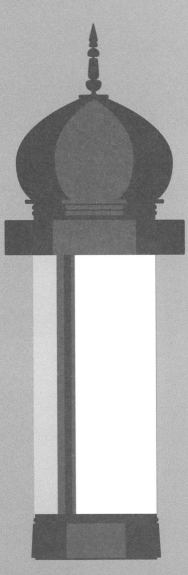

construction

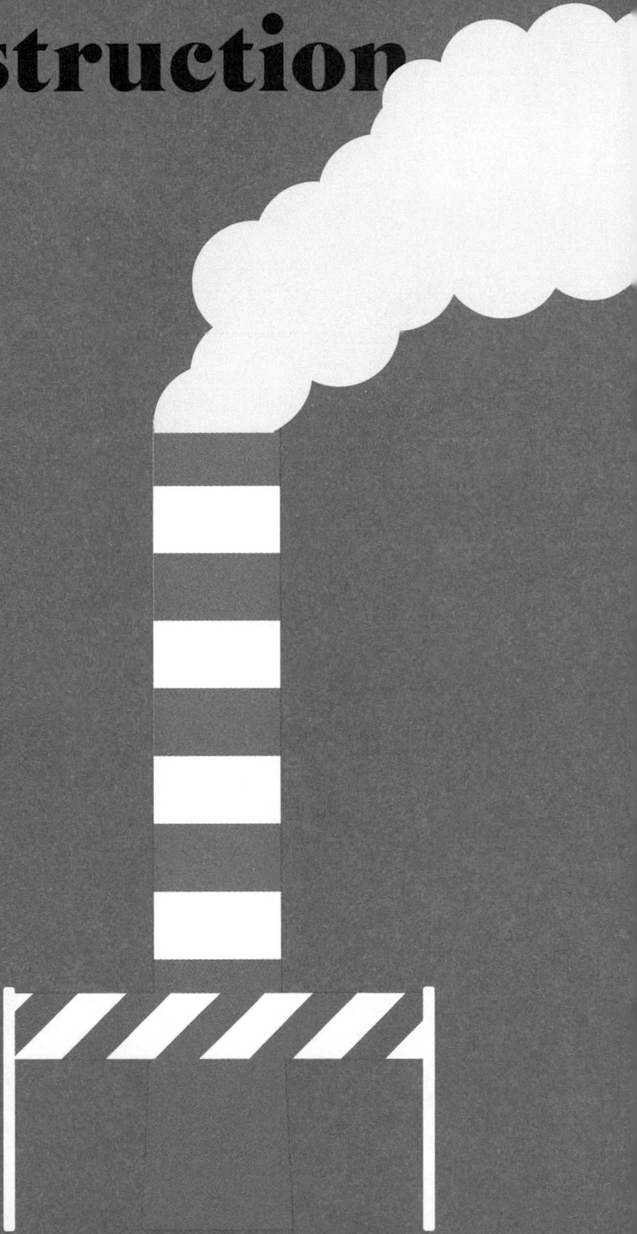

conversation

dialogue

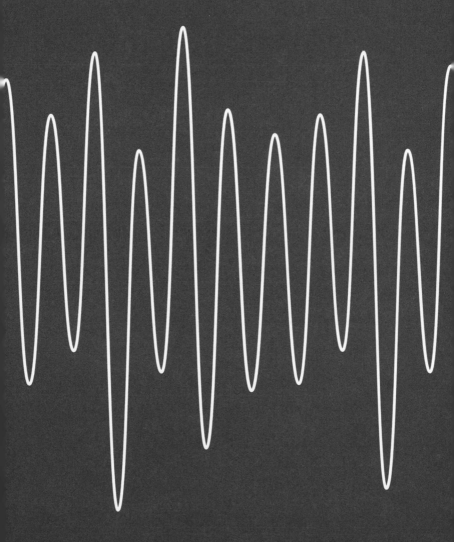

pâtisserie

pastrami

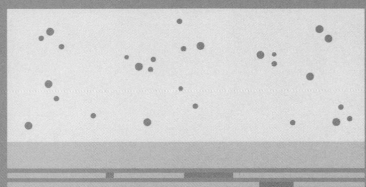

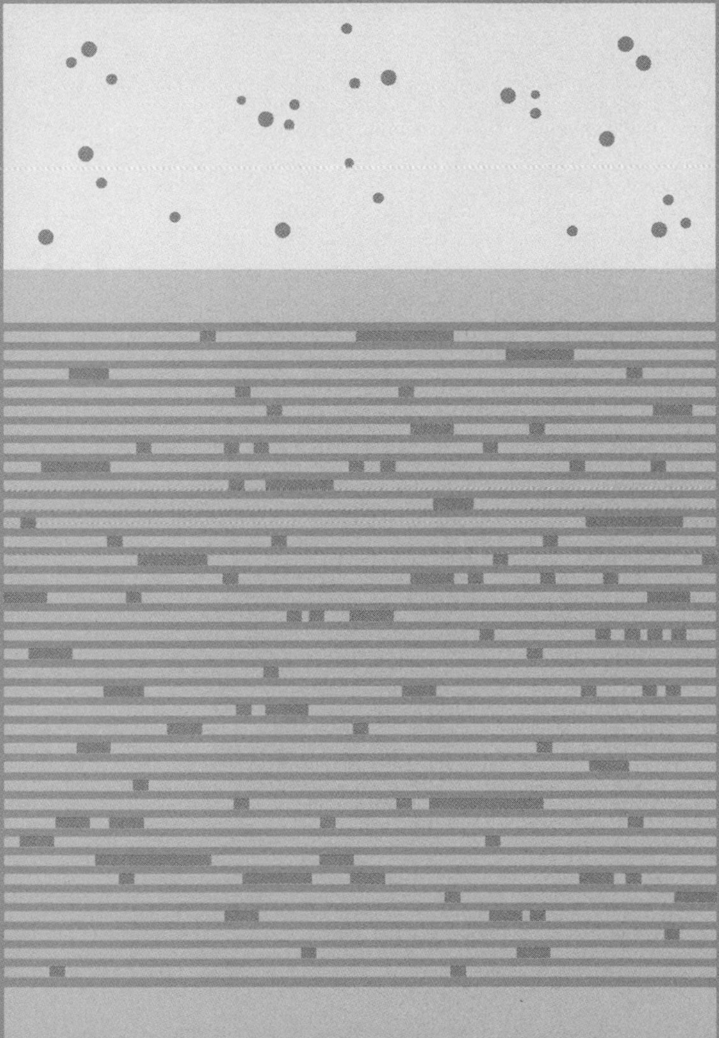

XS

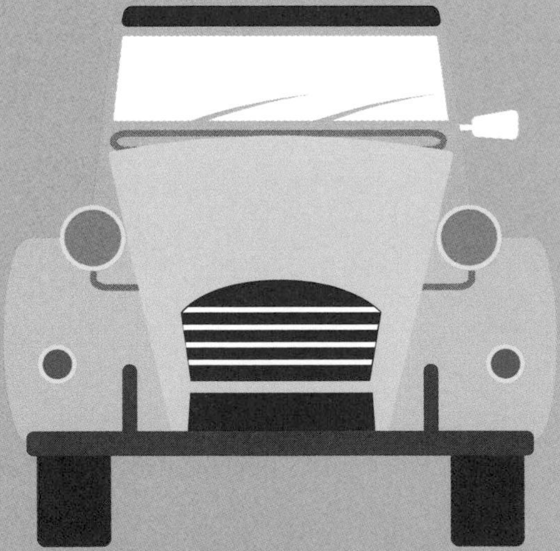

XL

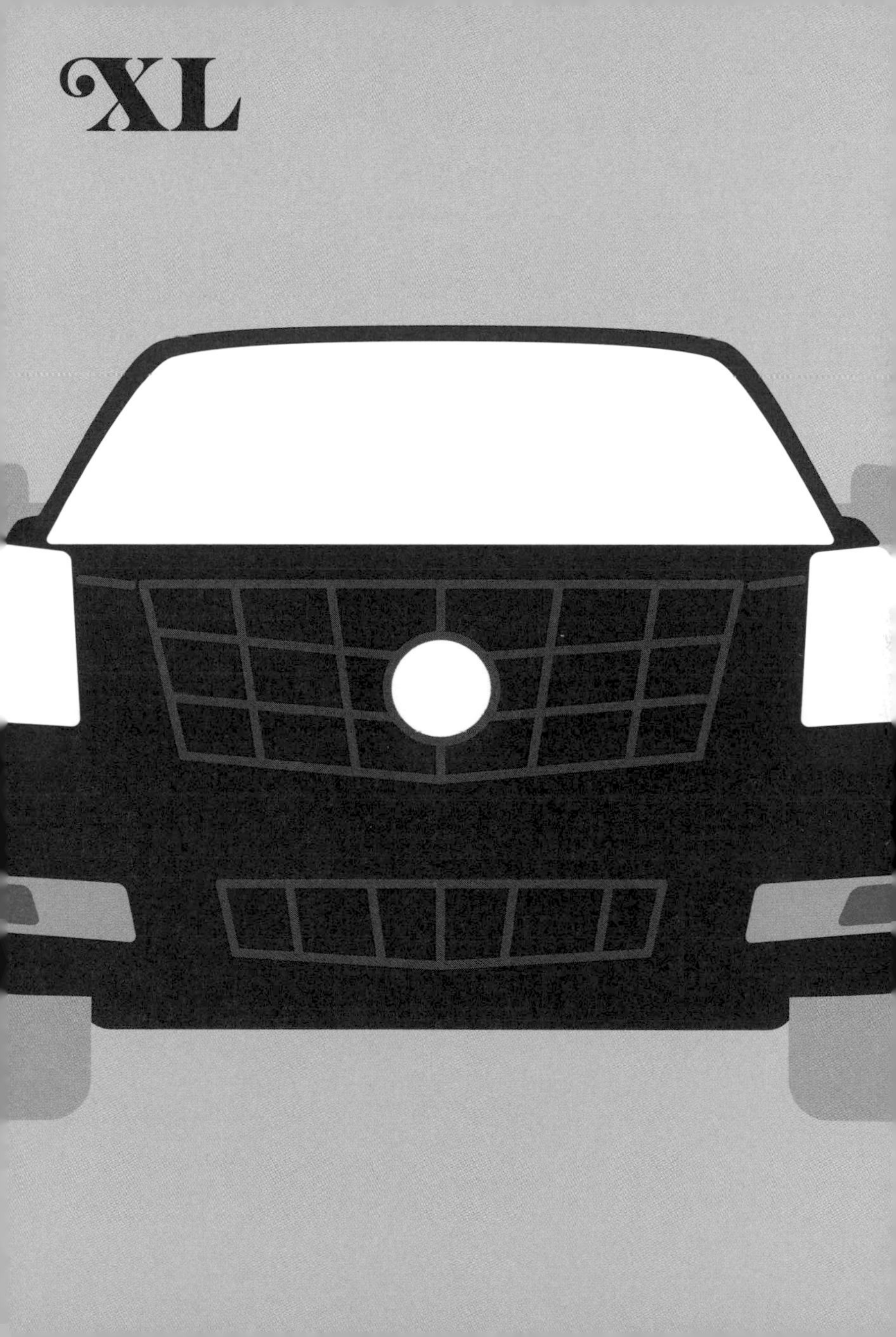

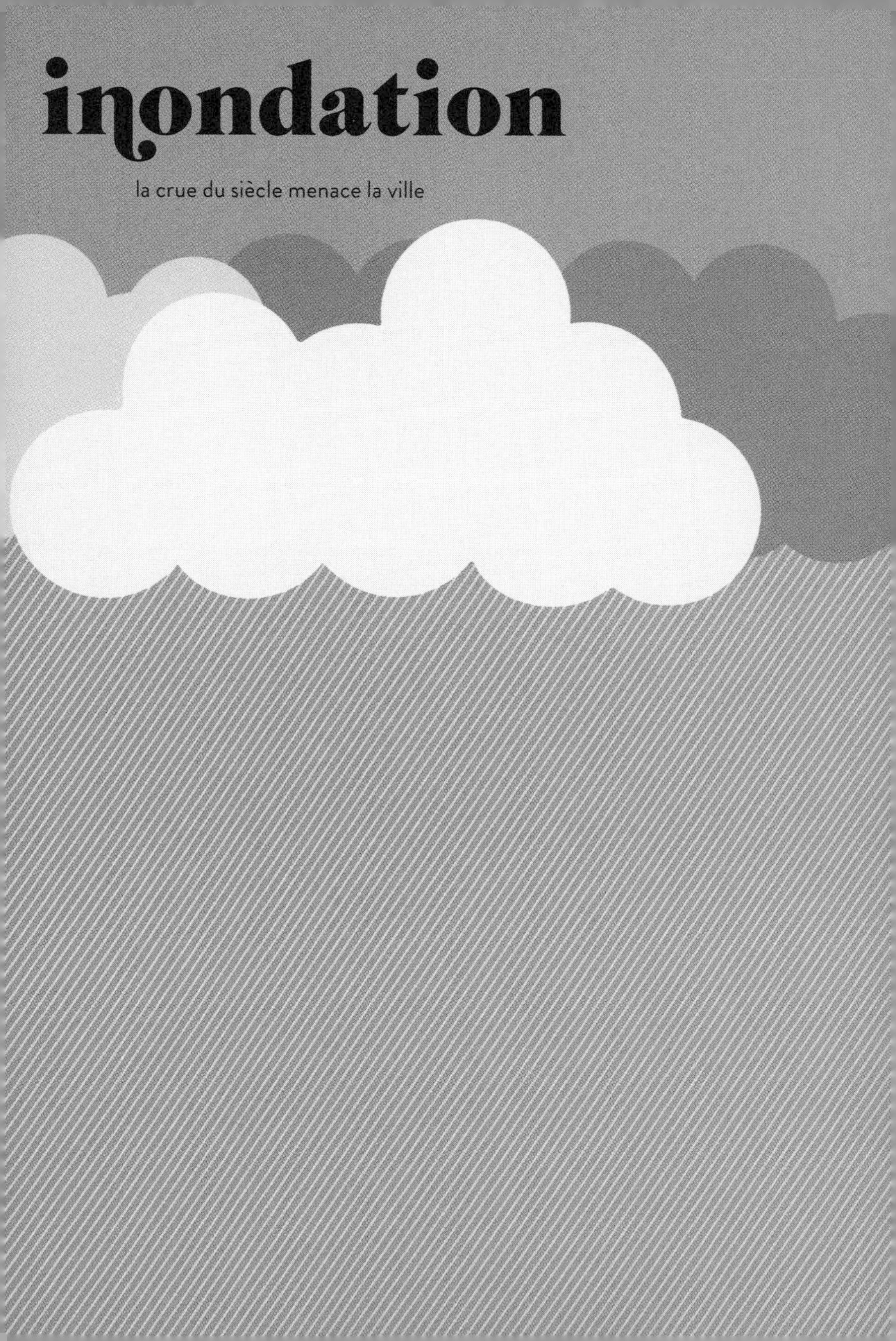
inondation
la crue du siècle menace la ville

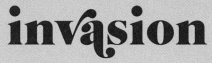

invasion

first aliens take manhattan

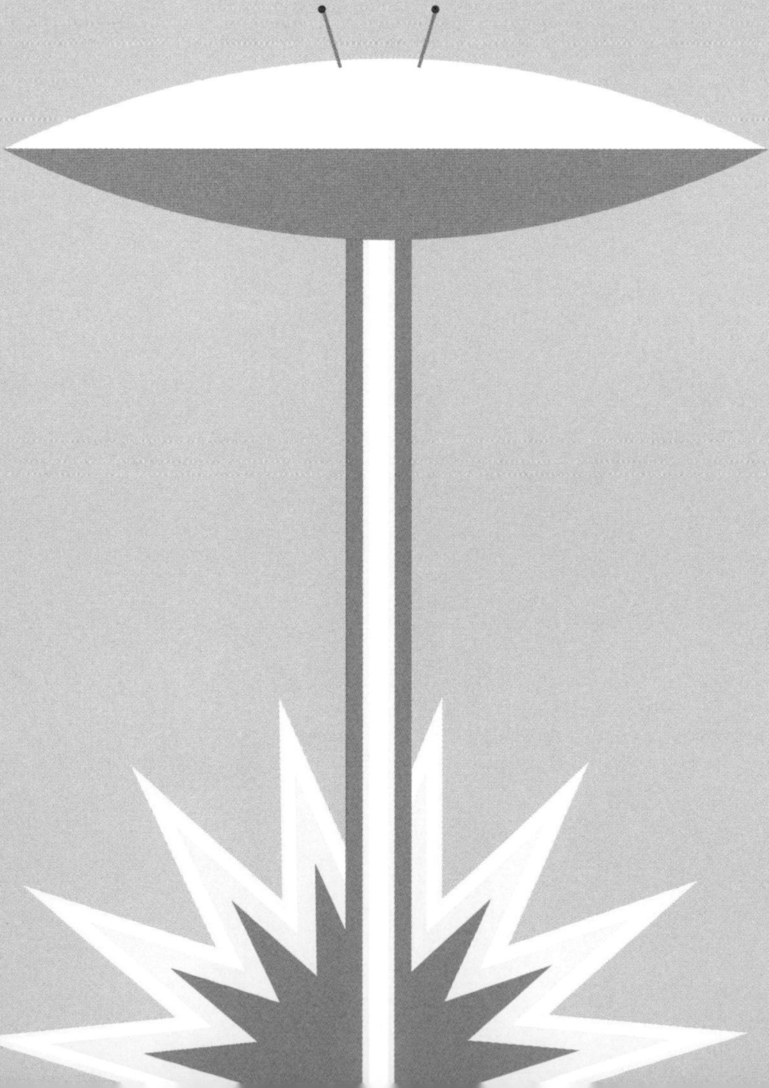

grand rex

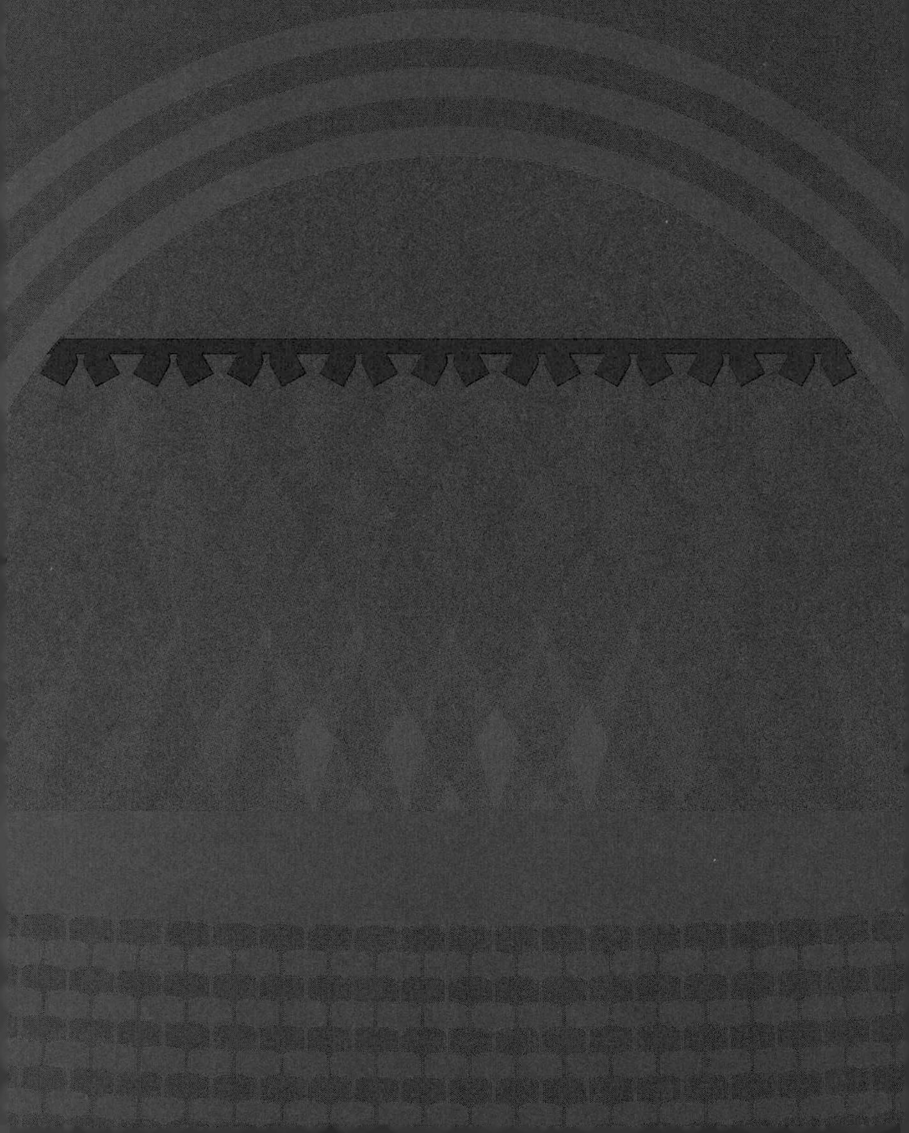

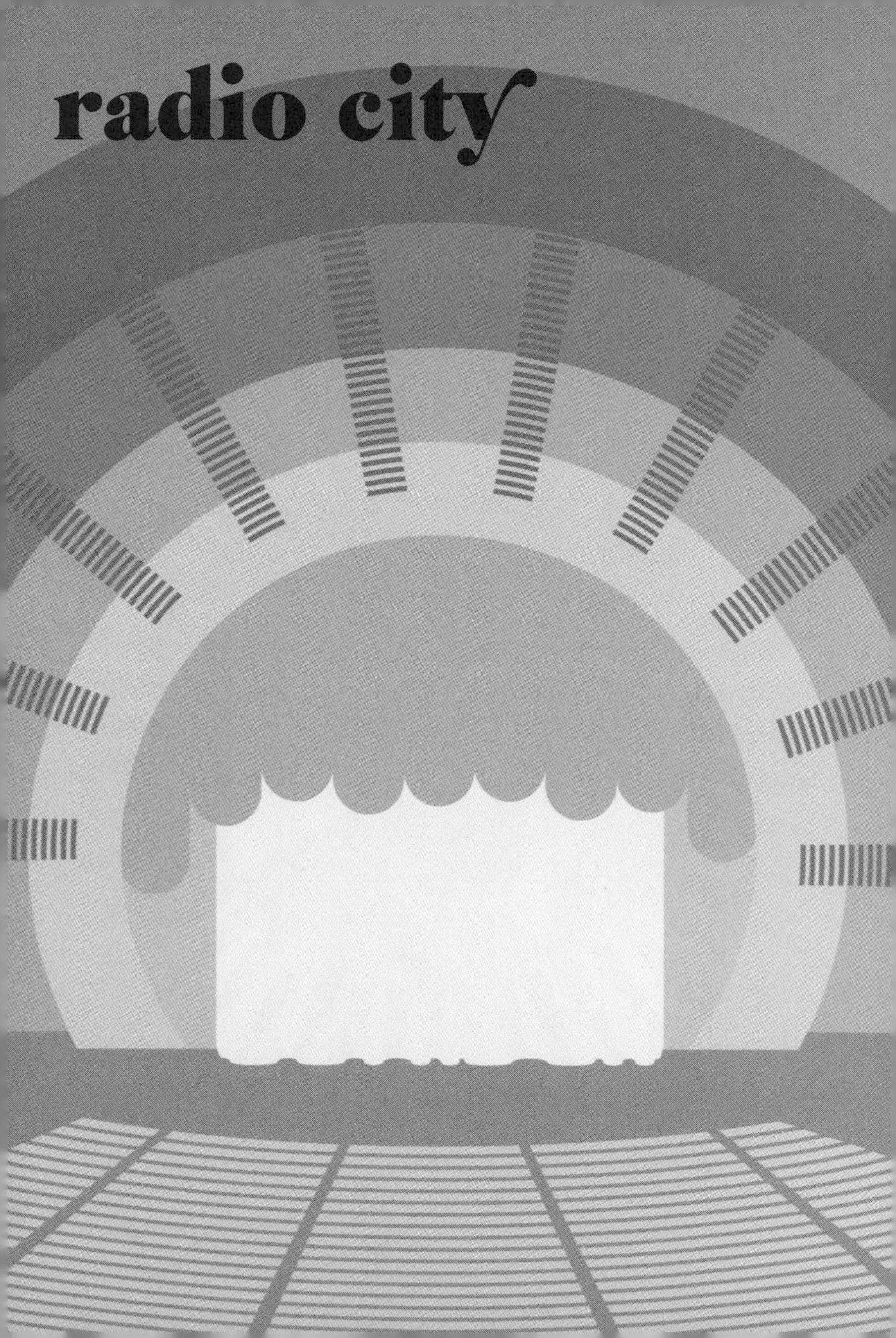
radio city

manif

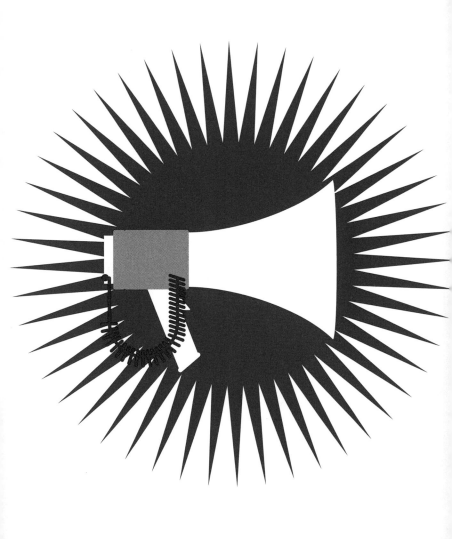

parade

disneyland

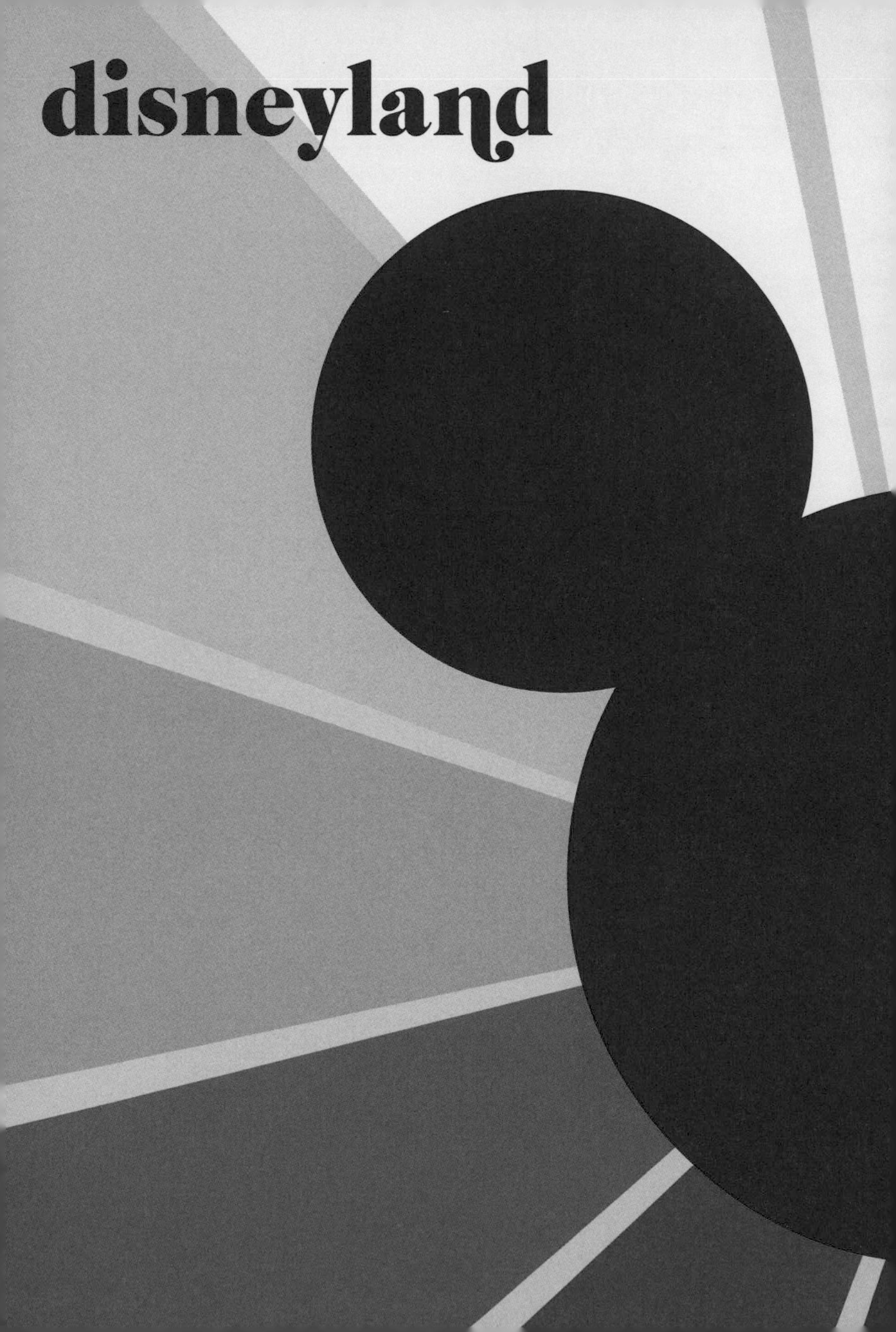

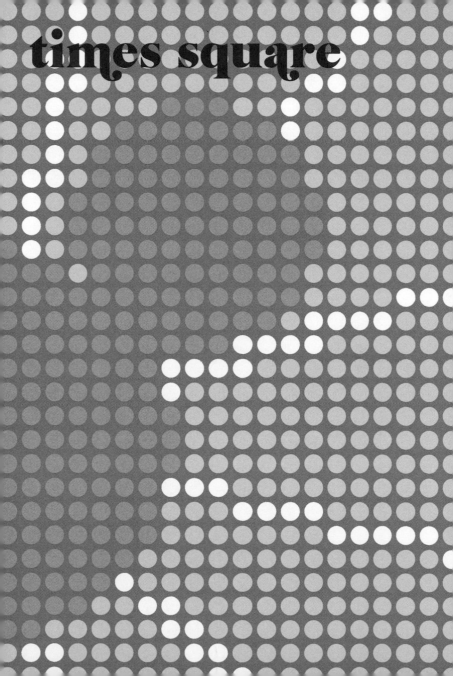

times square

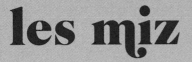

les miz

demain sera pour tous un lendemain

rent

no day but today

édith

voit la vie en rose

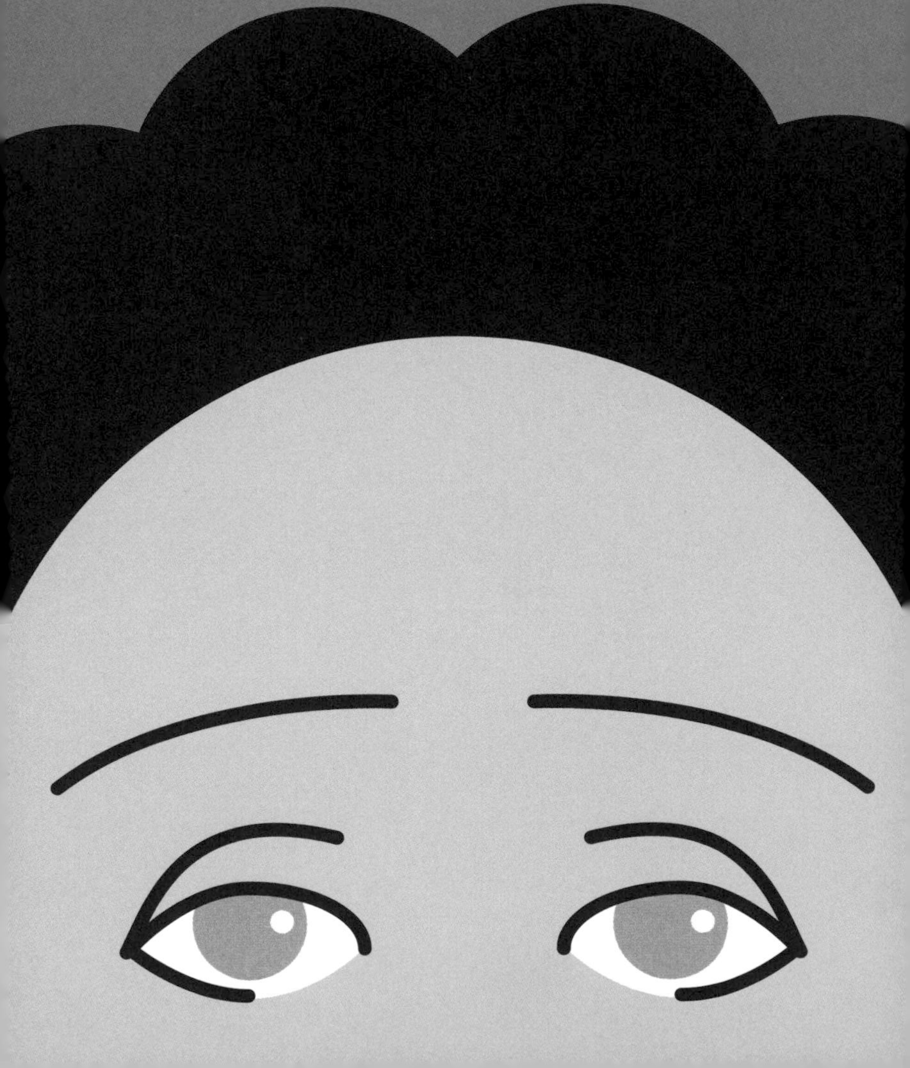

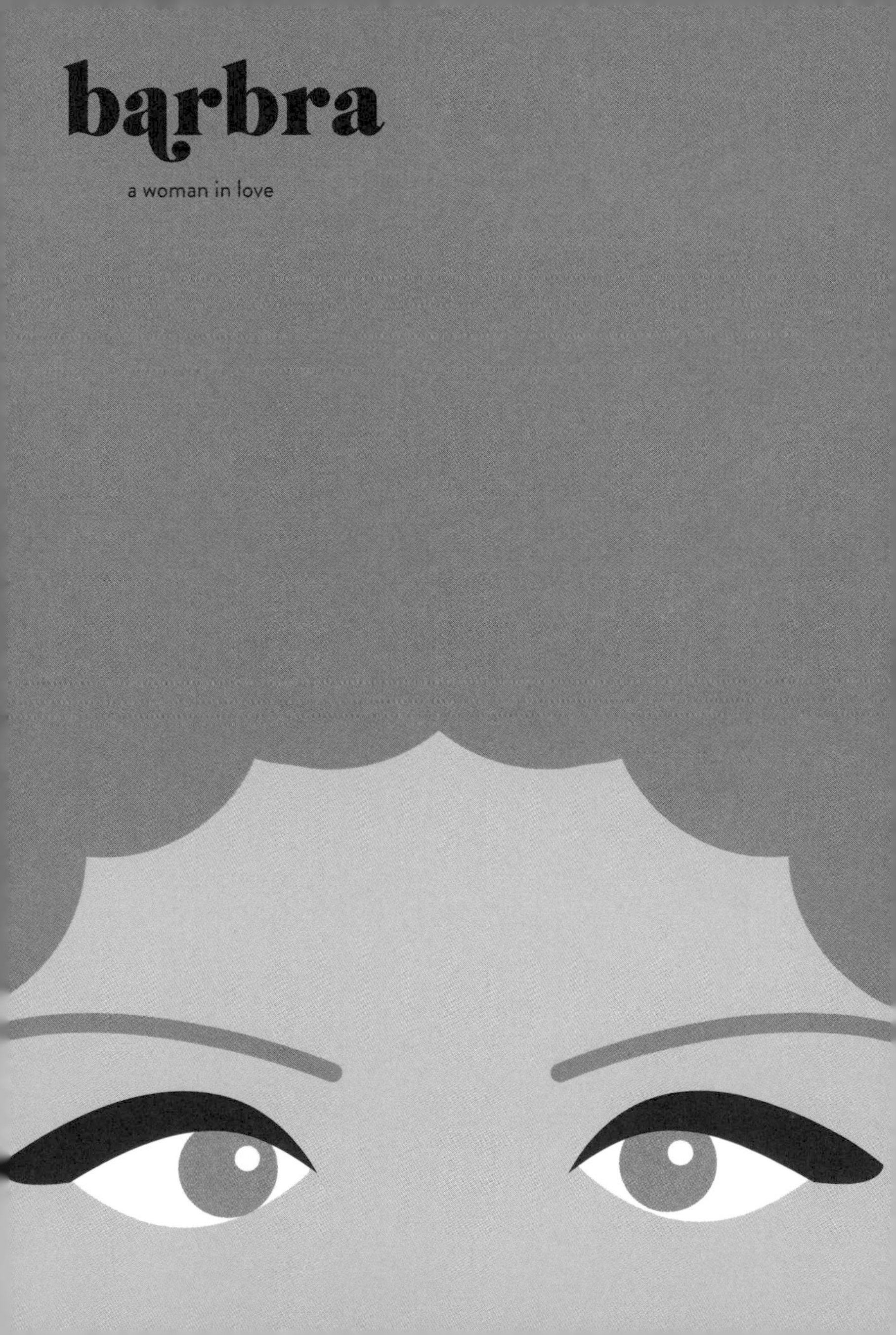
barbra
a woman in love

aznavour

se voyait déjà en haut de l'affiche

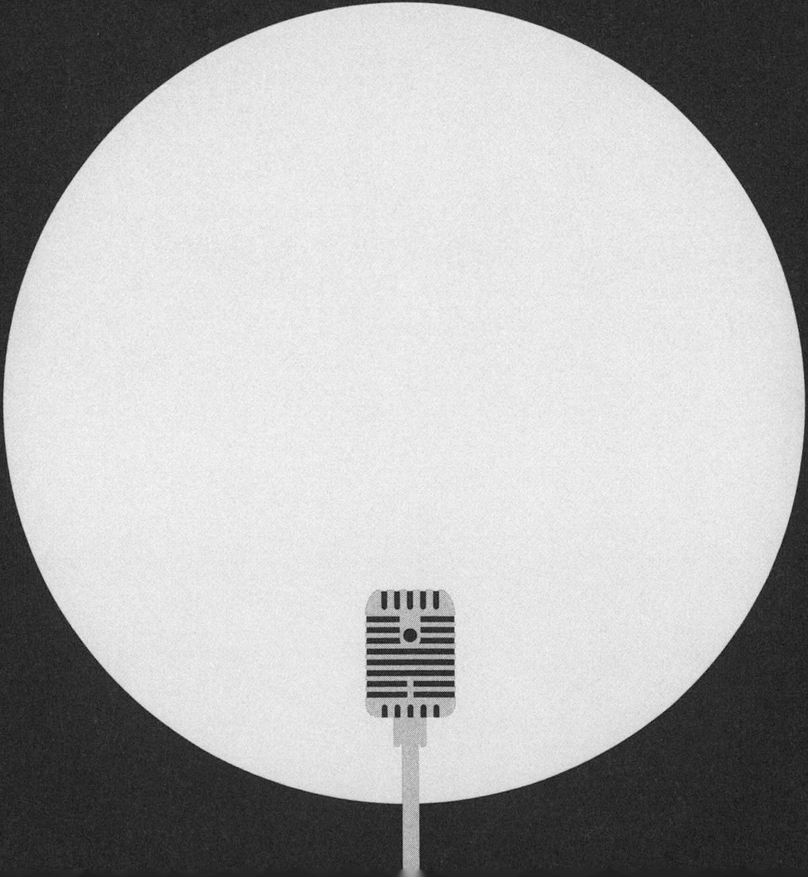

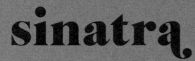

sinatra

if you make it here, you'll make it anywhere

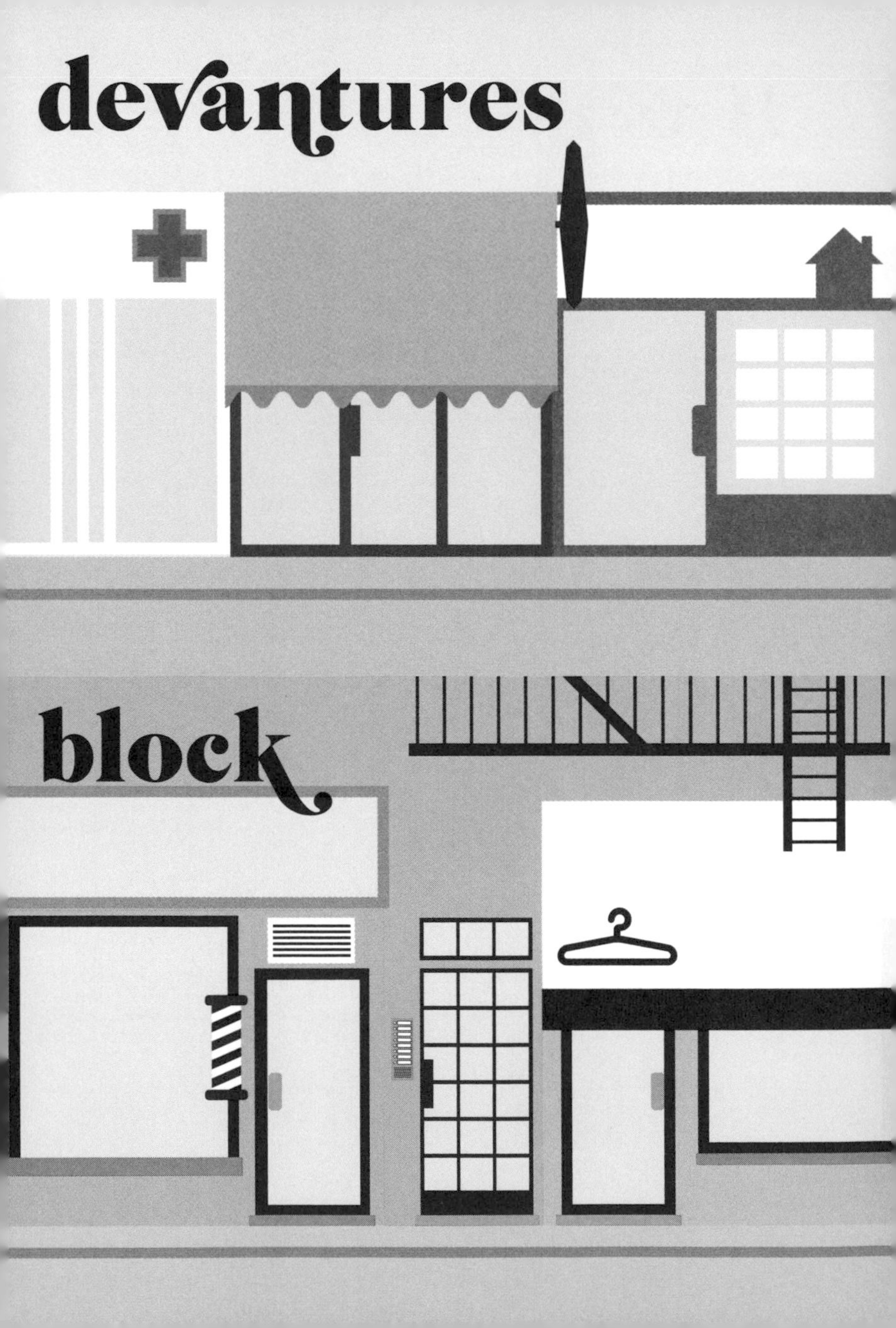
devantures
block

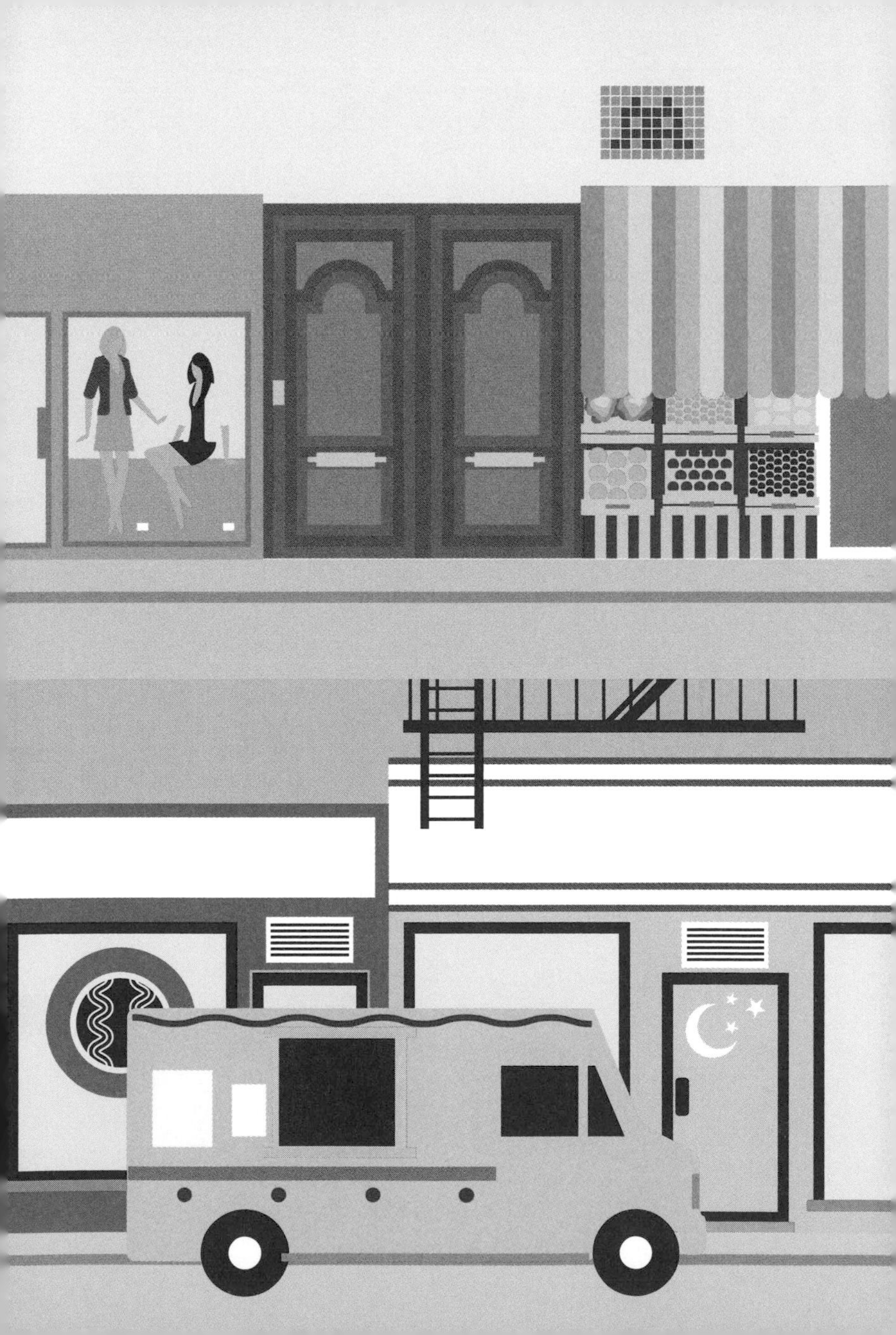

bordeaux

cosmo

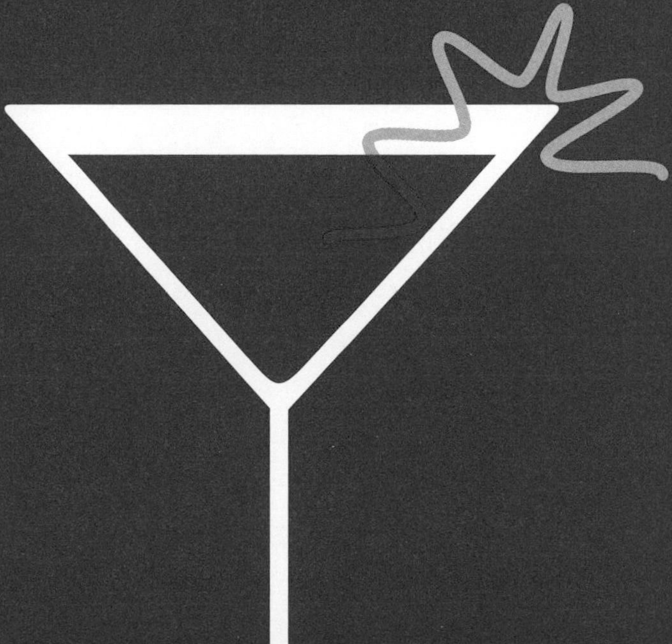

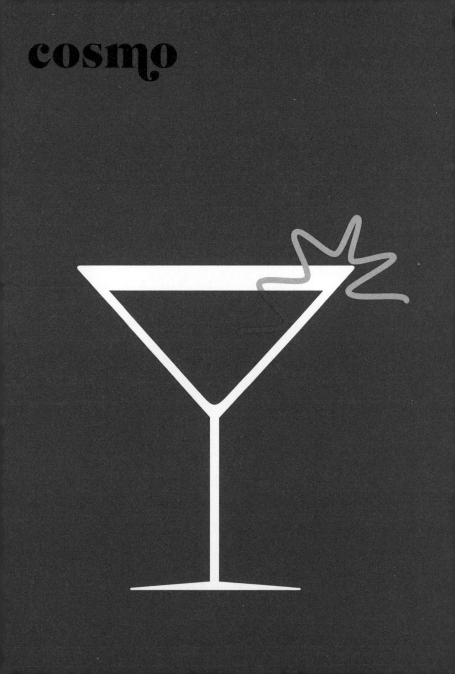

brasserie

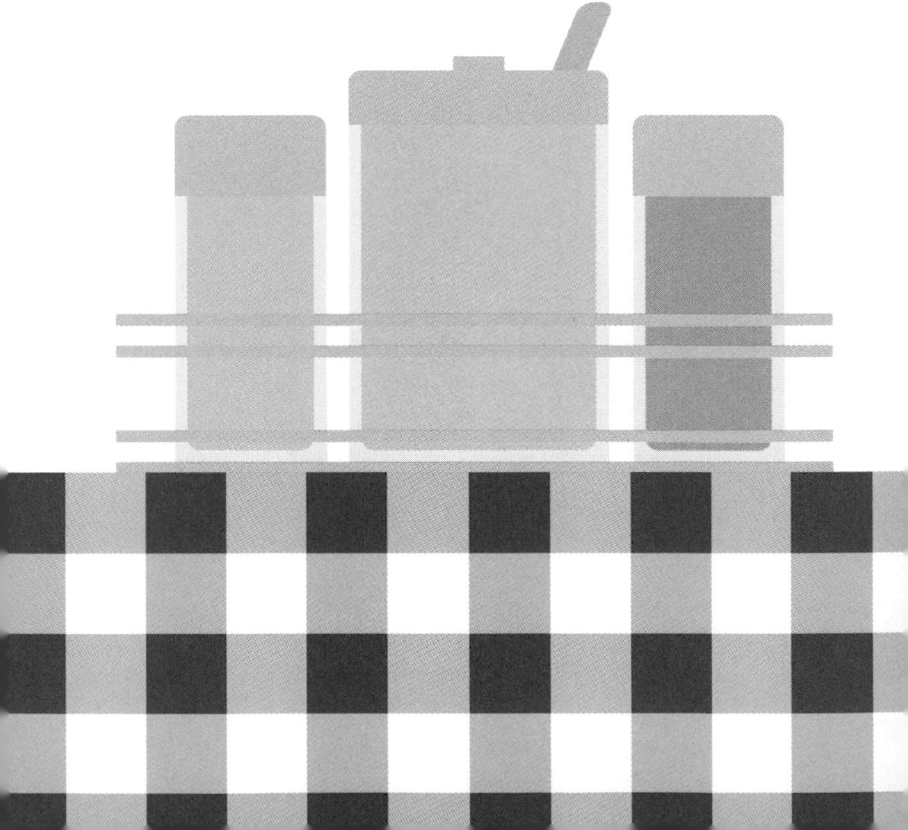

diner

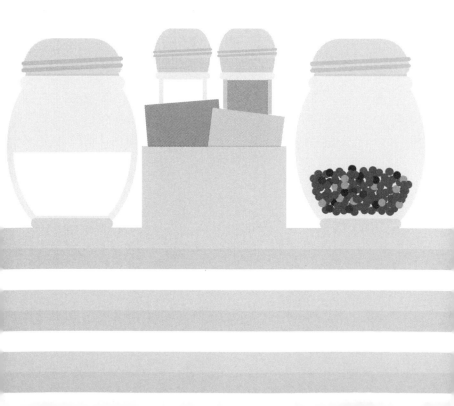

fromage

avec du pain, du vin, du raisin, c'est divin

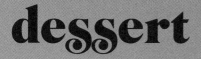

dessert

new york cheesecake is a real treat

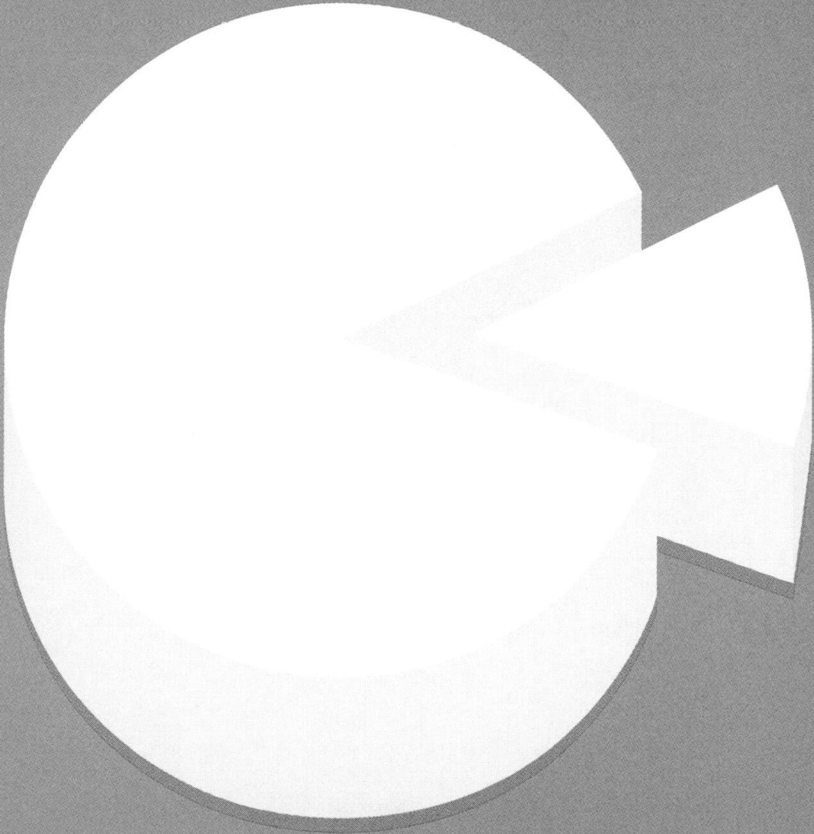

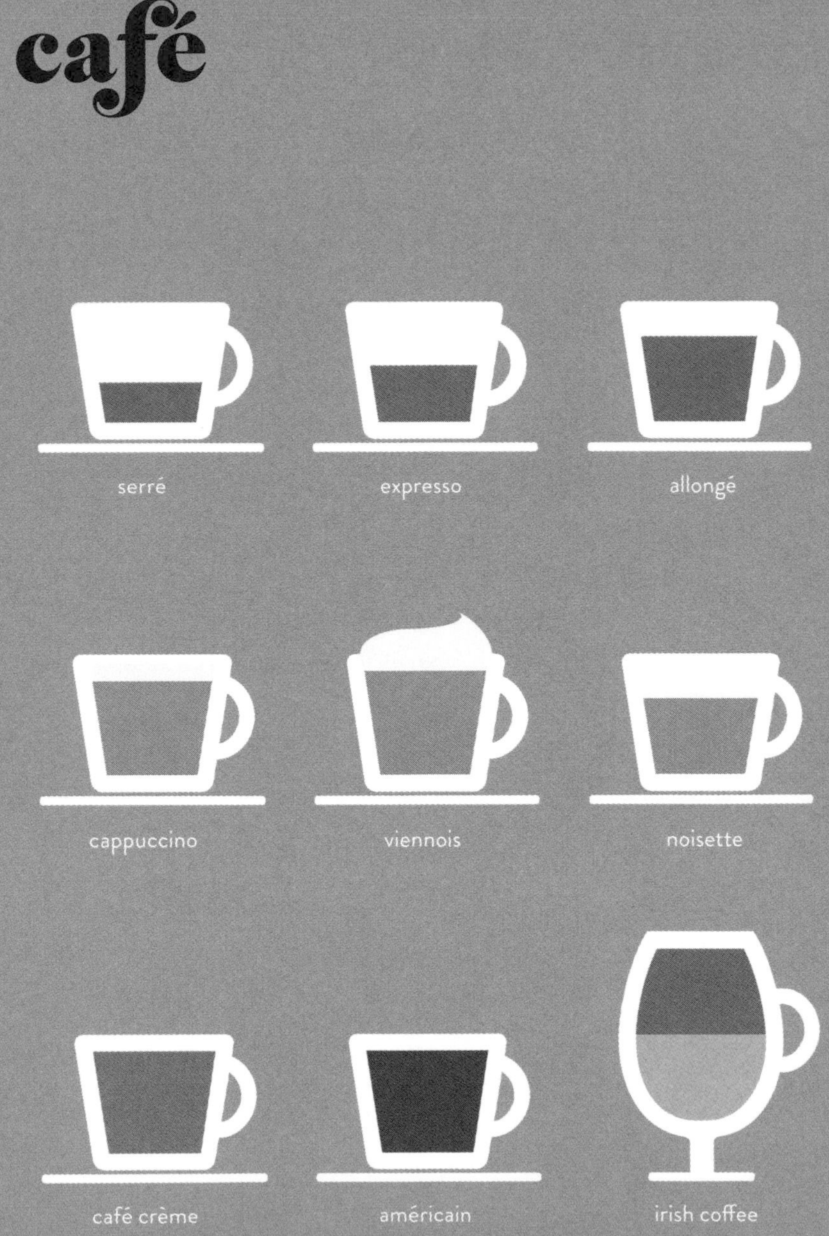
café
serré
expresso
allongé
cappuccino
viennois
noisette
café crème
américain
irish coffee

coffeehouse

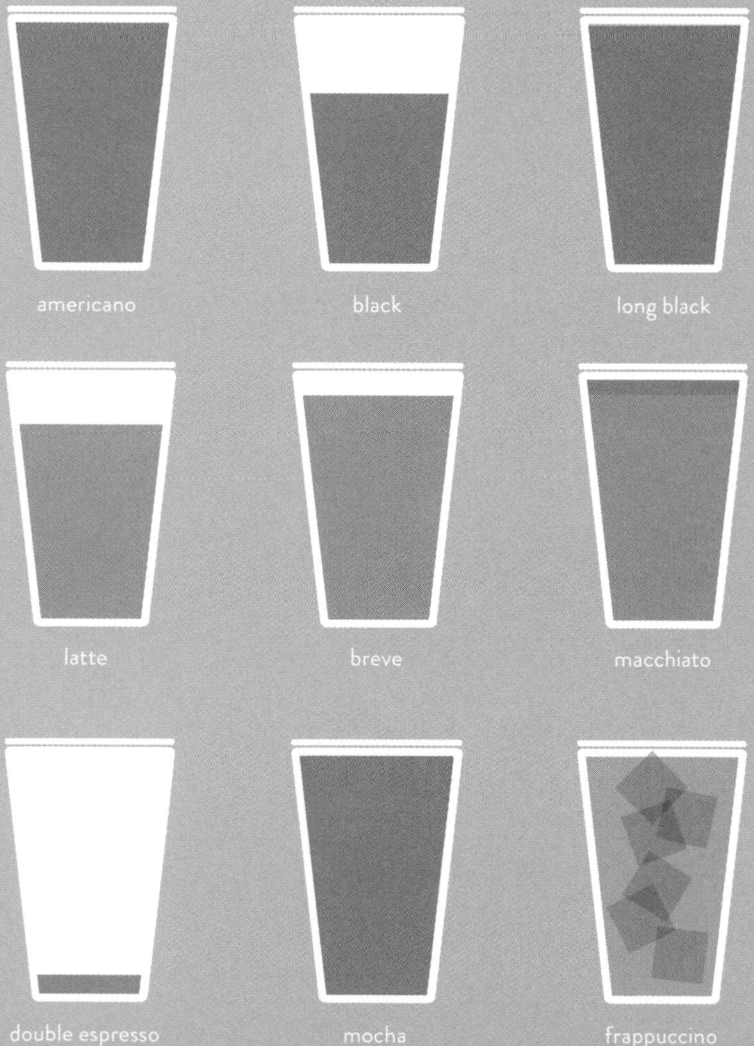
americano
black
long black
latte
breve
macchiato
double espresso
mocha
frappuccino

pourboire

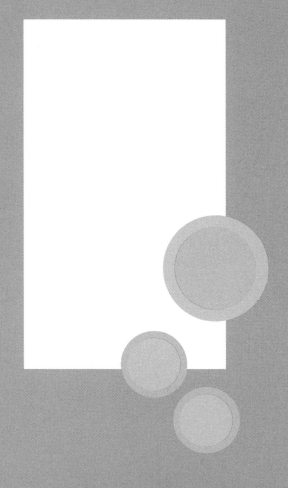

tip

10
10

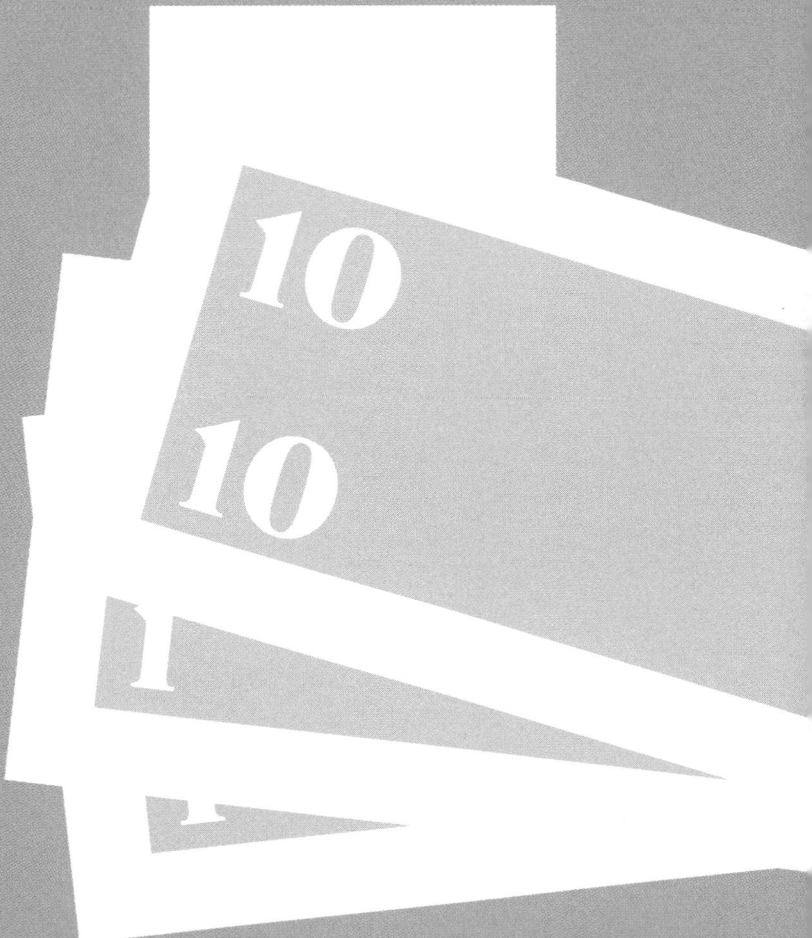

Paris je t'aime

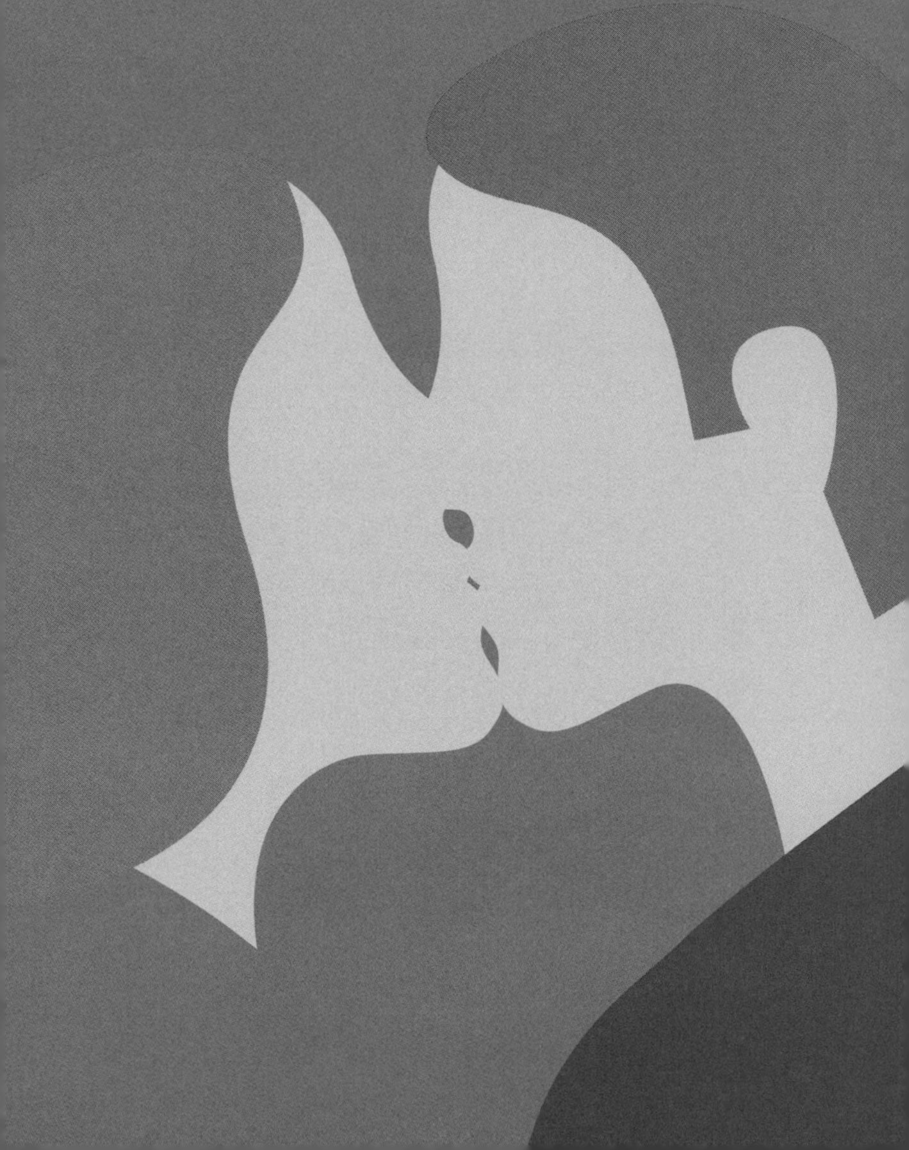

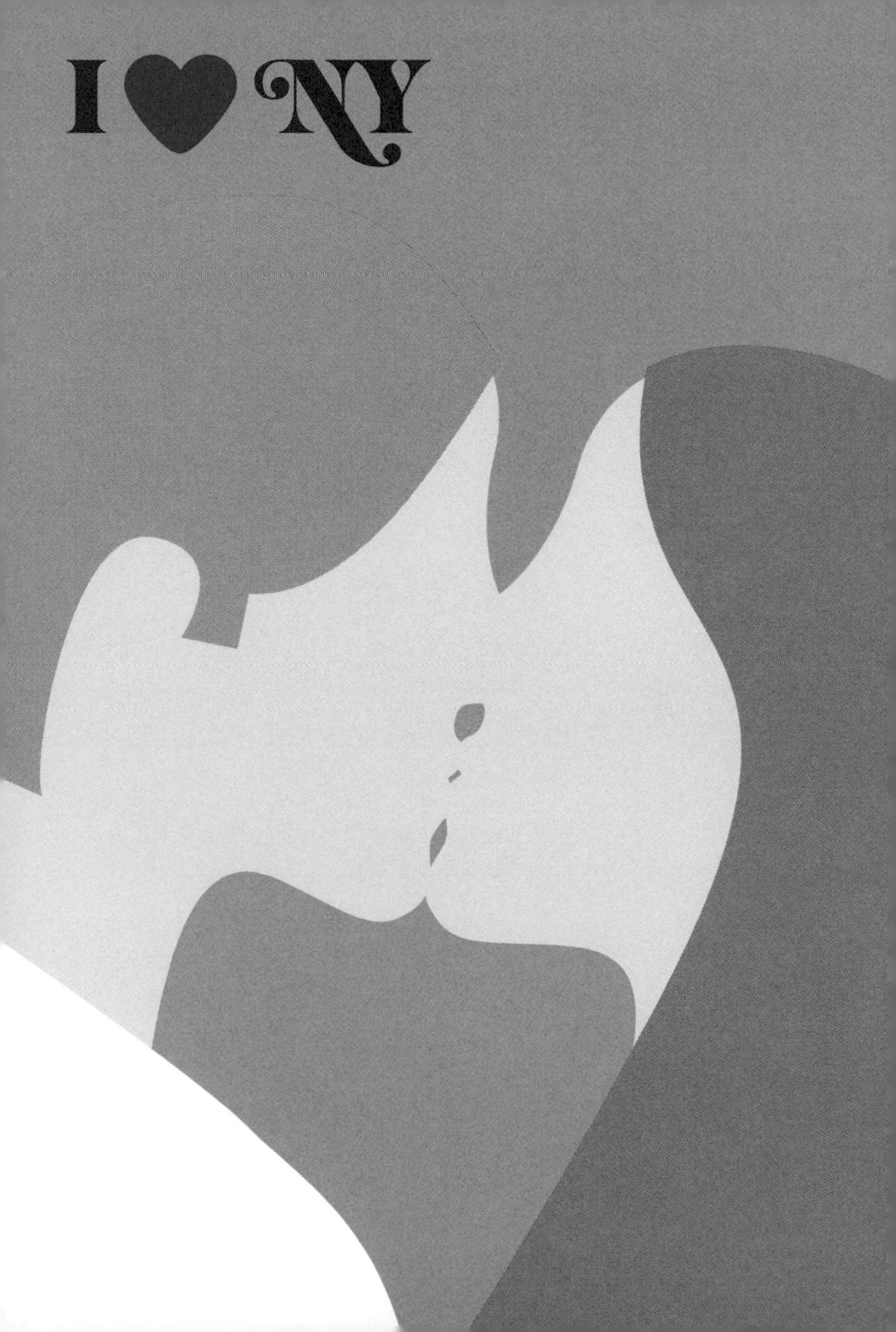
I ♥ NY

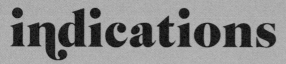

indications

libre — occupé — fin de service

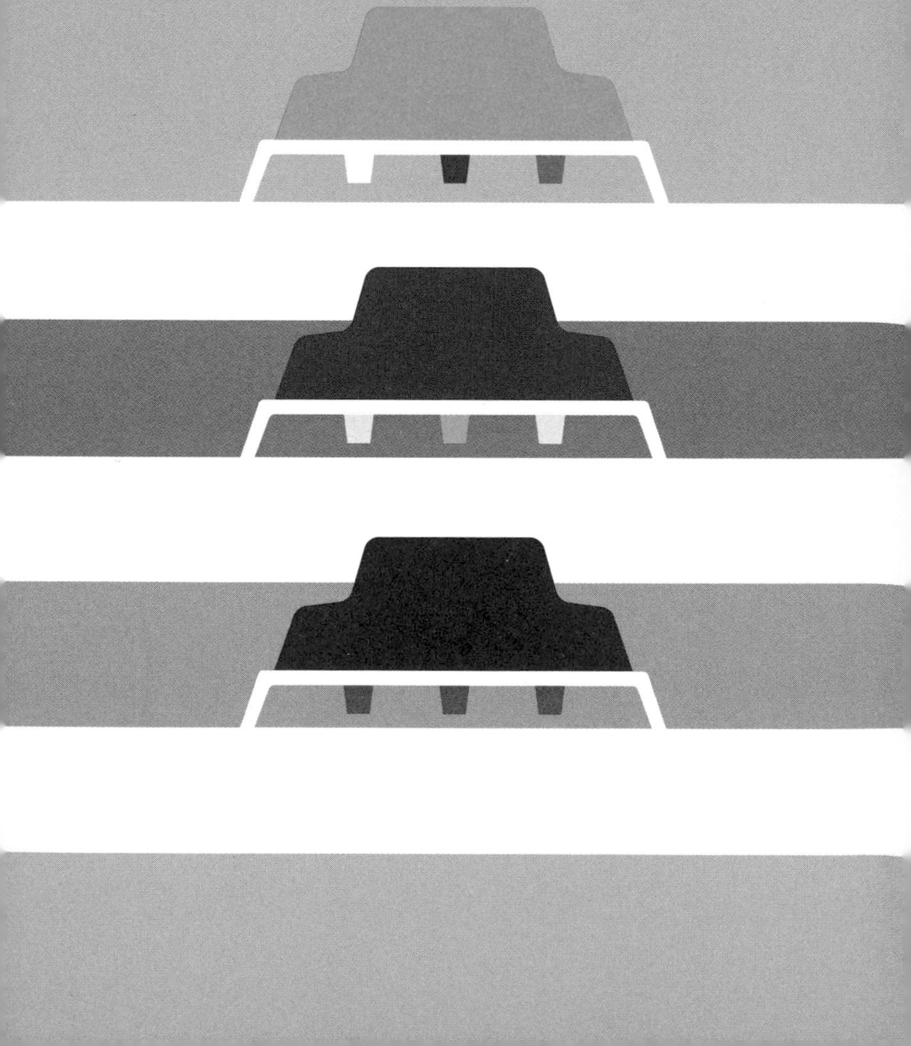

lights

free — taken — off duty

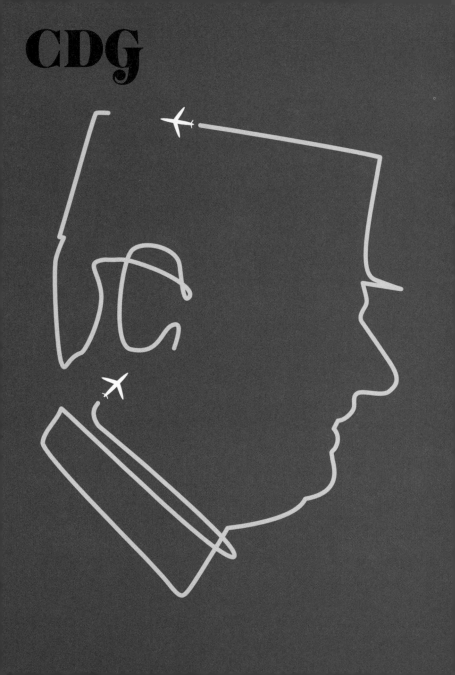

CDG

JFK

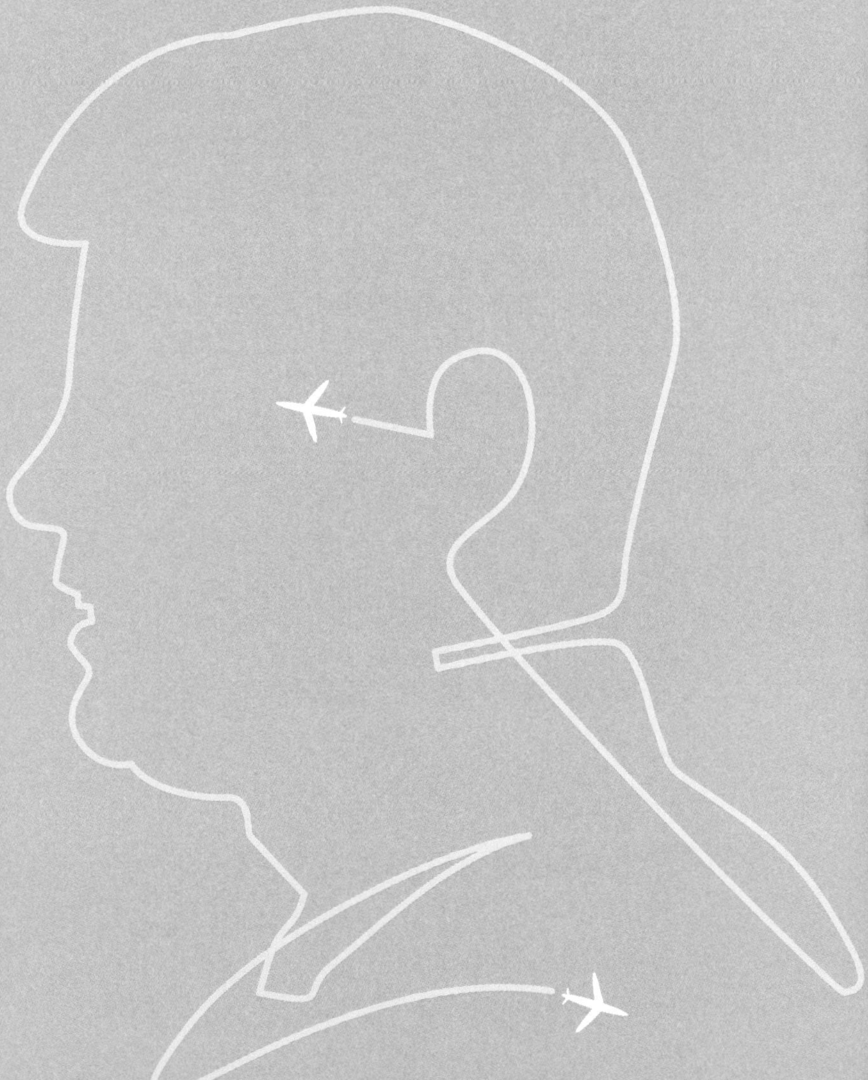

à bientôt Paris

londres
rome
berlin
barcelone
le caire
istanbul

so long
New York

san francisco
st. louis
cape canaveral
chicago
rio
mexico city

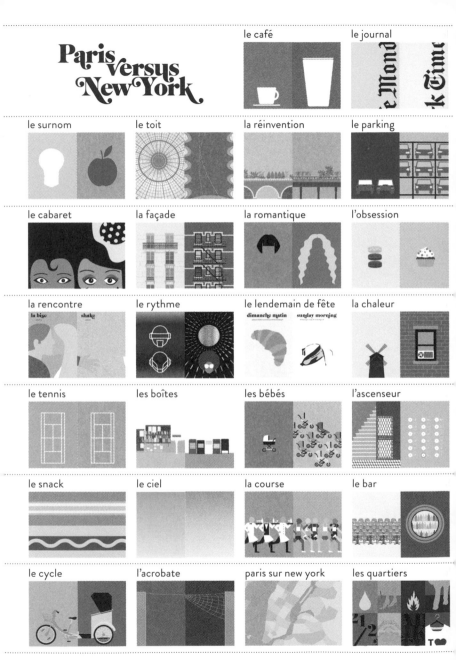

Paris versus New York

le café

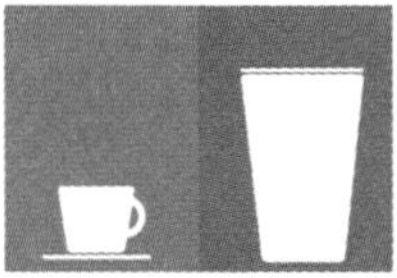

le journal

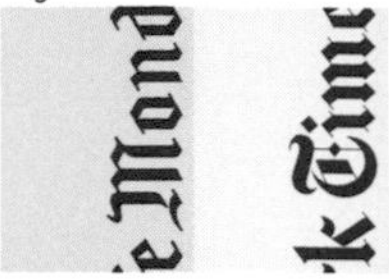

le surnom

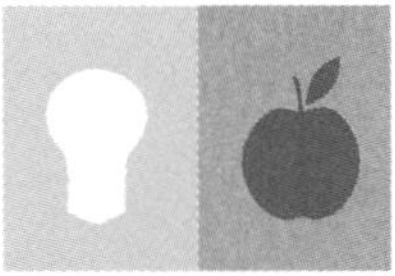

le toit

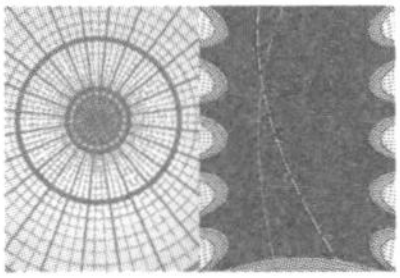

la réinvention

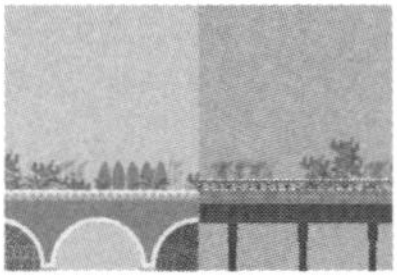

le parking

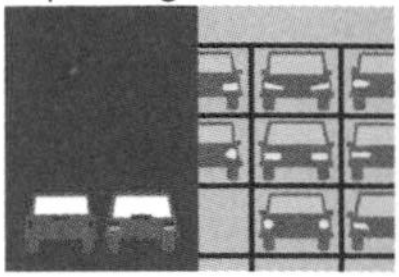

le cabaret

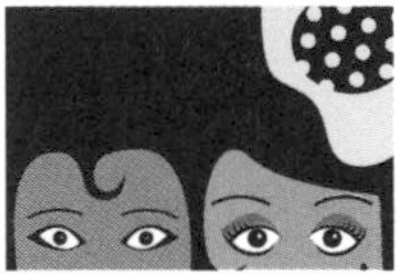

la façade

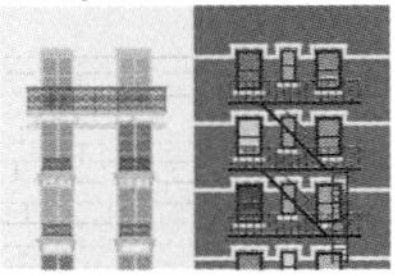

la romantique

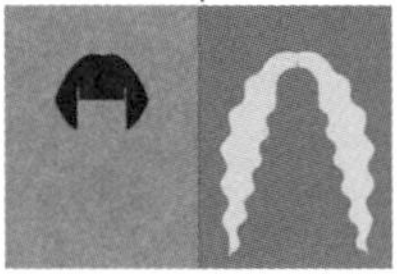

l'obsession

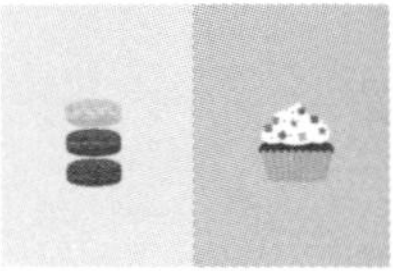

la rencontre

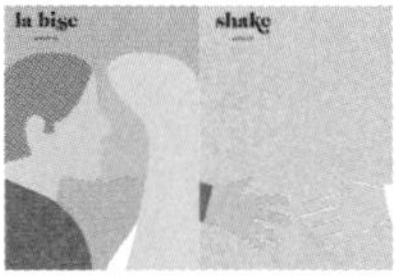
la bise
shake

le rythme

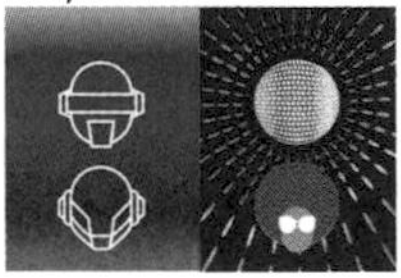

le lendemain de fête

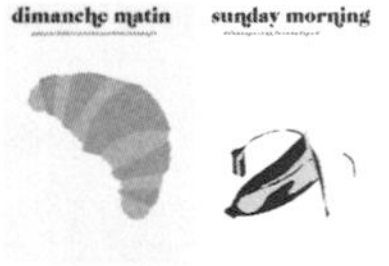
dimanche matin
sunday morning

la chaleur

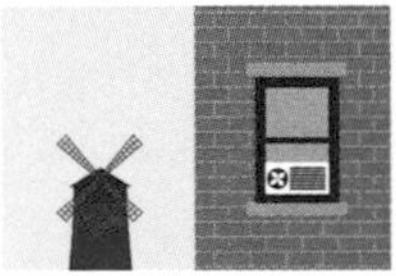

le tennis

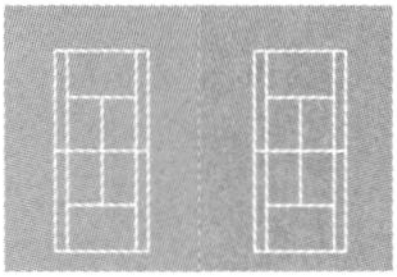

les boîtes

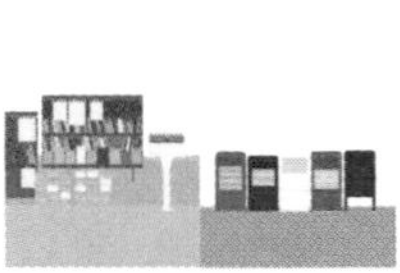

les bébés

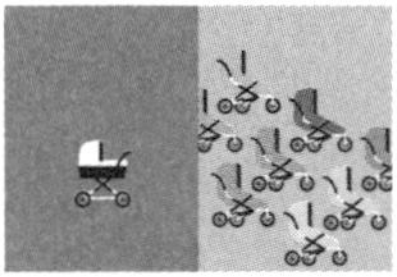

l'ascenseur

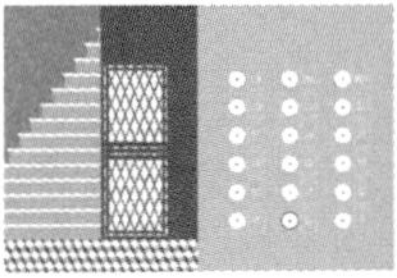

le snack

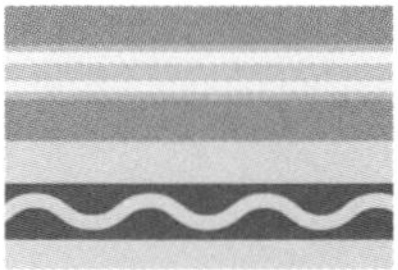

le ciel

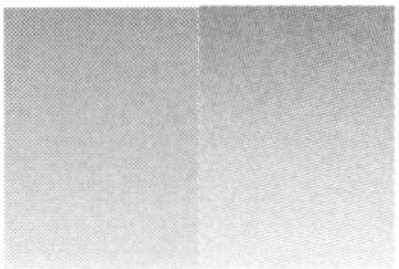

la course

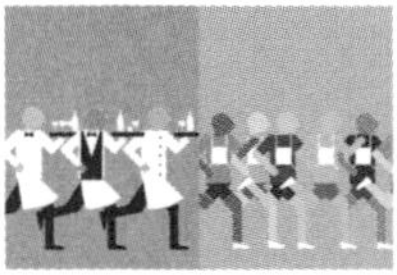

le bar

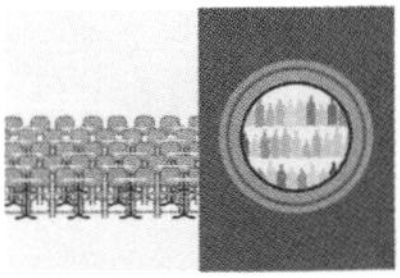

le cycle

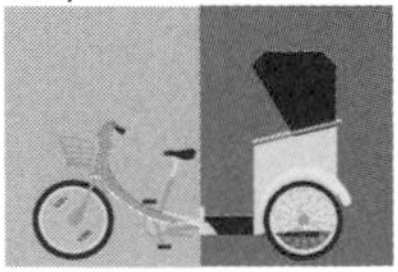

l'acrobate

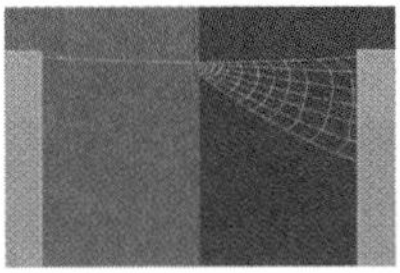

paris sur new york

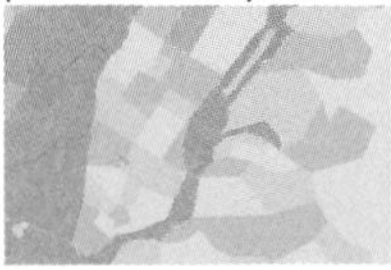

les quartiers

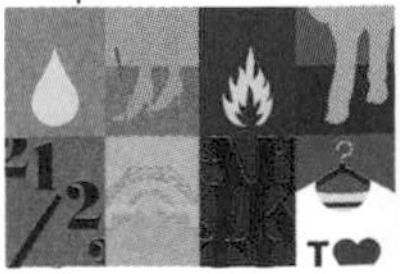

le pain

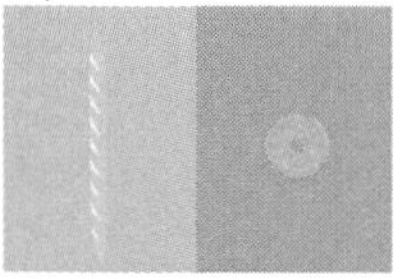

les rues

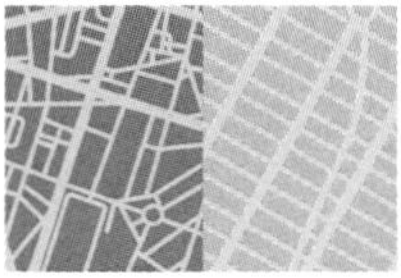

la détente

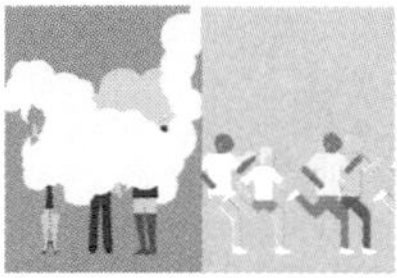

le ticket

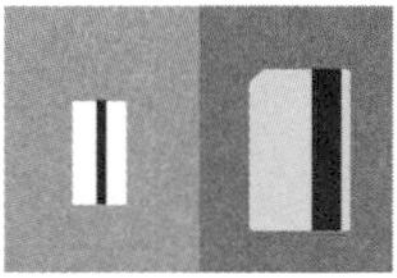

la neige

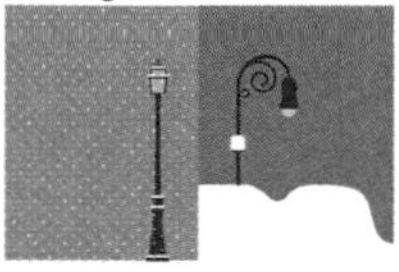

les mamies

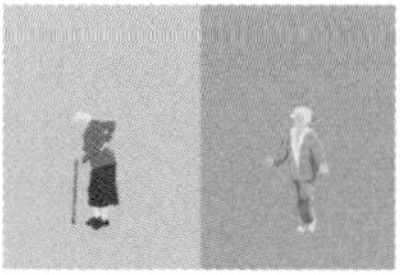

les piétons

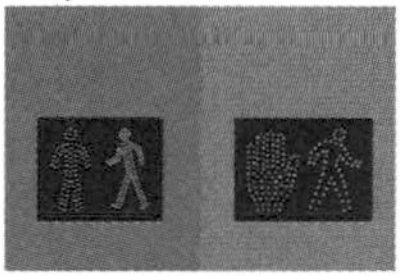

les clous

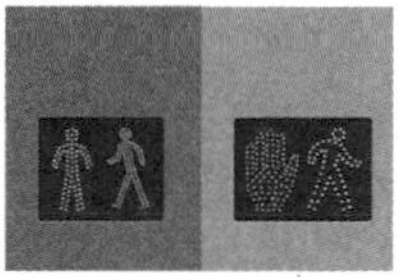

le taxi

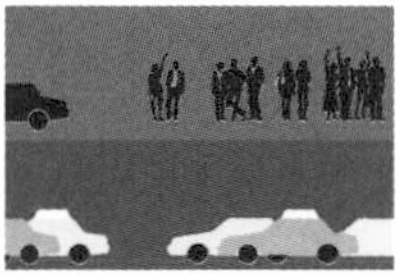

l'acteur

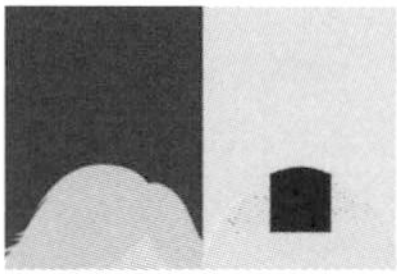

l'enfant terrible

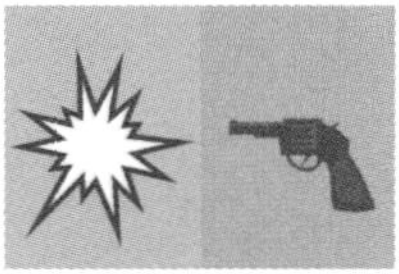

la fête

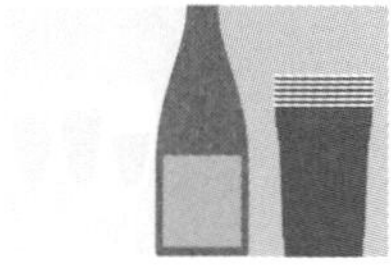

le show

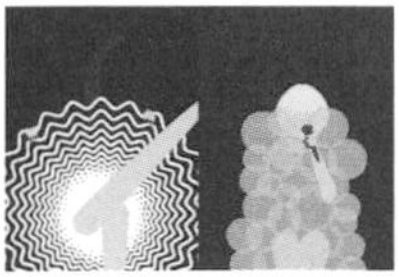

les mains

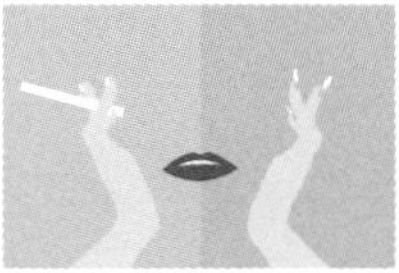

la mode

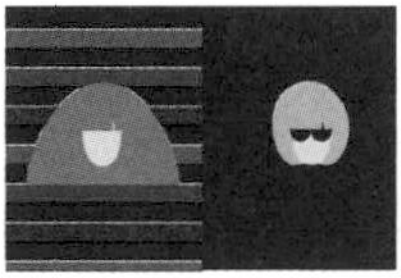

la barbe

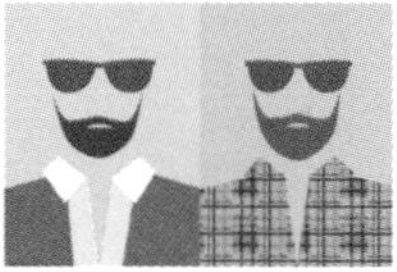

la créature

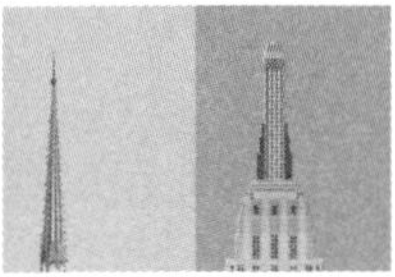

la verdure

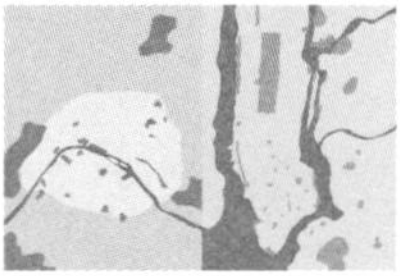

les anges

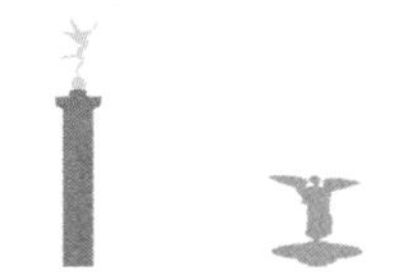

le coureur

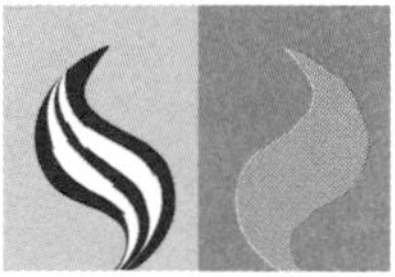

bon appétit

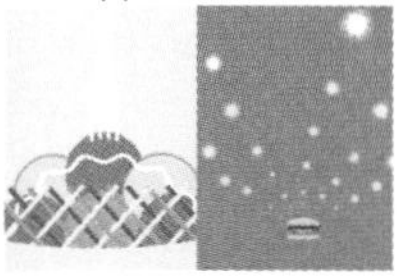

l'université

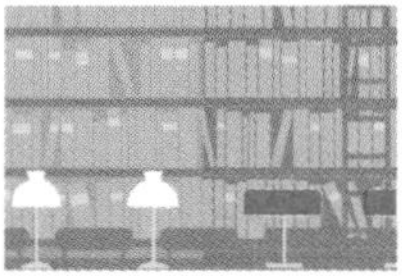

le réalisateur

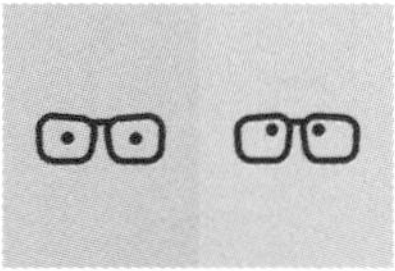

l'écrivain

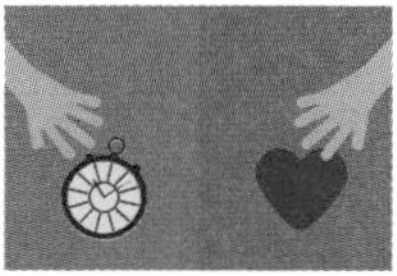

les tours

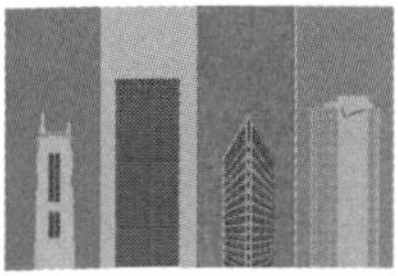

new york sur paris

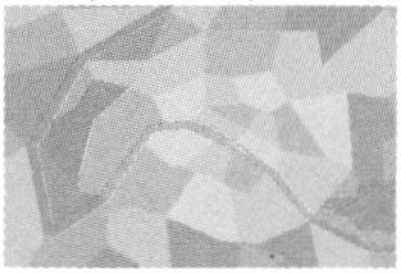

la banlieue

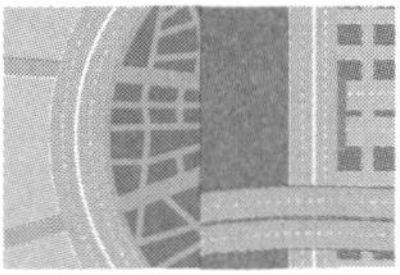

le train-train

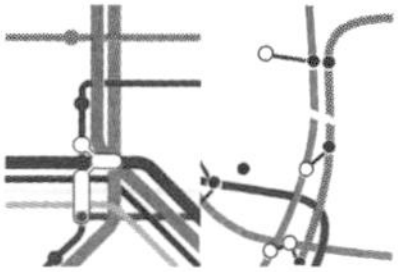

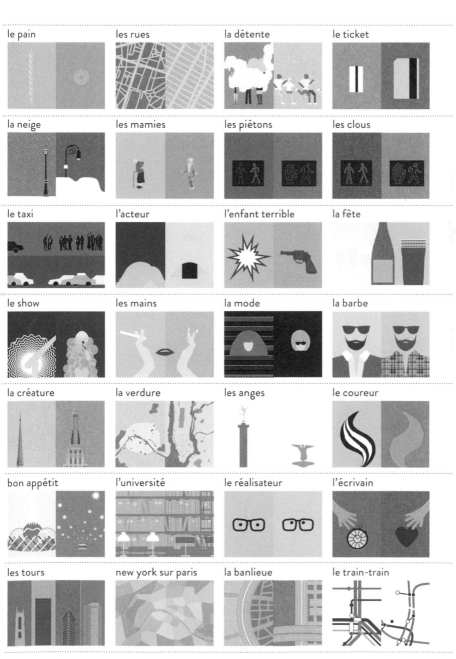

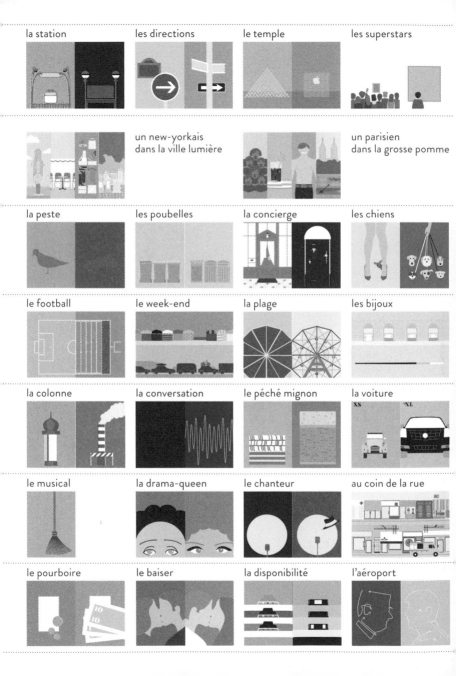

la station

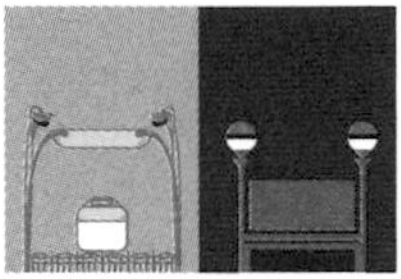

les directions

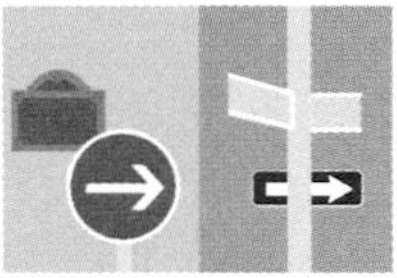

le temple

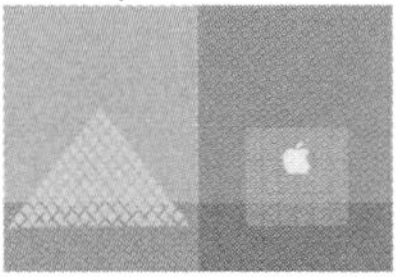

les superstars

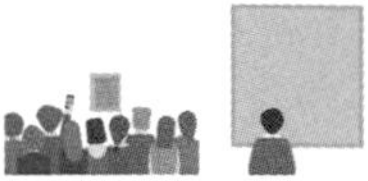

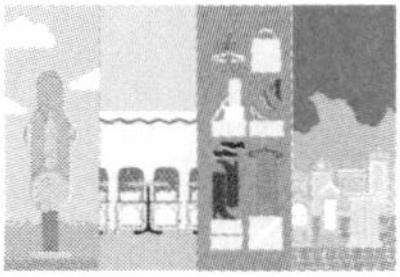

un new-yorkais
dans la ville lumière

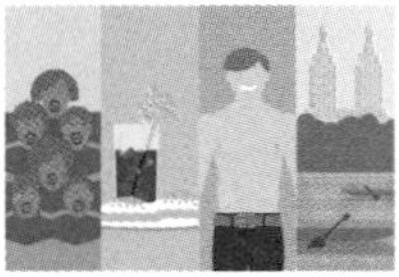

un parisien
dans la grosse pomme

la peste

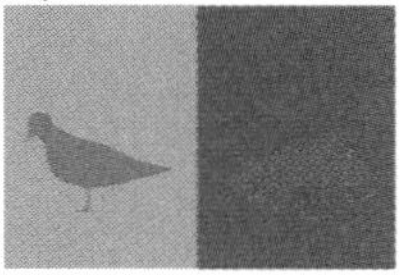

les poubelles

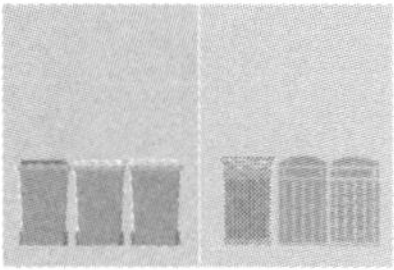

la concierge

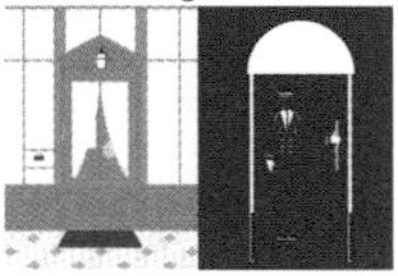

les chiens

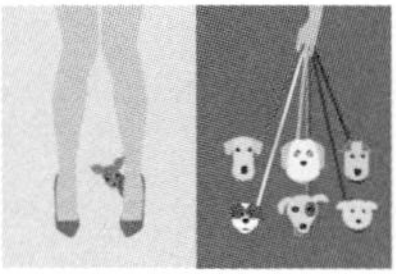

le football

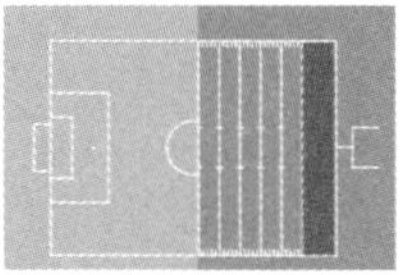

le week-end

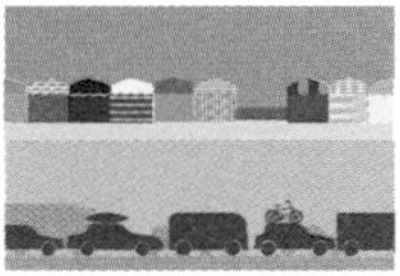

la plage

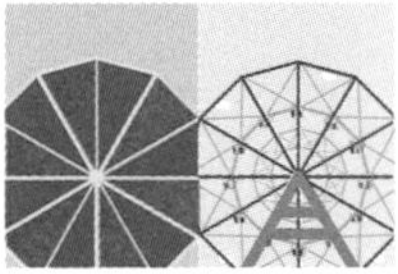

les bijoux

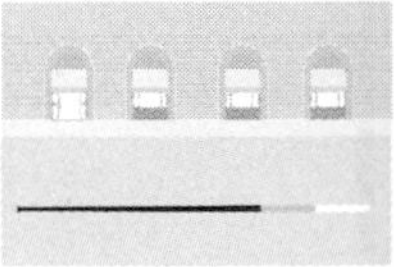

la colonne

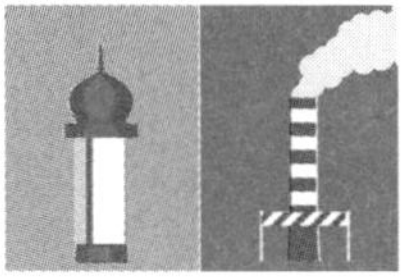

la conversation

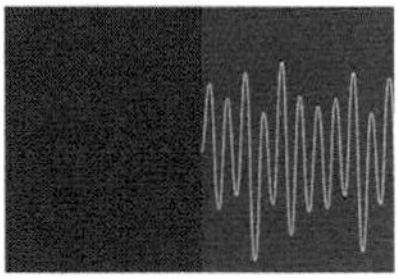

le péché mignon

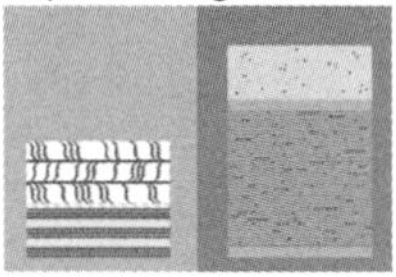

la voiture

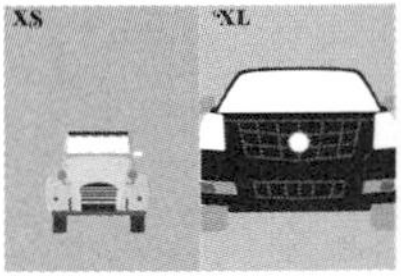
XS
XL

le musical

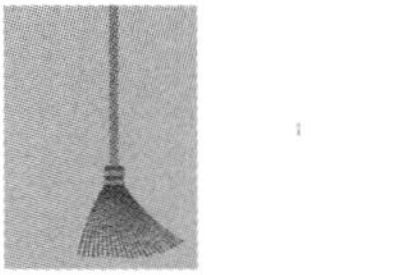

la drama-queen

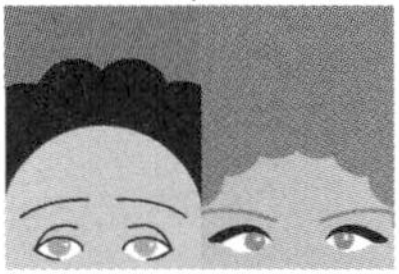

le chanteur

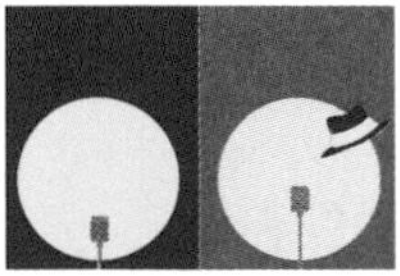

au coin de la rue

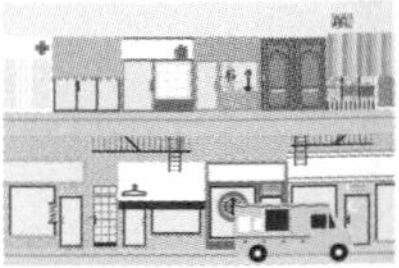

le pourboire

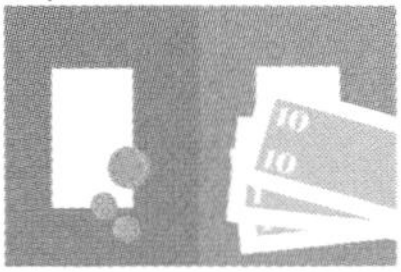
10
10

le baiser

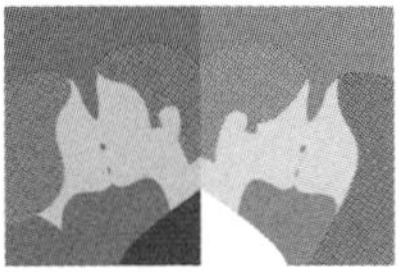

la disponibilité

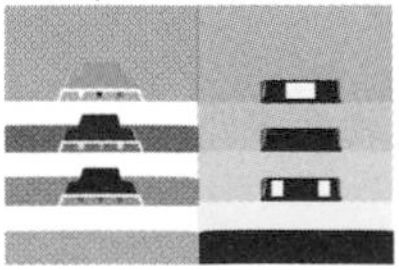

l'aéroport

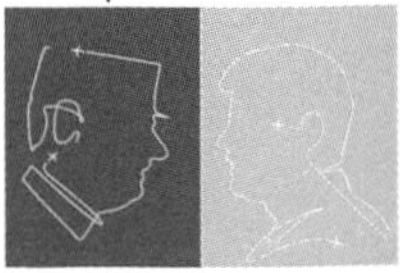

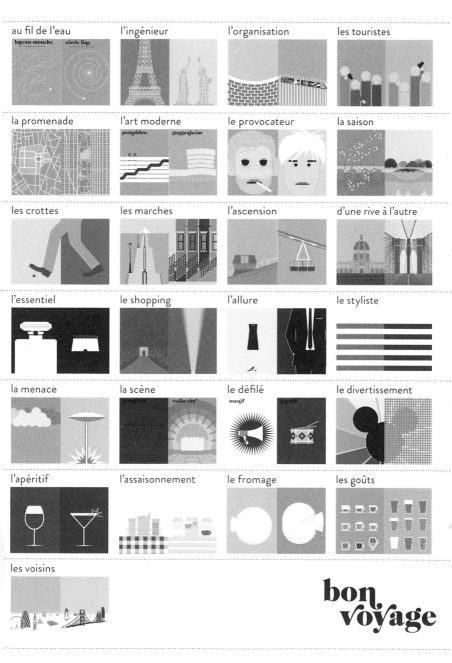

au fil de l'eau

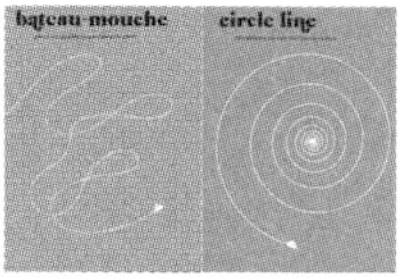
bateau-mouche
circle line

l'ingénieur

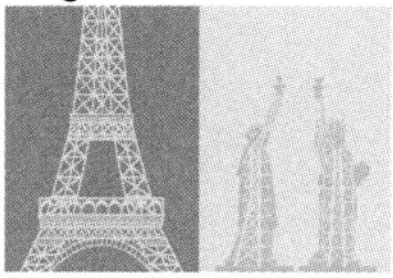

l'organisation

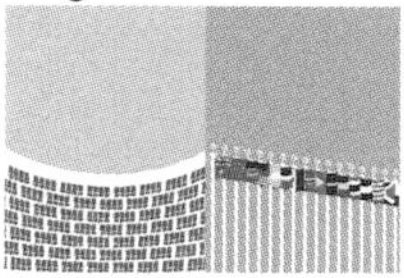

les touristes

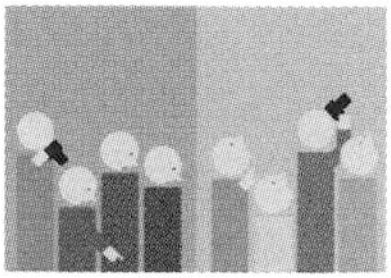

la promenade

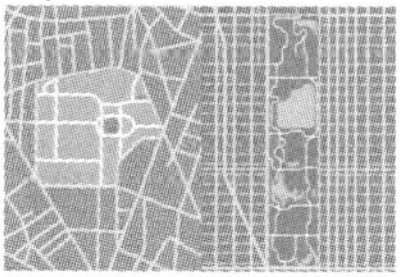

l'art moderne

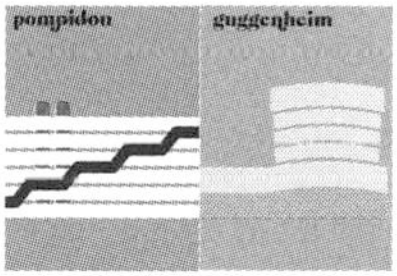
pompidou
guggenheim

le provocateur

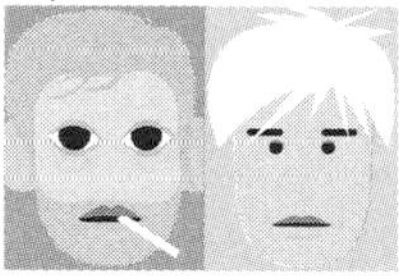

la saison

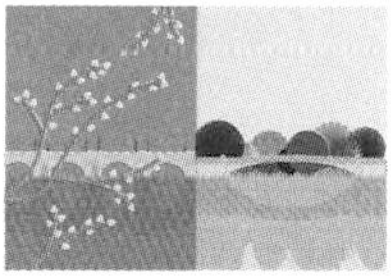

les crottes

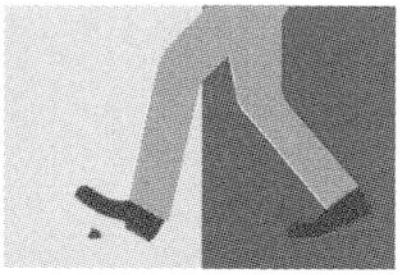

les marches

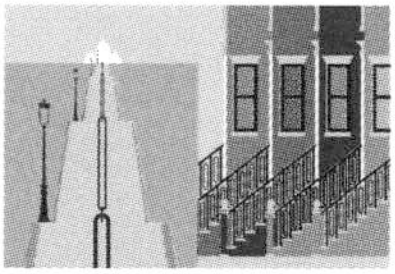

l'ascension

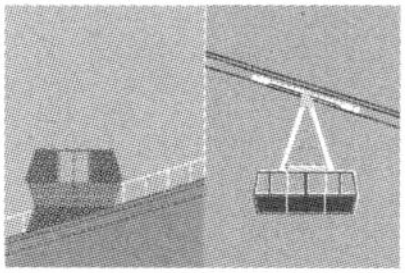

d'une rive à l'autre

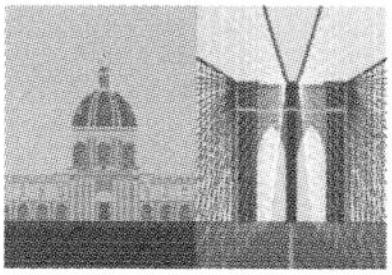

l'essentiel

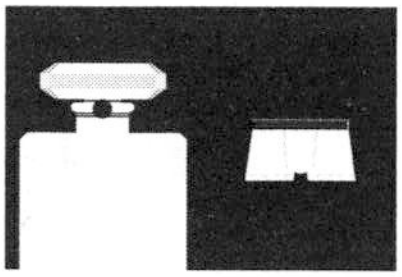

le shopping

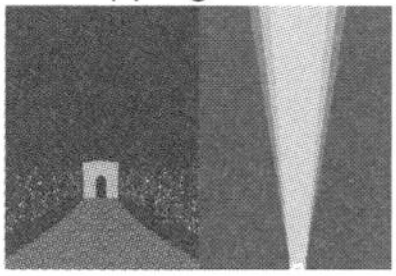

l'allure

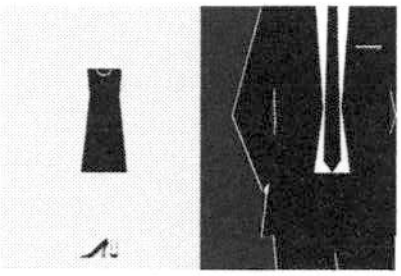

le styliste

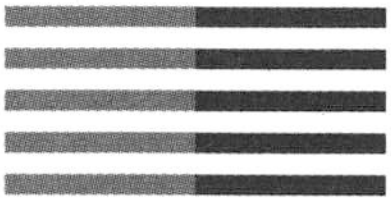

la menace

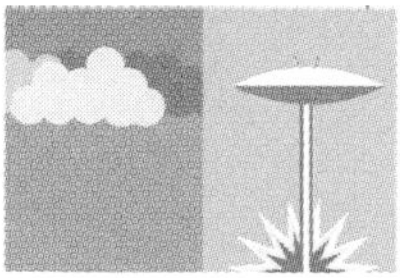

la scène

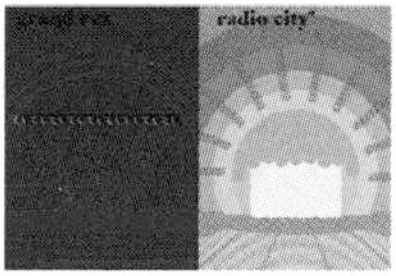
radio city

le défilé

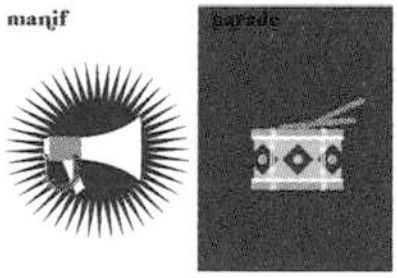
manif
parade

le divertissement

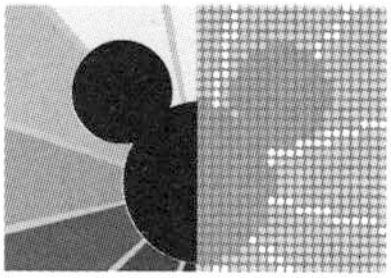

l'apéritif

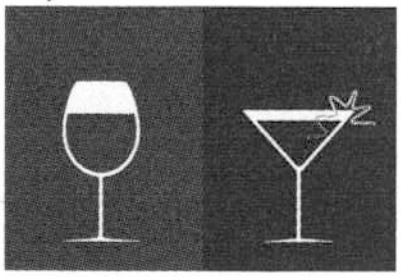

l'assaisonnement

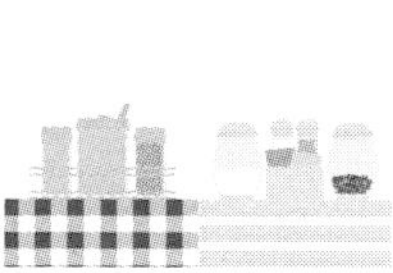

le fromage

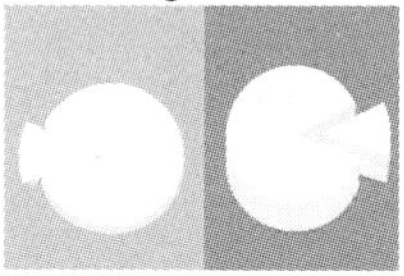

les goûts

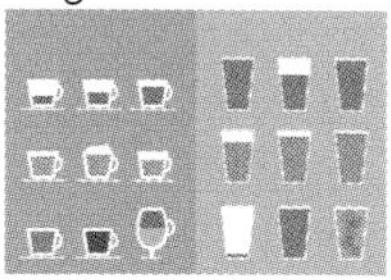

les voisins

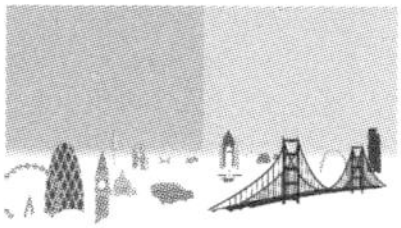

bon voyage

merci

to the American dream team from Penguin Books, especially Laura Tisdel, for being the first to say hi and never good-bye; Stephen Morrison, aka the eye of the tiger; and Sonya Cheuse, what a très chic flair. Brettne Bloom and Caroline Zimmerman—loved those overwhelming triangle conversations whenever-wherever-whatever the subject. Sandra Stark, my very own special tata d'Amérique; Jim Mersfelder, because it all happened at 52D; Eve Mersfelder, my great heart-twin sister; Meline Toumani, my insider on so many levels; Marie Cortadellas and les amis français de la Grosse Pomme, for their uplifting mood; the incredible share-retweet online community; and my number-one source of inspiration: New York and the people making it there.

thanks

to the other side of the pond, the Parisian publishing team 10/18-Univers Poche; Emmanuelle Heurtebize, being in love with Paris and New York has never been so apropos. Thiery Teboul Fontana, for his unbelievable sense and sensibility; Sonia Kalaydjian, the very first one to say GO!; Elodie Chaillous, for those crazy ViiiZ years; Bernard Baissait, revealing the concepts within me has paid off; Anouche Der Sarkissian, for the puns, idioms, and all our English love affairs; mes amis à Paris ou ailleurs, my super extra family; my brother Arnaud, for all the genuine advice; my grandparents, for drawing those paths of hope; my parents, Armand and Viviane, for giving me the chance to start creating this match in my head until I was able to share it with the world.